Policing the Factory

History of Crime, Deviance and Punishment series

Series Editor: Anne-Marie Kilday, Professor of Criminal History, Oxford Brookes University, UK

Academic interest in the history of crime and punishment has never been greater and the History of Crime, Deviance and Punishment series provides a home for the wealth of new research being produced. Individual volumes within the series cover topics related to the history of crime and punishment, from the later medieval to modern period and in both Europe and North America, and seek to demonstrate the importance of this subject in furthering understanding of the way in which various societies and cultures operate. When taken together, the works in the series will show the evolution of the nature of illegality and attitudes towards its perpetration over time and will offer their readers a rounded and coherent history of crime and punishment through the centuries. The series' broad chronological and geographical coverage encourages comparative historical analysis of crime history between countries and cultures.

Other Forthcoming Titles in the Series:

Deviance, Disorder and Music in Modern Britain and America, Cliff Williamson

The Forefathers of Terrorism, Johannes Dillinger

Policing the Factory

Theft, Private Policing and the Law in Modern England

Barry Godfrey and David J. Cox

B L O O M S B U R Y
LONDON • NEW DELHI • NEW YORK • SYDNEY

Bloomsbury Academic
An imprint of Bloomsbury Publishing Plc

50 Bedford Square
London
WC1B 3DP
UK

175 Fifth Avenue
New York
NY 10010
USA

www.bloomsbury.com

First published 2013

British Library Cataloguing-in-Publication Data
A catalogue record for this book is available from the British Library.

ISBN: HB: 978-1-4411-0752-7
PDF: 978-1-4411-5252-7
ePub: 978-1-4411-7688-2

Library of Congress Cataloging-in-Publication Data
A catalog record for this title is available from the Library of Congress.

Typeset by Deanta Global Publishing Services, Chennai, India
Printed and bound in Great Britain

Contents

Acknowledgements

Our interest in issues of private policing has developed over a long time, and we have accumulated a large intellectual debt over that time. This work originated as a PhD thesis under the supervision of Professor Peter King, a superb guide and ally in the quest to develop historical knowledge on crime and policing, as well as a great person to discuss all manner of ideas (historical, political, football. . .). Subsequently, we have learnt a great deal from academics working in the fields of police history, as well as postgraduate students past and present. In developing theories around the legal governance of private space and the relationship between labour and capital we have formed a happy coalition founded on differing areas of knowledge – David's research on entrepreneurial and public policing in the eighteenth and early nineteenth century, and Barry's research on workplace crime in the textile regions of the nineteenth century. We hope that our joint efforts have strengthened our work – which would not exist without the work of the archivists in various West Yorkshire repositories who cheerfully provided huge dusty-covered quarter sessions records, and huge very heavy volumes of Director's minute books. We would like to thank them, and all the other un-named but important people who have contributed to our thoughts and to our work, printed here.

Barry Godfrey and David J. Cox
August 2012

Foreword

The study of workplace appropriation and its policing offers windows in to many important historical concerns. Strangely, however, the vast majority of historians working on this topic have either focused on the eighteenth century or on the twentieth, and on areas peripheral to the fundamental regional transformations that formed the core of the industrialization process. The publication of a study centred on one of the heartlands of 'the industrial revolution' and on the century in which that process, whatever we might wished to call it, transformed many aspects of economic and social relations in Britain is therefore immensely welcome. The focus of many of the first generation of social historians that studied crime and customary rights on the pre-1800 period left a very considerable hole in the following century, and the conclusion of some of those authors that the eighteenth century witnessed a clear 'custom to crime transition' also seems to have led to the subject being much less well served by historians of the Victorian period. That transition was not, however, as clear cut as historians such as Peter Linebaugh chose to believe, and the continued battles over workplace appropriation in the nineteenth and twentieth centuries are an important testing ground for grand theories about 'the rise of the policeman state' and the about the extent to which more general structures of power and discipline were effective in the journey to modernity. In many contexts, and particularly in industrial locations such as the factory, we still know far too little about the nature of the normative orderings and sanctioning systems that actually constituted 'discipline' in this context. Workers showed a remarkable reluctance to keel over in the face of these new disciplinary agendas and we need to know much more about the array of sanctions available, about their depth of penetration, about the policing practices and resources (formal and informal), that supported them, about the modes in which they were subverted or overtly opposed, and about the compromises that emerged from the interplay of imposition and opposition.

The immensely discretionary nature of the practices found in the courts, the problems of defining what 'the law' was, and the complex and often flatly contradictory legal principles which seem to be embodied in the black letter law was the subject of much debate, and considerable criticism, when legal reformers attempted the task of systematising the criminal law in the second quarter of the nineteenth century. Historians have recently debated both the extent to which law was remade on the ground in the eighteenth and nineteenth centuries and (most notably in the heated debate between Bruce Smith and Norma Landau in the *Law and History Review*) the degree to which certain legal structures – including some of the laws related to the woollen industry – undermined (and indeed flatly contradicted) contemporary rhetoric about 'the presumption of innocence'. In the process, they have emphasized once again the vital importance of moving below the jury court records of the quarter sessions and assizes to study the petty sessions records, for this is where the vast majority of cases – including cases involving the appropriation of materials used in the woollen industry – were heard. While historians have rightly emphasized that the law and the summary courts themselves were used by all social groups in the eighteenth and nineteenth centuries this does not mean that, particularly at the more informal level of the justice's parlour or the petty sessions meeting, it could not be use strategically and effectively by employers to control their workers.

Examinations very rarely survive from the summary courts of the eighteenth century but those for the borough of Colchester, which had a large woollen cloth industry until the nineteenth century (when competition for Yorkshire and elsewhere destroyed it) indicate clearly how the law could be used by the clothiers against the weavers and other woollen-industry workers. In late June 1791, for example, the weavers struck for higher wages and large crowds destroyed the looms of those who refused to join them, and then subsequently rescued their leaders after they had been arrested. The clothiers immediately used the magistrates' courts to hit back, mobilizing accusations of receiving embezzled waste against a number of weavers and bringing strategic accusations of failure to complete work on time against others. The imprisonment of these men seems to have greatly weakened the strikers' resolve. By the end of the first week in July they were back at work, but the clothiers continued their attack in the ensuing months, using the summary courts to prosecute a further 10 workers for refusing to complete their work in time. In periods of crisis the Colchester courts were an important source of power for the clothiers even though, unlike the area studied in this volume, there was no specific woollen industry-based police inspectorate available to them.

Professor Peter King
Professor of English Local History
University of Leicester, UK

List of Abbreviations

Journal titles

BSSLH	Bulletin for the Society for the Study of Labour History
TNAPSS	Transactions of the National Association for the Promotion of Social Sciences

Record repositories

MCL	Manchester Central Library
WYAB	West Yorkshire Archives, Bradford Office
WYAC	West Yorkshire Archives, Calderdale Office
WYAL	West Yorkshire Archives, Leeds Office
WYAW	West Yorkshire Archives, Wakefield Office

Frequently cited records

DMB	Directors' Minute Books
PP	Parliamentary Papers
WCAB	Worsted Committee Accounts Book
WCMB	Worsted Committee Minute Book

Bibliographic references

CUP	Cambridge University Press
LUP	Liverpool University Press
MUP	Manchester University Press
OUP	Oxford University Press

1

Introduction

Background: Workplace appropriation in the factory system

Although the view of the nineteenth century as rushing headlong into an industrial 'revolution' with the factory system as its vanguard has been tempered by recent investigations, changes in industrial organization in the mid-nineteenth century undeniably had a profound effect on labour relations, social relationships and wider economic and political structures (Berg and Hudson 1992; Griffin 2012). Yet, one aspect of the relationship between the employers and the employed which was greatly changed by industrialization – the operation and control of workplace appropriation – has been almost entirely ignored by historians.

There have been many publications which have chronicled the rise of the factory system and of the textile factories in particular. Several contemporary studies were published in the nineteenth century, including Bischoff, J. A., *A Comprehensive History of the Woollen and Worsted Manufactories and the Natural and Commercial History of Sheep from the Earliest Records to the Present Period*, 1842; Baines, E. *An Account of the Woollen Manufacture of England*, 1858; James, J., *A History of the Worsted Manufacture in England*, London, 1857, Hodgson, J., *Textile Manufacture and other industries in Keighley*, Keighley, 1879; Ure, A., *The Philosophy of Manufactures, or an Exposition of the Scientific, Moral and Commercial Economy of the Factory System of Great Britain*, 1853 and Dodd, W., *The Factory System Illustrated*, London, 1842. The most comprehensive modern studies include Berg (1985), Jenkins (1975), Gregory (1984), Heaton (1965) and Hudson (1986, 1992).

Few historians, however, have discussed the organization and operation of the mature factory system. Of those that have, Joyce (1980) and Price (1986) have provided two conflicting views of the character of the mature factory system.

Other studies have examined facets of the social effects of the factory system, while pursuing other related subjects (see Jowitt and McIvor 1988; Ittmann 1995; Koditchek 1990; Chapman 1967; Clapham 1910; Firth 1990; Collier 1965). Despite the very detailed information provided by these studies, the focus for most of them has been the cotton rather than woollen factory, and again they tend to concentrate only on the pace of technological change.

There has been a good deal of work on the general disciplinary environment of the factory space (see Pollard 1993; Thompson 1967; Whipp 1987; McClelland 1987; Reid 1986; Roberts 1978; Lazonick 1978; Hopkins 1982; McKendrick 1961; see also contemporary documents which illustrate the development of factory discipline in Finer and Savage 1965; Flinn 1952). Not least, Foucault and those influenced by his work placed the factory as central to the 'disciplinary agenda' along with the clinic, the prison and military organization. However, none of those authors studied any particular factory system in depth (see Foucault 1977; Melossi and Pavarini 1981; Ignatieff 1979, 1983a, 1983b). Edward Thompson's work has enthused, informed and provided the starting point for the research of many social and labour historians. His work on factory discipline and the commoditization of time provides a valuable insight into the attitudes of both employers and labour to the dictates of industrial organization, as does the work of Eric Hobsbawm (1968).

Again though, neither historian has explained how the factory masters attempted to control workplace appropriation, which they saw as one of the major reasons for establishing that productive system, or how the workforce reacted to the new forms of control. Nor have historians explained how either the legislation passed in the eighteenth century or the private industrial police agencies that legislation helped to create were used by nineteenth-century factory employers to control the activities of their workforce.

Yet the taking home of workplace materials by employees was so commonplace as to be considered routine by many thousands of workers, and the gradual criminalization of the practice was a profound mechanism of labour control in the industrial age. It would be impossible to understand labour relations and the part played by criminal law in private spaces, or even what the lives of ordinary working people were like in the factory districts, without researching workplace appropriation.

While there are many studies of workplace appropriation in the pre- and proto-industrial era, together with several twentieth-century studies, notably those by Ditton (1977) and Mars (1983), the nineteenth century is not so well served. The existing studies of low-level minor crime in the mid- to late-nineteenth century contain little research which explores this very prevalent and 'ordinary' offence (Weinberger 1981; Emmerichs 1991). The few studies of workplace 'crime' that do exist, such as those by Davis (1984, 1987, 1989) and (in small measure) by Philips (1977), have been able to explore a number of dimensions of workplace appropriation in particular contexts. Philips has analysed prosecutions for appropriation in the ironworks, mines and workshops of the Victorian Black Country, for example. Jennifer Davis has examined employee appropriation in the London service and non-manufacturing industries. Locker and Godfrey (2006) and Robb (2006) have also explored white-collar frauds in the Victorian period.

However, the ways that the factory context of workplace 'theft' differed in significant terms from other forms of workplace illegalities has received little attention until this present study.

Definition of 'workplace appropriation'

It is first necessary to define what exactly we mean by 'workplace appropriation'. In this book, we use the term to refer to all those acts by which employees converted to their own use materials which they had access to by virtue of their work. Contemporaries rarely used the term, preferring more pejorative terms such as 'fiddling', 'workplace theft' and 'embezzlement'. However, workplace appropriation covered a broad set of activities ranging from simple theft to the exercising of customary rights within a work context. Those who appropriated workplace materials may or may not have considered themselves as indulging in criminal behaviour. The taking of materials, as perquisites or by simple theft, was often governed by rules of behaviour accepted by both employer and employed, although these boundaries may have overlapped for the various actors, and might have shifted according to changing circumstances (Behagg 1990, p. 5; Hobsbawm 1968). It also ranged from occasional minor appropriations of waste to wholesale thievery.

Prior to this study, one of the most discussed examples of workplace appropriation has been the taking of 'chips' (wood offcuts) from the Royal Dockyards. The taking home of wood by workers for their own use was at times condoned, and at times attacked, until the government succeeded in transforming the perquisite into a cash payment in 1801. This transformation was coincident with the introduction of a more regular system of wages payment in some industries. John Rule has pointed out that the system of money wage payments was not fixed or consistent in this period, perquisites and payment in kind existed alongside formal pay rates, and only in the nineteenth century were there efforts to transform the wage 'from a form in which money constituted a substantial part of the wage to one based wholly on it' (Rule 1992).

The lingering on of customary payments in kind in certain industries is evidenced by a case at Sheffield quarter sessions, when a cutler said he had taken some steel 'as part of wages' (Sheffield court, 1841, QS1/179/10, *WYAW*), and others have suggested that the perquisite remained an invisible component of the wage from the eighteenth century up to the present day, see Ditton (1977, p. 86), Mars (1983, p. 152), South and Scraton (1981, pp. 36–43), Henry (1978) and Harding and Jenkins (1989, p. 132).

Together with stricter supervision and police action, this probably did succeed in reducing the amount of material taken from the yards (Emsley 2010, pp. 153–9). There is however little evidence that the bulk of workplace crime was ever conceived as a protest against a new wage discipline and there is similarly scant evidence that customary rights were preferred to the new wages (presumably an estimation by the workforce as to which suited them best was a factor).

Appropriation of this type was not achieved simply by 'taking' raw materials. Emsley, Styles and Rule catalogue a series of out-worker appropriations, including 'bugging' by hatters and shoemakers whereby cheap material bought from carriers was substituted for the more valuable material received from the master, the more valuable material then being converted to the employee's own use (Rule 1992, pp.126–7, 130–3; Styles 1983, p. 204; Linebaugh 1972, pp. 237–41; Emsley 2010, pp. 147–77). Customary rights were also exercised by miners throughout the eighteenth, nineteenth and first half of the twentieth century, and it is likely that, as is the case today, most retailers regularly lost large amounts of stock to employee theft (nearly £700 million of losses was attributed to employee theft in 1993–4, see Speed et al. 1994, and in 2009 approximately 7 per cent of retail theft losses were caused by employees, according to the British Retail Consortium http://www.brc.org.uk/brc_stats_and_facts.asp).

Miners had another method of enhancing their wage rates through appropriation. They were paid by the filled corve, and were known to put large coals at the bottom leaving plenty of hollow spaces, so that when the top was filled with smaller coals it appeared to be full. The deceit was not one-sided, however; employers could weigh the corves and declare the coal load under-weight, which meant that the coal in the corve remained on the surface, and the miner remained unpaid for his labour. It would be surprising, under that system, if employers did not weigh the corves with one eye on the scales and the other on their profits (see Rule 1986, pp.127–8, Philips 1977, pp. 182–4). From these examples it is easy to conclude that most industries saw some form of appropriation of finished goods and/or raw materials.

The scale of workplace appropriation was 'rife' and of almost 'epidemic' proportions in the manufacturing industries of the nineteenth century (Randall 1990–2, p. 193; Soderlund 1993). Watchmen in factories, ironworks and other manufacturing concerns, whose job required them to apprehend 'embezzlers', admitted that they missed hundreds of workplace thefts for every one that they detected (Jones 1992, p. 124). In the textile districts, people complained that the problem was out of control:

> In the town and neighbourhood whence I write, the principal employment of the labouring classes is that of weaving, in which misery and vice abounds to a greater extent than among any other class of operatives, but one of its demoralizing effects is seen in the training of weavers from their earliest childhood through all their subsequent career, in the various practices of embezzling the raw material . . . Their dealings in embezzlement, in every variety of form, destructive alike to the morals of the operative and the property of the respectable manufacturer, were never more rife than at present, and considerable activity is being shown in detecting offenders, making seizures, etc. (*Justice of the Peace* 1843, p. 1243)

Some forty years later, James Naylor was convicted of inciting textile workers to steal from their employers. The factory lost about £500-worth of goods in six months (a considerable sum in 1883). Over a similar period, Thomas Monkhouse appropriated over £100-worth of waste, and in January 1885, a systematic robbery of goods was discovered to have been going on for seven years at one factory, causing huge losses (WCMB 56D.88/1/6, June 1881, January 1885). The list continues: a woolsorter appropriated 2,000lbs of wool in 1857; 1,000 fleeces were taken by a warehouseman; 500lbs of woollen waste were taken by a weaver in 1859; a twenty-three-year-old took 200lbs of shoddy in 1862 and the same amount of wool was appropriated by a warehouseman in 1880; in yet another case, a spinner was found guilty of illegally appropriating materials worth £260 in 1885 (*Bradford Observer* 8 October 1857; *Huddersfield Chronicle*

7 January 1859; WCMB 11 December 1862, June 1880 and 28 September 1885). For an explanation of specialist technical terms referred to within this book, see *Glossary*.

In Manchester, only sixty workplace thefts were indicted at the major courts per year between 1840 and 1855, but Philips' work suggests that, if summary data had been available for Manchester, those figures would be massively inflated (Philips 1977).The only surviving records of summary convictions in Manchester for the early-nineteenth century suggest that textile labour offences formed the majority of cases heard by magistrates (*Manchester Prison Calendars, Lancashire Records Office, QSB/1 379–447).*

For example, in the Black Country, by the mid-1850s, more than 500 'industrial thefts' a year were prosecuted. Between 1856 and 1860, an average of 479 workplace appropriators a year were convicted. Philips also states that there were at least 4,617 cases of 'industrial theft' prosecuted between 1840 and 1860 (Philips 1977, p. 190). Jennifer Davis' work on London also indicates that appropriations by employees were the most common form of theft brought to the magistrates' courts in the mid-Victorian period (Davis 1987, p. 401). Thus, it seems from this evidence, that, as was the case in the eighteenth century, the greatest possibility of a working person indulging in a criminal act was by the appropriation of raw materials or finished goods from their place of employment. The appropriation of work materials, in terms of the number of participants (although not necessarily in terms of numbers of prosecutions) may have constituted one of the largest categories of crime in the eighteenth and nineteenth centuries (Davis 1984). The classic age of the factory, with its new technologies of surveillance – the internal factory supervisory structure and the development of formal policing agencies – appears to have been steeped in eighteenth-century cultures of workplace appropriation.

Workplace appropriation – the historiographical debate

How far did the authority of the law permeate what was essentially a 'private' space – the factory environment? Second, to what extent was the law 'shut outside' the factory, and replaced by unofficial norms? Since the regular enforcers of the law (the borough or county police forces) were absent from factory interiors, did the employers rely on private forms of policing or new forms of organizational control? Parliamentary legislation, case law and unofficial factory regulations do not visit their power upon the guilty without the aid of human agencies. How did formal and informal methods of policing and punishment work together within the complex inter-relationships of competing norms inside the factory?

Two alternative conceptual frameworks have been constructed to explain the pervasiveness of both the ideology and operation of the law. The first suggests that the authority of the law made uneven, gradual but effective progress throughout the last two hundred years in impressing its codes of legitimacy upon increasing numbers of people in every sphere of public and private life (Gatrell 1992), a progression which extended from the streets to the factories (with the enforcement of factory legislation) and has now entered into individual homes (in attempting to combat domestic violence, for example).

Alternatively, in the second framework it is argued that the forms, codes and powers of the law were limited, enhanced or otherwise altered when they met new spheres of legitimacy (Allott 1980, pp. 16–26), such as the norms of the domestic household or internal orderings which governed the factory environment. This seems the more reasonable supposition since the operation of the law was, and is, undoubtedly different in quality depending on the social, political and practical contexts within which it acts.

A second site of historical debate is the location of the workplace offender within a criminal typology (For an overview of this debate, see Emsley 2010; Davis 1987; Taylor 2010; Stevenson 1986). It may be that employees' notions of customary or other rights normalized appropriation, so it was not seen by them as illegal or immoral. Conversely, it is possible that inequalities in the wage structure, exacerbated by economic downturns, provoked workers into periodically committing illegal acts which they knew and accepted as illegal, but which they legitimized to themselves because of the poverty they suffered. Crudely expressed, the question is whether the factory worker appropriated primarily through need and/or opportunity?

The administration of justice provides a third broad area of interest. Several historians have suggested that the administration of the law could be controlled in the interests of powerful local elite groups (see Hay 1983; Steinmetz 2000; Woods 1982). Since the mill owners were one of the strongest industrial power groups in England, this volume examines the extent of their participation on the local benches, and the decisions taken in court by these magistrates when trying workplace illegalities. Some have attempted to contextualize these questions by juxtaposing modern and historical studies of fraud, white-collar and corporate crime (Karstedt et al. 2006; in particular see, in that volume, essays by Locker and Godfrey; Robb; Wilson).

Rationale

In this book, by concentrating on workplace appropriation within the worsted industry from the late-eighteenth century to the mid-twentieth, we attempt to answer four central questions:

First, did workplace appropriation, which was widespread in the eighteenth-century domestic industries, continue at the same level in the nineteenth-century factory system, where a more disciplined environment existed?

Second, what form did appropriation take, and which groups within the factory exercised opportunities to take home workplace materials?

Third, how was appropriation controlled by both internal and external agencies, and what legal and organizational weapons were used against workplace appropriators?

Fourth, how did private policing such as that practised by the Worsted Inspectorate develop generally in the eighteenth and nineteenth centuries, and what was its relationship with public policing forms such as the Parish Watch and the New Police?

The answers to these four questions overlap somewhat of course, but they together contribute to several important historical debates about crime and authority in the industrial age.

Before concluding, the book also addresses one further broad area of historical enquiry, investigating the impetus towards organizing workers within large, heavily supervised and policed, centralized production areas (see the interesting debate between Marglin 1976, 1984; Landes 1986; Berg 1984; and also Dandeker 1990; Lyon 1994 and Dickson 1981) and whether the control of workplace theft underlay that movement to the centralized factory? Our last question is one which would have been of great interest to nineteenth century factory owners and employees alike – did the factory actually help to control appropriation or simply provide a different context for workplace theft? This is a deceptively simple question which spawns an interesting and complex set of answers.

The worsted acts and workplace appropriation

The worsted industry of northern England was chosen as the subject of our detailed enquiry for a number of reasons. First, the industry was one of the most important in the development of industrialization and the factory system; textile manufacture was in the vanguard of the change from a proto-industrial, home-based underpinning of the English economy to a full-blown factory-based regime in which every aspect of workers' lives could (at least theoretically) be regulated and controlled by the employer. Secondly, it was a huge employer of both men and women; throughout the period under discussion, many tens of thousands of people passed through the numerous mill gates, and consequently a great deal of contemporary interest and concern was generated about the industry. Much of this documentation is still extant and as such, the worsted industry is one of the best documented in England. This wealth of primary sources has proved to be invaluable in our study (see *Bibliography* for a full list of sources).

Although a number of anti-appropriation acts were passed in the eighteenth century, just three acts, one passed in 1749 (22 Geo.II c.27) and two in 1777 (17 Geo.III c.11 and 17 Geo.III c.56) – collectively known as The Worsted Acts – changed the *character* of the fight against workplace appropriation. Moreover, the 1749 Act has been seen as the *key* moment when the English criminal law announced its presence in the sphere of industrial relations, when breaches of trust were considered as equally deserving of carceral forms of punishment as were felonies (Stephen 1890, pp. 150–1; Ashton 1955, p. 210; Wadsworth and Mann 1931, p. 396). From 1749, the law acted against the 'theft' of manufactured goods, or goods in the process of being manufactured, whether they were taken from the street directly outside the factory, from the warehouse or from inside the premises where the goods were made. Workers were essentially subject to the same laws of larceny inside the workplace as they were on the streets.

Thompson never addressed the effect of the 1777 Worsted Acts. Nevertheless, he was correct in identifying the 1749 Act as paving the way for all such further acts which criminalized appropriation from the workplace: 'What was now to be punished was not an offence between men . . . but an offence against property' (Thompson 1975, p. 207). Styles doubts the dramatic nature of this change, stating that there 'never was a once-and-for-all transition at law from restitution to punishment' (Styles 1983, p. 191). He is correct to reason that few convicted embezzlers would have been able to pay the compensation demanded by the acts of 1703, 1726 and 1740. The offenders, in default of payment, therefore tumbled into gaol long before the 1749 Act. However, the 1749 Act did alter the relationship between working people and the law in at least two key areas:

First, it extended the scope of legal action against employees by allowing the prosecution of domestic workers who had failed to return the materials given out to them within twenty-one days, later reduced to eight days by 17 Geo.III c.56 (1777). The Act was designed to enable the prosecution of those workers who were believed to have sold the materials entrusted to them to other parties, where no real evidence existed other than the absence of the material itself, but it also struck hard at those workers who had pawned materials but who could not afford to redeem them.

Second, the Act extended the power of surveillance into hitherto private areas. It permitted the houses and outbuildings of suspects to be searched by a policeman, accompanied by other interested parties. Of course, the issuing of a search warrant had previously allowed law agencies to enter and search a suspect's house, but now the victim or their agent was allowed to accompany the legal officers. Any suspicious goods that were found were confiscated by the authorities and could then be claimed by the owner. Alternatively, proof of purchase could be given by the accused within twenty-one days. If, however, the goods remained unclaimed by any party which could prove ownership, the goods were publicly sold, the profits going to the parish.

The acts passed in the mid-eighteenth century generally increased the penalties for workplace appropriation (although the 1774 Act reduced the punishment for short-reeling to a small fine) and strengthened the manufacturers' grip over the domestic productive process. The Worsted Acts passed in 1777 continued this process by further increasing the punishments for workplace appropriation, but they also refined the techniques of prosecuting the law in significant ways. To briefly summarize the clauses of the Worsted Acts, by 1777 the law forbade the embezzling of worsted waste or finished cloth, or the selling and/or buying of the same. It also made it illegal for workers to take a job in a false name, to be employed by more than one master, to wilfully damage their work, to leave their work uncompleted for eight days or to be found carrying suspicious goods after sunset.

Most importantly, 17 Geo.III c.11 (1777) also established an employer-organized policing and prosecution agency financed in its operations by Yorkshire, Cheshire and Lancashire manufacturers from the rebate which they received relative to the amount of duty they had paid on soap used in the manufacturing process (from 1712, a heavy tax on soap had been introduced, continuing in various guises until 1853, and worsted manufacturers were able to claim a rebate on at least some of this tax).

The Worsted Inspectorate

This policing and prosecution agency took the form of a number of paid Worsted Inspectors employed directly by the Worsted Committee to investigate, detect and prosecute any infringements of the anti-appropriation laws, and allowed the houses of anyone suspected of purloining goods to be searched by the Inspectors unaided by police officers. If any of the materials found could not be accounted for to the satisfaction of the Inspector (no matter how small the amount), the suspect could be seized and taken to the magistrate who had granted the search warrant. Then, if the material's owner or the Worsted Inspector wished it, the suspect could be tried by two magistrates at petty sessions, such as those regularly held in the textile districts of Bradford, Halifax, Leeds, Huddersfield, Keighley, Bingley, Skipton and Otley.

Indeed, it seems that workplace appropriation suspects passed almost daily through these courts – for example, Wakefield House of Correction received appropriators on 6, 7, 8, 10, 13, 17, 26, 27, 29 and 30 December in 1842 (General Reception Book, Wakefield House of Correction, October 1842 – April 1843 *WYAW*, C118/99). If the suspect again failed to provide proof of ownership, either with a receipt or a witness to the purchase, the magistrates were required by 17 Geo.III c.56 (1777) to punish the suspect with a £20 fine or a month in gaol in default. Although these laws were felt to be sufficient for the legal control of workplace 'theft', there were other laws which, although not designed for this purpose, could also be applied to appropriators.

Structure

Chapter 2 outlines the legal background to the various attempts to stem workplace appropriation, examining whether legislation aimed at eighteenth-century domestic workers was also applicable to the nineteenth-century factory worker.

In Chapter 3, we look at the background to workplace appropriation, including the reasons why so many individuals took the risk of carrying out such crimes, the varied methods utilized in the taking of employers' property, who was involved in such appropriation and what was taken.

Chapter 4 examines to what extent rules, the disciplinary culture of the workplace environment, and the nature of authority in the factory, were used to control appropriation. Two key issues will be addressed. How and in what circumstances was factory authority exercised and did it have a legal foundation, who were the agents that administered discipline within the factory and how successful were they in controlling appropriation?

In Chapter 5, the growth and functioning of the Worsted Inspectorate is contextualized by placing it within the wider field of police history within the past two centuries. It is compared and contrasted to the numerous other forms of private policing that emerged from the late-eighteenth century onwards. The methods employed by both the Worsted Committee and its Inspectorate are then examined in detail, together with a debate concerning public versus private policing.

Chapter 6 investigates the changing relationship between the Worsted Committee and its Inspectorate with the emergent public police forces. From the 1830s onwards, the growth of county and borough police forces, maintained and paid for by public rates, resulted in a change of emphasis of policing and had concomitant effects on the work of the Worsted Inspectorate. The response of the Worsted Committee to these developments is discussed in detail.

In Chapter 7, we examine the structure behind the punishment of workplace appropriation offences, including problems of perceived judicial bias/impartiality and the ways in which offenders were sentenced.

Chapter 8 discusses the social meaning of workplace appropriation and the Worsted Acts within the wider criminological debate concerning changing notions of customary right, morality and control in the factory system, the interaction between private and public forms of control, the changing relationship between law and capitalism and industrial change and the disciplining of working people.

Chapter 9 provides a conclusion in which we summarize our findings and reflect upon the four main questions, which we set out to address in our study of workplace appropriation and policing of the factory system.

2

Customary 'Rights' and Workplace 'Theft'

Workplace appropriation and the law

In the woollen and worsted industries, appropriation had a well-established tradition and history. Clothiers frequently complained that the trade in 'slinge' (as embezzled wool was known in the West of England) constituted a major threat to their income. If the evidence given to the 1774 Parliamentary Committee is correct, then illegal perquisites added approximately 20 per cent to the wages of Gloucestershire spinners and weavers (Styles 1983, p. 181). Some of the most prevalent forms of appropriation used in the West Country were what might be termed 'offences of weight': wetting the cloth with water or oil so that it weighed heavier on the scales (estimated to cost the clothier four shillings per pound), suspending the wool over steam so that it weighed heavier (thereby embezzling one pound in every twelve) or filling the cloth by rubbing it with chalk. These short-weight offences were fairly easy to detect, although finding the evidence to prove the offence was more difficult. Short-reeling was more likely to escape detection, since it was usually more trouble than it was worth to unravel all suspicious reels. Consequently, it was claimed in 1776 that worsted yarn in Yorkshire was reeled on average 6.5 per cent short (Styles 1983, p. 177).

Short-reeling was acknowledged as an illegal activity by employers and workers alike. Other retentions by workers however were asserted to be part of the semi-legitimate and secretive world of customary perquisites. Weavers, for example, were used to keeping 'thrums', those ends of warp thread left on the loom after the finished cloth had been removed, just as other workers retained flock and fluff. To try and stop the excessive waste which masters claimed was made in order to increase the number of thrums, groups of Yorkshire manufacturers advertised the penalties for the retention of waste in 1764, 1765, 1770, 1812 and 1819 respectively, but the right to keep these scraps of cloth was fiercely defended. Collective protests at the imposition of penalties against those convicted of workplace appropriation occurred at Manchester in 1750, at Norwich in 1753 and at Stockport in 1772, and there was a bitter weavers' strike in 1758 which followed the Colchester clothiers' demands for the return of waste (Philips 1977, p. 285).

The creation of waste was an inevitable consequence of most manufacturing processes. In some industries, such as textiles, the waste could be valuable, although often it consisted merely of scraps. The property rights to the waste products often rested on unspoken customary agreements between employers and employed, with periodic redrawing of the boundaries. These customs were sometimes spoken of in court by the accused as explanation for their behaviour, for, as outlined in P. B. Bicknell's *The New Police Manual*, the prosecution had to prove that the accused meant to commit the theft, thereby demonstrating 'felonious intent'. In other words, the goods must have been taken without any claim or right, for if they were taken by mistake, or under a *bona fide* claim of right, though unfounded, it would not be a felony (Bicknell 1877, p. 43). If the waste product itself acquired value, as it did in the textile trade with the growth of the recovered wool industry in the latter half of the nineteenth century, then the redrawing of the customary line usually became final, and in favour of the employers.

Often after periods of labour unrest provoked by the employer's attempt to prosecute appropriators, masters tried less confrontational methods, such as offering to 'buy out' thrums by increasing the piece-rate by a sum they considered a fair equivalent to the value of the appropriated materials. These attempts to standardize the form of wage payments were then either accepted or rejected by the workforce. Of course, the workers could simply accept the perquisite buy-out, without curtailing their appropriative habits. Certainly the appropriation and utilization of workplace materials was considerable and became a normal part of many working people's lives in the eighteenth century.

How did textile employers combat these losses? Soderlund (1992), Linebaugh (1972) and Hobsbawm (1968) have all asserted that both the eighteenth and nineteenth centuries saw the employers attempt to criminalize customary rights within the workplace, while other historians have argued that a parallel process was also occurring in the countryside. Linebaugh and others (Bushaway 1982; King 1989) place the large body of eighteenth-century legislation against workplace frauds within the context of what they believe was a defining character of eighteenth-century criminal law – the transformation of a large number of infractions that had previously been violations of trust or corporate obligation into criminal offences against property. This view is typified in the work of Rusche and Kirchheimer (1939), Snyder and Hay (1987), and Hay, who wrote that:

> The custom of . . . payment in perquisites, either part of the product or raw materials, became the subject of extensive penal legislation. Employers did not always want to eliminate perks: allowing such appropriation by employees could be a way of escaping employers' wage-fixing agreements in times of labour shortage, and also a way of avoiding monetary wage payment during downturns in the trade cycle. At such times both capital and labour tacitly agreed on the custom, within limits, of taking perks. But those limits were always contested, and in the long term, with expanding inventories, larger workforces, and a sharpening interest in accurate book-keeping, employers requested, and received, criminal legislation that designated such appropriation as theft. (Hay 1975, p. 5)

There have been many attempts by parliament to legislate the appropriation of work materials out of existence, the first dating from the early seventeenth century. For example, James I made it criminal for any person in the wool industry to 'imbezil any wool or yarn delivered to him to be wrought.' (7 Jac. 1 c.7). It was the eighteenth century, however, which not only witnessed a general growth in criminal legislation, particularly against property offences, but also a plethora of anti-embezzlement laws (Hall 1952, pp. 34–58). In the eighteenth century, fifteen acts were passed which were designed to outlaw workplace appropriation and related practices in many industries. Many of these acts merely extended protection to manufacturers who were not covered by the existing anti-appropriation legislation. Shoemaking and watchmaking, for example, were brought into line with the already protected textile industries. 9 Geo. I c.27 (1722) extended protection to shoemakers that 1 Anne s.2 c.28 (1703) had extended to textile and iron masters; similarly 27 Geo. II c.7 (1754) extended the protection to clock and watchmakers that 13 Geo. II. c8 (1740) and Geo. II. c.27 (1749) had afforded textile producers.

It must be noted that the passing of these anti-appropriation laws did not necessarily imply a deluge of workplace criminality, but does, as John Styles notes, reflect the growing influence of manufacturers over the legislative process. Many acts were private bills proposed or campaigned for by manufacturers, see Styles (1983, pp. 188–200), and also Wadsworth and Mann (1931, pp. 396). Similarly, in continental Europe, when manufacturers exercised power in parliament, legislation favourable to them was enacted, as well as court decisions going in their favour, see Hanagan (1989); also Gruttner (1982).

In 1820, persons who privately and feloniously stole goods or wares valued between 5 shillings and £15 from a warehouse could be convicted at quarter sessions and transported for from seven years to life, or imprisoned for up to seven years with or without hard labour (under 1 Geo.IV c.117). Seven years later, legislation introduced by Home Secretary Robert Peel stated:

> That if any person shall steal, to the value of 10 shillings, any Goods or Article of Silk, Woollen, Linen or Cotton, or of any one or more of these Materials . . . whilst laid, placed, or exposed, during any Stage, Process or Progress of Manufacture, in any Building, Field, or other Place, every such Offender, being convicted thereof, shall be liable to any of the Punishments which the Court may award (7 & 8 Geo.IV c.27).

The case of R. v. Woodhead (1 MOO & R.549) established that goods may be still in 'process or progress of manufacture though the texture be complete, if they be not brought into a condition of sale'.

Another law, brought in by Gladstone in 1843, appeared to further secure manufacturers' property. The act may have been intended to reassure textile masters, who had found that workplace appropriation had not been eradicated by factory style organization, that the government shared their concerns. However, as *Justice of the Peace* (7,1843) observed, 'the new provisions in the Bill condense and re-enact nearly all the enactments in the acts proposed to be repealed', and, although the editor of the journal did go on to commend the utility and sentiment of the legislation, it scarcely altered the legal landscape. When the manufacturers cried for legal aid in their war against appropriation, it was not new acts they desired but the full and regular implementation of the existing legislation, a view concordant with that of the magistrates. When, in the mid-century, a Bradford magistrate stated that 'the evil has risen to such a great extent that the provisions of the Act will be carried out to the full effect in every case', he surely spoke both for the magistrates and also for the manufacturers (*Bradford Observer* 26 November 1840).

The 1820, 1827 and 1843 Acts could all have been used to enmesh appropriators. Nevertheless, it seems that these Acts lay mostly redundant as far as workplace appropriation was concerned. It appears that the vast majority of cases prosecuted by the Committee were taken to petty sessions under the Worsted Acts. Critically, after the decision to prosecute had been taken, some calculation was made as to which act was best to proceed under. Felony prosecutions at quarter sessions may have ensured a 'stiffer' penalty for the guilty, but it also introduced the uncertainty of jury trials, whereas summary proceedings at the petty sessions offered a greater hope of conviction. The choice of which act to prosecute cases under, and therefore the type of court that heard the case, also rested to a great extent on the evidence offered.

For example, if the cloth found in a suspect's possession was anonymous, with no markings which directly linked it to the suspect's employers, then it would be more difficult to gain a conviction for larceny at quarter sessions. The same evidence would almost guarantee conviction under the Worsted Acts applied in a magistrates' court. However, if the evidence was strong enough, and there was a need to force an exemplary trial, the aggrieved victim would launch a felony prosecution. This level of ability to control which court heard a prosecutor's case was unusual in the English legal system. It was not possible for most victims of crime to decide whether a major or a minor court would hear their case, and this system placed a good deal of power in the hands of the textile masters.

So, although the acts passed between 1820 and 1843 could have been used extensively against workplace appropriation, in reality the Worsted Acts remained the preferred route for such prosecutions throughout the nineteenth century. A full count of all the quarter sessions depositions relating to workplace appropriation between 1840 and 1875 reveals that only about 5 per cent of such cases were tried as felonies. The other 95 per cent were brought under the Worsted Acts. Approximately 5 per cent of quarter sessions depositions do not survive for the 1840–75 period. However, it appears that only 4.7 per cent (98 cases) of workplace appropriation were dealt with at quarter sessions. The remaining 1857 cases were dealt with at summary courts under the Worsted Acts.

Criminal or civil legislation?

Is it possible that civil legislation, or master and servant laws were used as an alternative or as a supplement to the criminal code? The 1823 Master and Servant Act (4 Geo.IV c.9) had made it illegal for a worker to break his or her contract, and the 1867 Act (30 & 31 Vict. c.141) increased the penalty for 'Misconduct or Misdemeanour' within the factory to three months' hard labour. The enforcement of contractual obligation may have extended to infractions of the factory rules, which might have made it possible to prosecute appropriators. Certainly master and servant laws were regularly used. Between 1858 and 1867 there were on average '9,000 prosecutions a year and 5,800 convictions and in the peak year of 1872 there were 17,082 prosecutions and 10,359 convictions'

(PP Judicial Statistics, 1858–1875), see also Woods (1982); how many were appropriators?

West Riding master and servant records are not sufficiently detailed to determine whether appropriators were dealt with in this way, but the evidence from newspapers suggests that master and servant cases were mostly brought against those who left their work without giving the agreed period of notice. Master and servant legislation may have offered a way of prosecuting groups who were seemingly immune to criminal legislation, such as women, and it may have been the legal entity which enforced contractual agreement, but there is little evidence that a significant proportion of appropriators were dealt with under its clauses:

> The offence of embezzlement is one which seems to be the most frequently before the courts in one shape or another, and the variety of circumstances under which it is committed leads to endless niceties. And as this offence is constantly appearing at sessions to perplex the justices, it is well always to keep one's memory well posted up with the latest contributions from the Court of Crown Cases Reserved. Even by the third-quarter of the century, matters had not improved as the editorial suggests (*Justice of the Peace*, 7, 35, 1871).

Problems of interpretation

The justices' confusion over the application of legislation stemmed from a number of sources. The first of these was caused by the ambiguous terminology of both common-law doctrines and anti-appropriation legislation. For example, the anti-appropriation laws could only be applied to 'servants' and not 'agents' of the employer. This distinction, which prompted many discussions in court as to the contractual status of the accused, was meant to separate those employees who acted under the direct supervision of the employer, from those who had some autonomy. In the second of these categories were the textile agents who toured the region on their employer's behalf, often collecting money from clients or showing them samples of wares. Since these samples of material had been freely given over to the agents, they were able to successfully claim that the employer had given over the constructive possession of the materials, and that any appropriation of such goods must be considered a breach of contractual obligation rather than a criminal act (see *Justice of the Peace*, 7, 35, 1871; Philips 1977, p. 223). This was an important distinction for the judicial authorities to make, as the accused had to merely disprove the alleged work relationship between themselves and their employer to instigate a new trial, with all of the expense and delay that involved. However, greater confusion lay with the application of the possessory immunity doctrine to both domestic and factory workers. In essence, the question was whether the goods given to employees to work on were still in the possession of the employer, or whether possession had been freely given to the employee?

Hall's work suggests that 'out-worker embezzlement scarcely ever reached a trial on indictment at Quarter Sessions because the out-worker came into possession of the materials with their owner's consent as a necessary part of fulfilling the work contract' (Hall 1952, p. 37). Hall thus asserts that the criminal code could not be applied to contractual wrangles, and that the appropriation of goods entrusted to the factory worker, who was an employee of the victim, must be treated as private and civil 'breaches of trust' (Hall 1952, p. 37). After all, what public harm was perpetrated by embezzlers, and what public good served by their criminal prosecution?

However, Hall's arguments do not hold true for the West Riding in two respects. First, civil legislation provided the means to pursue embezzlers, but so did the criminal code. For example, hundreds of domestic spinners and weavers were routinely prosecuted every year. Between 1777 and 1786, prosecutions averaged over six hundred per year, and between 1844 and 1876 over six hundred workers were prosecuted for 'embezzling' materials, or having illegal possession of worsted goods (see Memorandum of Summary Convictions, 1777–86, *WYAW*, QE15/1–29; Cheshire Quarter Sessions, *CRO* QJF212–215; An Account of Frauds and Offences, 1778–83, *MCL*, ms.338.4 w.1; *LM*, and *LIYP*, 1777–1886; WCR, *WYAB*, 56D.88/1/2–3).

Second, Hall asserts that workers who had been entrusted with materials could not be prosecuted since they had, albeit temporarily, been given possession of the goods. However, the Worsted Acts cut across possessory immunity clauses. It is clear that the West Riding benches acted as though the employers had not relinquished constructive possession, and that as soon as the employees acted to appropriate the goods they were legally culpable. By doing this, the magistrates acted in accordance with the common law doctrine of 'forcible taking' or *vit et armis*. It seems that magistrates considered the property within the factory to be at risk of being taken by stealth, and that the employer had a reasonable right to claim protection from the courts, even to the extent that goods could be said to have been appropriated when they had not even left the factory (see Baker 1979, p. 433). Hall also contends that the eighteenth-century embezzlement laws narrowed the notional conception of a breach of trust, while expanding the possession of the master to include all properties distributed to others for the purpose of manufacture (see Hall 1952, p. 37; Styles 1983, p. 188; Pritchard 1875, p. 420). For example, James Cain, a doffer at James Haley's worsted mill at Bradford, had been employed for three days when he was seen hiding some brass parts under old machine drive bands in a corner of the factory. When he went for dinner his bag was searched and 14lbs of brass was found by the overlooker. A constable was called and, after being questioned at his work-desk, Cain was searched. When more brass pieces were found in his pocket he was arrested, and later imprisoned for one month, although the brass had never left the room (27 July, Leeds Quarter Sessions, 1844, *WYAW* QS1/183/14). At other times, the magistrates would not entertain rather similar cases. For example, Rebecca Petts, aged 17, and employed by Thomas Willet and Co., 'was charged with having collected together a quantity of worsted waste with the intention of taking it away from the premises. The Inspector proved finding the waste, tied up in a handkerchief belonging to the prisoner; but as it had not been removed from the premises, the magistrate considered there was not a case to convict upon – she was discharged with an admonition.' (*Bradford Observer* 28 January 1841).

The conundrum of whether goods inside the factory, which had been freely given over to the employees to work on, could be said to have really been appropriated grows more complicated when one also considers the common law doctrines of 'taking' and 'carrying away'. For a conviction to be made, the accused had to have both 'taken and carried away' the goods. These rather vague requirements proved problematic for the courts when trying workplace appropriation. To 'carry away', there had to be an actual severance, a complete removal of the goods by the offender from the place they occupied, 'though the time of possession, be it instantaneous only, and the extent of dislocation so as it is complete, are of no import'(see Burn 1837, pp. 627–34). For example, if an employee cut a piece of cloth with the intent to steal a part of it, and it fell to the ground, but the employee did not pick it up, there was no 'taking', and consequently, no felony (*Justice of the Peace*, 7,28, 1867). But if the weaver, spinner or whoever picked it up and put it in their pocket, and had it in their possession even for a moment, the offence was complete. This was the case because the second clause of the larceny statutes was fulfilled: the appropriator had 'carried' away the goods. The contemporary journal *Justice of the Peace* saw 'carrying' as an inevitable consequence of the process of 'taking', and gave the following example to illustrate the point:

> Where a quantity of linen cloth was packed up in a wrapper, in the form of a long square, and laid length-wise in a waggon, and the prisoner set up the long square on one end in the waggon, in order more conveniently to get at the linen, and cut the wrapper all the way down for that purpose, that this was no removal, and therefore no felony (see Williams, 1794–5, pp. 361–72; see also Burn 1837, pp. 613–41).

However, if the material was notionally the property of the employer at all times, and in all areas of the premises of the employer, at which stage was the material 'carried away'? For if one takes the factory to be no more than the wagon enlarged, the goods stolen from the factory would have to be completely removed from the premises and not merely secreted on the person within the factory. Hence, perhaps, the introduction of perimeter fencing, walls, gatehouses and counting houses, a phenomenon discussed in Chapter 6. The moment the offender stepped outside the physical boundaries of the factory with any workplace material would appear to be the moment the felony was committed. However, as was previously stated in the discussion of 'possession', many appropriators were also stopped inside the factory.

Lastly, there was the problem of 'larceny by finding'. In nineteenth-century English criminal law, in respect of most cases of theft, the mere possession of stolen goods was not sufficient to guarantee conviction. Even if proof of ownership could not be provided by the accused, the prosecution would need to find the 'real' owner. If that was not possible, circumstantial evidence would be considered – the place of apprehension, the accused's explanation of their actions, the nature of the 'stolen' property and so forth. It appears that the quality of circumstantial evidence could place the accused in the clear or deep in trouble. The *Justice of the Peace* twice explained this point:

> 1) If a party finds goods which have the appearance of being lost, without having at the time ready means of knowing to whom they belong, his taking and converting them to his own use will not amount to a larceny; but if, on the other hand, the party so finding the goods know to whom they belong, and without making any effort to restore them to the rightful owner, deal with them in such a manner as to show that he intends to withhold them from the proprietor, and apply them to his own purposes, he will then be guilty of the offence of larceny. (*Justice of the Peace*, 1843)

> 2) The broad distinction under such circumstances is, that if he really believes at the time of taking possession of the goods that the real owner cannot be found he is not guilty of larceny; but if he takes them with the intent to appropriate them to his own use, reasonably believing that the owner could be found, that would amount to larceny. This species of defence in answer to a charge is always open to considerable suspicion, and it would be best supported by showing that the accused had made no secret of his possession of the property, or that he had used every exertion to discover the owner.
>
> *Justice of the Peace*, 1864

The accused, therefore, needed merely to prove that he had attempted to find the true owner of any goods he had found, to be innocent. If the goods were labelled or marked in some way, then the accused's failure to find the true owner could be held to be suspicious. Both defending and prosecuting advocates would then rely on their interpretation of circumstantial evidence being accepted by the court. This has obvious implications for workplace appropriation. It has been suggested that the basic characteristic of most goods appropriated from employers was their anonymity, and whether the materials be coal, grain or cloth, the necessary proof of ownership was deficient. Sweeney ignores the practice of stamping and marking goods, although they were crucial to the prosecution's case (see Sweeney 1985). The stamping and marking of finished cloth went some way towards establishing ownership, but the majority of stolen goods were unmarked, and 'anonymous', or were made that way by offenders cutting off identifying marks (which was made punishable with one month's imprisonment in 1774 under 14 Geo. III c.25, s.1). Similarly, employers in other industries took care to mark their goods in some way that is the stamping of initials on items of cutlery. If ownership could not be established, the prosecution's case was severely weakened, especially if the circumstantial evidence was also weak. The Worsted Acts, however, in direct opposition to generally held legal principles, placed the onus of proving ownership on the accused.

Those charged under the Worsted Acts had to account for any material on their person, and failure to do so rendered them open to prosecution and conviction. The appropriator who could claim they had found the material outside the factory was at an advantage (if only a slight one) over those who were caught inside the factory with workplace materials, since it weakened the circumstantial evidence of the case. Accordingly, the hiding of goods for a later collection by the accused or their accomplice became a *modus operandi* of the embezzler (*WYAW* QS1/191/15, 17 September 1852). Police occurrence books also reflect the frequency of goods being 'found'. Police Officer Gammell in one case received information from Mr James Key, Independent Minister of Batley:

> That he found on the top of his Ash Pit Wall on Sunday morning . . . four Knots of Red, four Knots of Black, two of Green and two Knots of Mauve Berling Wool wrapped in a parcel all of which I took possession of.
>
> (Batley Constabulary Occurrence Book 21 December 1875; see also entries for 11 November 1873; 25 November 1873; 24 March 1874; *WYAW* A229/79)

It seems likely that these were left by someone to be picked up at a later occasion. Thomas Fowler, an engine-tenter, was one man who might have wished he had also been denied the opportunity of 'finding' some goods. He was seen in the early evening on a piece of waste ground near the factory where he worked. Previously, four brass pieces had been found buried there by a man while out rabbiting. After Fowler had picked up the brasses, he was apprehended, questioned, searched and arrested, despite his protestation that he had found the brasses and intended to inform 'somebody'. Later the brasses were found to be part of a set of twenty-two made for a particular job and stolen from a shelf in Fowler's place of work. (*WYAW* Bradford QS, 29 Sept 1845).

The claim that stolen goods had merely been found by the accused was, of course, not exclusive to workplace appropriation cases, but, before the Worsted Acts, appropriators asserting this defence were aided by the anonymity of the goods they took. The Worsted Acts cut away that help to a very great extent by forcing the accused to account for any goods in their possession or in their homes. Workers in the courtroom who had previously been protected by a common law defence were now forced to depend on the skill of their advocate in the unlikely event that they had one, and the sympathy of magistrates.

Conclusion

If these matters appear problematic to the modern historian, were they more easily understood by nineteenth-century magistrates and prosecutors? Philips suggests they were, and that the factory system simplified matters for the courts, because the question of the ownership of raw materials was now coincident with the possession of them. 'Once all the material was worked up within the factory or workshop', Philips asserts, 'this legal confusion disappeared.

As larceny prosecutions were becoming much more common and easier to bring, employers naturally prosecuted for larceny in these cases' (Phillips 1977, pp. 224–5). However, the confusion remained. The *Reports of the Criminal Law Commissioners* from 1833 to 1843 (supported by the magistracy which had actively campaigned for all larceny cases to be tried summarily since the 1830s) suggested that the offence of embezzlement be submerged, alongside other species of larceny, into one general law in order to simplify affairs (see also Hostettler 1992, pp. 113–127).The editorial columns of the *Justice of the Peace*, in 1841, still campaigned for reform, but grew ever more despondent of their prospects of success. This extract from the 1837 Report was reprinted in the *Justice of the Peace*, so relevant was it considered to be for magistrates:

> We have thought that the preferable course . . . might be, to include all cases of fraudulent misappropriation of property within one general description, or at most two, which should directly comprise all offences that are now brought within the description of larceny by construction, and all others to which the same principle ought to apply. For example, a general law, including all agents entrusted merely with the custody or application of specific property, would supersede the necessity for special enactments in the cases of clerks or servants receiving money on account of their masters, and would remove all the difficulties which have been experienced in bringing carriers, or other bailees, who misappropriate property of which they had originally had lawful possession, within the scope of the ancient law of larceny; and would supersede the nice distinctions . . . between a special use, or bare charge, or mere custody of goods, and such a possession of them, as, in the case of fraudulent appropriation, exempts the offender from punishment altogether, or reduces the offence from a felony to a misdemeanour. *Justice of the Peace*, 1837

The Commission's suggestions were not taken up, however, and this reform never became law.

The imprecise 'fit' of anti-appropriation legislation to the circumstances and methods of workplace appropriation, as well as to the existing common law doctrines, caused confusion among the magistrates, but was a source of power to manufacturers. Not only could employers choose from a number of acts when they prosecuted their workpeople, but, perhaps more importantly, they could also choose the court which tried the accused. This was achieved because the Worsted Acts allowed victims to try offenders in the summary courts, whereas other larceny statutes were applied at quarter sessions. This meant that employers could choose to have the case heard at the nearest petty sessions by magistrates who may well have been fellow industrialists or even friends and colleagues of the prosecutor. This may have had a considerable impact on the chances of conviction, not least because magistrates also held a good deal of discretionary power in cases prosecuted under the Worsted Acts.

For example, the Acts listed specific materials to which they applied, but also stated in addition that *all* materials involved in the manufacture of cloth were covered. This power to interpret the Worsted Acts – to decide which materials were covered, whether the accused was a servant or an agent and whether circumstantial evidence was strong enough to convict in cases where the materials were alleged to have been found – allowed the magistrates to include or exclude cases under the Worsted Acts almost at will. How the magistrates exercised their discretion, and to what end, will be examined later. As for legal definitions of embezzlement, it is clear that there were many legal categories under which crimes of workplace appropriation could be dealt with, and a multiplicity of complex and seemingly paradoxical legal principles which were addressed in such cases. These complexities inevitably affect any attempt to measure the scale of appropriation using the national and local series of criminal statistics. Nevertheless, these statistical series must be considered, if only to reject them as being too unreliable to be used to accurately measure the scale of workplace appropriation.

3

Why Take the Risk? Workplace Appropriation: Motivation and Method

When William Hardaker spoke in court in the trial of his friend Robert Wilby for having 50lbs of embezzled wool in his possession, he brazenly declared that 'he had as good a right to rob his employers as they had to rob him'. Both men had been weavers, but had been dismissed from the factory after the theft was discovered. While only Wilby was sentenced to a £20 fine or one month in gaol in default, the judge remarked that Hardaker, too, left court 'with the character of a thief' (*The Northern Star and Leeds General Advertiser*, 10 December 1842). Like many convicted workers, thirty-four-year-old father-of-seven Robert Wilby struggled to pay the fine rather than go to prison. But Worsted Committee registers show that many of the offenders were unable to bear any financial penalty imposed, let alone the huge amount demanded by the Worsted Acts: £20 from men and women who earned less than £1 per week. Consequently, less than a fifth of those prosecuted between 1840 and 1880 were able to discharge their liability by paying off the fines, and were subsequently imprisoned for a month in default.

Those who paid the sum (£20 until 1885, when it was reduced to £5) were often reliant on financial help from friends and parents, or selling whatever goods they owned. One offender had been obliged to sell the family furniture and leave the neighbourhood (WCMB 25 September 1882). A minority may have preferred to go to gaol rather than sacrifice their life-savings. To choose to be sent to a gaol renowned for its rigour rather than paying the fine must have been a difficult decision, and the majority of those who ended up in Wakefield House of Correction must surely have been incapable of paying a fine, which was the equivalent of several months' wages. Wakefield had a repressive silent system, and required its inmates to do large amounts of demanding labour tasks (see 1834 Rules of Wakefield House of Correction, Nottinghamshire Records Office, QAG 5/83); McConville (1981).

Why did workers take the risk of appropriating their employer's goods when the penalties could be so severe? Was it simply to take advantage of opportunities when they appeared to present themselves? Or was it financial desperation? Did the prosecution rate for workplace appropriation reflect the poverty experienced by textile workers, and is there evidence that economic trends dictated levels of workplace theft? This chapter addresses these questions and also looks at gender differences in offending patterns.

Crime and economic cycles

When social commentators posited a relationship between poverty and criminal activity, their views were based on their experiences, observations, intuition and political orientation. The Chairman of Bradford Court closed the 1855 Christmas quarter sessions with the observation that the court had more work to do now that the times of peace and plenty had passed (*Bradford Observer* 4 January 1855). The *Bradford Observer* agreed, and further asserted that the eradication of poverty would lead to a more just society:

> The general increase of the material prosperity of the people and the rise of wages relatively to the cost of the necessities of life, will exert an important influence in diminishing pauperism, and fostering those habits of thrift and economy which it is so desirable to encourage; so that before very long the time may come when the worthy magistrate may no longer have to tease his legal mind with the painful alternative of punishing a starving man, or letting the guilty go free, since he will administer equity in a land where there is little pauperism and less crime' (*Bradford Observer* 8 October 1873).

However, those views were contradicted by the Wakefield magistrate who, in commenting on the fact that the number of court cases he had dealt with was less than in the previous year, said 'So far this was favourable, considering the prosperity of the country, for it was a melancholy fact that prosperity did not diminish crime, rather it increased it, thus showing that crime did not so much result from poverty as temptation' (*Wakefield Examiner* 3 March 1860).

Opinions were heard from other counties. The Chief Constable of Manchester, for example, in greeting the publication of the 1847 Manchester crime statistics, rejoiced in the fact that:

> During the latter portion of the past year, and especially during the last three months when trade has been exceedingly depressed, and great privations have had to be borne by the working classes, in consequence not only of the shortness of work, and consequent diminution of wages, but also the high price of all sorts of provisions, the apprehensions have been fewer than they have been during any three months since the police force was first established in 1839. (Chief Constable's Reports, 1847, *MCL*, F942.7389 M442).

Although the Chief Constable was commenting on a time when poverty was rising, and crime rates falling, whereas the magistrate spoke of a prosperous period when crime rates rose, both men agreed that poverty was not the dominant motivation for criminal action. Of course, all of these views portrayed 'crime' as a homogeneous whole, rather than an extremely diverse range of offending behaviour committed for numerous reasons. Nevertheless, although flawed in many ways, some interesting research was carried out on the reasons why some started a criminal career.

For example, Reverend Henry Lettsom Elliot, Chaplain of Birmingham Borough Prison, traced the reasons why a thousand inmates had turned to crime, and his research revealed that criminal associations, not poverty, were the largest influence. He alleged that 'bad company' was responsible for over half of the inmates ending up in gaol. He further broke this figure down into two categories. 36 per cent of those imprisoned first experienced 'the criminal classes' in the factory, workshop, street or at home, and a further 15 per cent were persuaded into criminality by those they met in public houses. 30 per cent of the inmates ascribed their behaviour to drunkenness (which may reflect the number of persons imprisoned for drunk and disorderly offences), and 11 per cent stated that the temptation arising from opportunity 'did for them'. Only 7.5 per cent believed that poverty had led to their downfall.

These figures may, however, reflect the difference in attitude between those already committed and those awaiting trial and/or sentencing, the latter of whom were much more likely to plead poverty (Elliot 1868, p. 327). Unfortunately, the rather similar research carried out by Reverend Clay at Preston Gaol is also unreliable, since it was undertaken to 'prove' that immorality caused crime, because this conclusion suited his ideological stance (Clay 1846). Clearly there was no uniform view about the dominant cause of crime among criminal justice administrators in the nineteenth century, but the belief that fluctuations in the trade cycle 'drove' crime to a significant extent continued to be a dominant theme.

Fluctuating trade conditions

Bradford's 'high-pressure' employers were extremely sensitive to changes in the trade cycle. Power-loom shed after power-loom shed arose when trade was brisk, but when trade fell, many of their owners were bankrupted within weeks (*Bradford Observer* 13 December 1849). Manufacturers sailed close to the profit/loss margins, navigating by the rumours concerning continental wool prices, and using the raising and lowering of wages as a rudder. Rises in the cost of raw materials and the lowering of the price of worsted goods both provoked a proportional drop in wages. With wages very responsive to the fortunes of the industry, it is possible to explore the lives of the worsted workers through the study of fluctuations in the worsted trade cycles. So, in order to examine whether economic conditions affected rates of appropriation in the clearest way, this section will examine the period 1844 to 1852, during which Bradford worsted manufacturers experienced extreme economic conditions. For these years, there is accurate information available concerning the number of appropriation prosecutions, and newspaper reports of the volatile worsted market. By comparing workplace appropriation figures and worsted trade data, an analysis of how economic trends might have affected rates of prosecution can tentatively be made. Of course, there are detailed economic and criminal statistics available for later periods, and indeed throughout the nineteenth century, but use of the Worsted Committee figures becomes problematic after 1853, for reasons explained below.

At the beginning of the 1840s, Hamer Stansfield, a stuff manufacturer and a Justice of the Peace, was moved to declare that 'the capitalists are approaching impending ruin, and the operatives suffering under starvation and want' (*Bradford Observer* 21 July 1842). To those living and working in Yorkshire during the 'Hungry Forties', his words would have seemed measured and considered. The context for the conditions suffered by those affected by the Yorkshire textile slump is provided by Ittmann (1995). The classic texts concerning the standards of living of industrial workers in the early to late-nineteenth century are reviewed in Hobsbawm (1957), Hartwell (1961) and Neale (1966). Large numbers of woolsorters, weavers and combers were under-employed or unemployed. For textile workers, and their employers, 'all was gloomy and dark. Manufacturers on every hand are struggling with large stocks and a cheerless prospect' (*Bradford Observer* 15 January 1843; 1 January 1844). In 1844, both worsteds and woollens experienced some trade difficulties, although they maintained average prices for the first half of the year, and even managed better than average prices for finished cloth in February (The *Bradford Observer* gave monthly descriptions of the state of the woollen, worsted and cotton trades in the town from which these general remarks have been drawn). The downturn reappeared, however, in September. The market remained sluggish throughout 1845 and the manufacturers complained that they could not even recover the costs of labour. At one meeting, a manufacturer gave a list of 888 operatives who now lived in poverty (*Bradford Observer* 26 February and 5 March 1845).

This trade slump coincided with the mechanization of combing, which caused the unemployment of thousands of hand-combers. Those hand-combers who stayed in work or learnt to operate factory combing machines laboured in miserable conditions and toiled for very low wages. They also suffered from work-related illnesses, poor living conditions and chronic poverty. Through the slackness in trade generally in 1846, a large number of workmen of all trades joined the hand-combers in great distress. These firms had all of their frames standing idle: Duckett, Beecroft, Prospect Mill, Leeming, Smith/Illigworth, Ogdens, Daniel Illingworth, Titus Salt, J. J. Greenwood, Calvert and Sons, Milnes/Brown, J. Ackroyd, Laycock, Allans and Ellis/Priestman. Rouse had 200 frames standing, as did a number of smaller manufacturers (see 'Circulars to Millowners concerning the Trade Slump', 21 September 1846, *WYAB*, DB30/3/4). The manufacturers' reaction was to draw government attention to the textile trade slump and to set up ameliorative organizations to relieve distress, for example the 'Committee of the Unemployed' which met at Bradford court house (*Bradford Observer* 26 February 1846). However, none of the manufacturers knew how to bring about the one thing which would provide lasting relief to these workers – the recovery of trade (see the despairing comments of John Rand for example in 'Circulars to Millowners concerning the Trade Slump', 21 September 1846, *WYAB*, DB30/3/4). The slump continued and deepened in 1847, especially in the mid-year when there was a sharp dip in the already depressed market. The larger manufacturers tended to blame the new Factory Acts for this, while the smaller masters blamed machinery for stopping production, although their reasoning was never spelt out (*Bradford Observer* 22 January 1846, 2 March 1848). The market recovered at the beginning of the next year, before falling dramatically in March and staying at a low level for the rest of the year. However, although the poor economic conditions affected all worsted manufacturers, the impact of poor trade on the industry was uneven. Some of the larger factories had full employment throughout 1848, but most mills were not running at anywhere near their full capacity (*Bradford Observer* 15 January 1848).

The existence of severe short-term dips in the market makes general statements about the state of trade in the 1840s problematic. However, it is safe to say that for most employers and employees this period was a trying one. Many mill owners went out of business, and many working people suffered deprivation and want. The situation improved gradually from 1849 until the spring of 1852, when market prices (and profits) rose quickly with trade reaching a high point over the summer. This trend could not be sustained and the industry suffered a sharp and disastrous fall in the autumn, continuing through to Christmas. These convulsions in the market, of course, resulted in periodically acute bouts of high unemployment and low wages when times were bad. Conversely, at times when labour was in short supply, workers' wages rose rapidly and significantly. Many historians have contributed to the debate about working-class living standards. Divided into 'pessimists' and 'optimists', the two sides have argued whether or not the lot of the working classes was improved by the industrialization of England (see Hopkins 1979, pp. 97–100).

Presented in general terms, most commentators believe that whatever the case in the first half of the century, all classes benefitted from a long period of prosperity which ran from approximately 1850 to 1870. The validity of these arguments will not be addressed here. Nevertheless, it must be stated that the position at the regional level cannot be understood through the general assertions of these historians. Nor can the experiences of workers in individual industries be summed up in these general terms. For example, the wages of all Bradford worsted workers did not rise continuously after 1850. They ebbed and flowed with trade circumstances, and lost or gained value in 'real' terms depending on changes in the cost of living. Moreover, sections of the workforce continued to labour for low wages when other workers had their wages raised, since a large reservoir of reserve labour was available for their jobs. Large numbers of textile workers therefore lived on low wages, which sometimes kept them above the poverty line, and sometimes did not.

Poverty as motivation for workplace appropriation

Some of the larger-scale appropriations that occurred in the nineteenth century have already been mentioned. These substantial appropriations were widely reported in the Yorkshire newspapers, but small-scale appropriations were equally damaging to employers. The majority of cases dealt with at petty and quarter sessions involved the taking of a mere few pounds worth of cloth. However, if appropriations like these were repeated over the days and weeks of the working year, by even a tiny percentage of the employees, then employers would suffer considerable losses. For the employee, conversely, appropriations of whatever scale meant a wage-supplement, and an increase in their financial well-being. For people engaged on low wages, even small appropriations could make a valuable contribution to family finances. The reeler who took small pieces of yarn home every day for a fortnight, for example, could triple or even quadruple her wages (Leeds QS QS1/179/9 8 August 1840). The taking of a couple of stones of waste could add an extra three or four shillings to the monthly wage (enough to buy an extra pound of butter, cheese and flour in 1861, see Garrett 1988). The value of woollen and worsted waste was a shilling per stone in 1840, and two shillings per stone in 1869 (*Leeds Mercury* 11 April 1840 and 15 December 1869; DMB, 1868–1877, Holly Mill Company, *WYAL*). These additions were perhaps crucial in the endemic low-wage system of Bradford (Richardson 1976, Cudworth 1887, Ittmann 1995).

In his analysis of the 'types' of crime, Rudé explored the motivating effect of poverty on those who committed acts of larceny. To support his argument that poverty bore a causal relationship to the amount of property crime, he provided a list of the pathetic statements of those indicted during the worst years of the 1830s and 1840s (Rudé 1985, pp. 81–5). One can find similar statements in the West Riding quarter sessions' depositions of appropriators. The cry of desperate poverty can be heard in David Illingworth's court declaration, 'I am tired of my life' (Bradford QS1/179/6 30 May 1840). It is again echoed by the weaver who reasoned it was 'better to take warp, weft and gears and all, than go on the road and rob. There was not as much paid for weaving as would keep a family alive, so he did not care' (*Bradford Observer* 16 January 1840). The *Bradford Observer* went on to record that he received three months' imprisonment. Mary Milnes was also imprisoned after a magistrate disregarded her plea that she 'could not make a wage' from her work. The apparent 'need' of people to appropriate is also seen in the appropriations made on behalf of needy friends, neighbours and relatives. For example, the septuagenarian who brought home stocking-wool for his 'lame' daughter who could only obtain her livelihood by knitting for neighbours, or the mill-firer, who occasionally gave a handful of coal to a widow he knew. Both men were arrested, prosecuted and convicted (*Bradford Observer*

23 November 1848; Wakefield QS1/212/4 15 February 1873). Whatever their real reason for taking these things, most offenders stressed economic need as their motivation on the deposition sheets, or in the courtrooms. For this reason a study of the remarks of offenders made in these places will always be biased towards the view that appropriators were poor, and that their crime stemmed from genuine need.

It is, however, very difficult for modern researchers to determine any sense of the poverty that offenders may have felt. What was an adequate wage for one man may not have been for his neighbour. Nevertheless, fragmentary records such as Worsted Committee records, court reports and gaol records can offer some perspective. When prisoners entered Wakefield House of Correction, certain information about them was recorded in the 'General Reception Book': age, educational ability and number of previous convictions, for example; unfortunately only two volumes (1842–43) of the 'Reception Book' series survive (Wakefield House of Correction General Reception Books, C118/99-100).

Few workers imprisoned under the Worsted Acts seem to have had 'criminal careers' in the way that many nineteenth-century commentators liked to believe was the case with most offenders. William Proctor, for example, had been already twice convicted for poaching, and also for wilful damage, assault and exposing his person, and had, thus far, spent exactly one year in gaol; factory labourer, John Magson, aged fifty and married with twelve children, had similarly already been convicted of neglecting his family, bastardy and poaching. However, the others in this cohort present a more pathetic picture. They include a seventeen-year-old mill labourer and sometime vagrant who was convicted of felony for stealing lead from his employer, and sentenced to one year in Wakefield Gaol; Sam Field, aged thirty-three, an illiterate man who lived with his mother, was convicted of embezzling 4lbs of wool; Hannah Bateman, a widow with three children; Jonathon Webster, aged seventy, who was convicted of the illegal possession of 6lbs of waste and a man suffering from rapidly advancing blindness, who was a widower with two children in the workhouse.

A summary of this small group finds that two-thirds were married, with the same proportion having had one or more children; approximately three-quarters of them had no previous criminal convictions, nine of the prisoners were illiterate, seven were semi-literate, six could read but not write and only one could read well. This rate of literacy accords with those prosecuted at quarter sessions where only a quarter of those accused of appropriation signed their voluntary depositions. Interestingly, three quarters of the witnesses who spoke against them signed their names. For a discussion of repeat offending, see Godfrey et al. (2007, 2010). They seem to be, collectively, a less-educated and less criminally active group than other convicted prisoners; by comparison, in Gloucestershire, 1815–50, 41 per cent of prisoners could read and write, 28 per cent could read but not write and 30 per cent were illiterate (Rudé 1985:46). Similarly, the *Manchester Guardian* 25 April 1838 published the following literacy rates for convicts:

Convicts unable to read or write – 35.85%
Read and write imperfectly – 52.08%
Read and write well – 9.46%
Received superior instruction – 0.43%
Unknown standard – 2.18%

As with all property offences, the majority of prosecuted appropriators were from the lower stratum of society, and those in the Wakefield Gaol Reception Book seem to have been some of the most pitiable of the poorest working class. Motivations can rarely be quantified (Rule 1981, p. 143). Without wishing to 'weigh' motivations or rank one above another, it is true to say that many textile workers lived in unremitting poverty for the whole of their lives, and that these people constituted a large proportion of those prosecuted for illegal appropriations. The workplace situation seemed to give employees the opportunity to improve their lot, but prosecution figures stand witness to the fact that such opportunities were sometimes illusory.

In conclusion, it would be surprising if there was not a more marked increase in offending behaviour during slumps. Since wages were reduced in line with falling profits, the employees could have viewed appropriation as a way of maintaining their standards of living. At the same time, the market for embezzled goods increased as well- and low-paid workers, the unemployed and small masters could all have been keener to buy appropriated materials in times of trade hardship.

As can be seen from the evidence presented above, it is not easy to chart how trade fluctuations affected workplace appropriation because so much depended on how employers reacted when thefts were discovered.

Poverty, prosperity and prosecution policy

Styles (1983) and Pollard (1963) both stated that during periods of industrial prosperity, employers in the eighteenth century were often more tolerant of appropriation (WCMB June 1865). For example, in 1776 (a prosperous year),

Yorkshire worsted manufacturers did not dare to prosecute false reelers 'for fear of becoming unpopular among the spinners and losing their work,' a justified fear in an industry with a 'great number of . . . master manufacturers and rival ship consequential thereon' (*Leeds Intelligencer and Yorkshire Post*, 24 September; 26 November 1776). When the severity of the punishment was reduced in 1774, the text of the statute clearly indicated the underlying reasoning. The Norwich master manufacturers who had sponsored the 1749 reforms had come to regret the severity of that law which had discouraged 'many honest and industrious persons from taking up the by-employment and deterred numerous employers from under-taking prosecutions for fear of losing their workforce' (Harding and Jenkins 1989, p. 132). Toleration of small appropriations may also have been a small price to pay for good industrial relations, until harder times when labour need not be kept.

Upon the stagnation of trade, however, the prosecution or dismissal of workers was more likely. The cotton manufacturers McConnel and Kennedy regularly replaced spinners who had not turned up within two or three hours of starting time on Mondays (their average turnover was about twenty a week or 1,000 per year) (Pollard 1963, p. 256). Employers who dismissed employees so easily for breaches of work-discipline (in this instance, the observation of the customary practice of starting the week slowly and building up the work rate towards the end of the week, or 'Saint Monday' as it was known) would experience few qualms about dismissing appropriators. This accords with the records of the body established in 1777 to combat illegal appropriation, the Worsted Committee. Their Inspectors were convinced that poor market conditions led to a real fall in offending behaviour. For example, one Inspector stated that, 'The trade having been quiet causes both embezzlers and receivers to be very cautious' (WCMB 20 December 1867). Similar remarks were made in 1874 when it was said that, 'Trade not being good, the weavers and the other hands behave themselves better than they did', and further remarks along those lines were made in the following years (WCMB March 1874, June and December 1877). The power of the employers, and the fear of unemployment, is revealed, for example, in an entry by an Inspector in March 1886:

> Eliza Dallert, a drawer in the employ of Jonathan Exley who was caught by the manager taking a piece of Backing from a quarter to a half pound in weight. Mr Exley wished me to go up and frighten her a little. I went and took her to her mother and told her I should have to make an example of her – her mother said do as well as you can, there are only two girls out of the family of eight who were

> working, her husband had nothing to do – I stopped 3/- from her wages and she thanked me for so doing (WCMB March 1886).

Sydney Pollard, with remarks about work discipline which are equally relevant to the control of workplace appropriation, stated that 'when a buyer's market in labour returned, a sigh of relief went through the ranks of the employers at the restoration of their power' (Pollard 1963, p. 261).

Assessing the statistical and qualitative information, it can be tentatively concluded that workers were less likely to commit appropriations in times of high unemployment, but employers were more likely to prosecute any appropriators they caught. Therefore, the proportion of workplace offences that were prosecuted rose in slump periods, and fell in boom times. However, it must also be remembered that the persistence of low wages may have served to undermine the influence that economic trends had on the rate of appropriation prosecutions, since many workers lived in economic hardship regardless of the trade cycle. These people may have needed to subsidize their wages through appropriation regardless of minor and/or short-term improvements in their pay. In any case, the underlying reason for employers to choose either prosecution or other forms of punishment remained unchanged during times of boom and slump – the need to eliminate severe and damaging long-term losses caused by illegal appropriation. It is clear that legal remedies were but one alternative among a number of control options of which informal punishment, the dismissal of an offender or inaction were others. Which of these options was used partly depended on trade cycles in the woollen and worsted industries, the nature of internal supervision in the factory and also the gender of the accused.

Gender differences

If national data is used as a yardstick, it appears that female factory workers were not strangers to the courts. Between 1867 and 1878, women constituted 27 per cent of the factory workers prosecuted in the United Kingdom (according to annually published judicial statistics). Unfortunately, figures which detailed the proportions of committed female factory workers were not compiled by county. However, detailed statistics were kept by the main gaols of the West Riding. Since it was rare for summary-level offenders to be sent to a prison far from where the crime was committed, the Wakefield and Leeds gaol statistics accurately record the numbers of West Riding operatives being incarcerated. It appears that female factory workers made up approximately a fifth of those imprisoned in those gaols between 1870 and 1875.These figures were compiled and published only for the period 1870–75. The figures are further broken down into skilled and unskilled, but these are of little use since women's work was often deemed unskilled by definition, and the criteria under which the skilled/unskilled categories were defined are unknown.

Although this is a significant figure, it does not prove that factory women were disproportionately likely to commit crimes. For example, between 1857 and 1880, nationally, 9 per cent of imprisoned women had formerly been factory workers, compared to 9 per cent who had formerly been domestic servants and 26 per cent who were formerly (non-factory) labourers (Zedner 1991, p. 321; Milne 1870, pp. 210–12).

The surviving petty sessions records show that few women were prosecuted for workplace theft in the minor courts. Wakefield petty sessions between 1805 and 1808 saw only three women, but twenty-three men prosecuted for false and short-reeling (these cases involved some of the dwindling band of hand spinners in that district). In the same court in the 1852 to 1860 period three women, but thirty-four men were prosecuted for the same offences (Wakefield Petty Sessions, 1805–8, 1839–80, *WYAW*, P7/1–28). In the Worsted Committee registers, only 15 per cent of those prosecuted between 1844 and 1876 were women. West Riding quarter sessions tell a similar tale. In those records, only 7 per cent of those tried for appropriation were female (QS1840–5 *WYAW*). These figures cannot be explained by any imbalance in the proportions of men and women who toiled in the West Riding textile industries.

Female labour was consistently important to textile employers throughout the nineteenth century. For the larger factory masters, women represented a cheaper and more docile workforce than men, and were to be employed as machine-minders whenever possible. For the smaller masters, who lacked capital resources, a female workforce was often the only means of competing with the large fully mechanized concerns. The tendency to employ female labour was a national phenomenon, but in the West Riding the effect was very marked. Women constituted 60.0 per cent of Bradford's worsted factory employees in 1841, and 73.7 per cent in 1850. A similar set of figures was recorded in the borough's woollen factories where a predominantly male workforce was replaced with a predominantly female workforce between 1830 and 1850 (*Bradford Observer* 22 February 1850). Together these two industries employed 35.0 per cent of the female working population of Bradford. Many contemporary commentators regarded these women factory workers as a group 'at risk'. Articulated through journal articles, the fears of middle-class reformers concentrated on the moral wellbeing of female factory workers fearing that 'natural femininity' would be perverted by the corrupting effect of factory toil and workplace associations:

> They listen to the gossip of experiences which are criminal from ignorance . . . evil communications . . . It is never so much the men that corrupt the women, but the women the women; and thus the cycle goes on from year to year. Experience shows the sisterhoods of vice are as strong as adamant.' (Baker-Smith 1868, p. 539).

A survey of general contemporary criticism of women's employment in (mainly cotton) factories appears in Pinchbeck (1930, pp. 196–201). Baker-Smith was a member of the influential discussion group, the National Association for the Promotion of Social Sciences, which met frequently in the manufacturing districts in the nineteenth century.

Such 'sisterhoods' were cited by the defending advocate of Fanny Whitehead, a power-loom weaver who had been 'encouraged by some evil advisers, ignorant of the Worsted Acts, not to return her work' (*Bradford Observer* 1 July 1852). The newspaper also warned of 'the corrupting associations into which they [female weavers and spinners] are necessarily thrown by their occupations' (*Bradford Observer* 8 October 1847). In the previous year, the 'Committee for Improving the Morals of Female Factory Operatives' had been set up in Bradford to improve and preserve good behaviour inside and outside the factory. Together with other members of the NAPSS (National Association for the Promotion of Social Sciences), Mr Baker-Smith used his lectures to discuss sexual morality within factories and the neglect of the children of factory workers, a regular concern of these commentators and others – see *Half Yearly Reports of the Factory Inspectors*; Saunders (1844); 384 Vol. 11, *Report of the Select Committee on the Health of Towns and the Effect of the Internment of Bodies in Towns, Report of Williamson, 3 April 1840,* Q1937. See also Parkes (1862); Faithfull (1862); Tabor (1862).

Baker-Smith's colleagues took up the baton in 1868, listing the problems that women could encounter in factory labour. First, the women were subsequently impossible to train in domestic duties. Second, the women were introduced and brought into companionship with people of bad character. Last, the workers lost their feelings of modesty and purity, through being obliged to work under immoral supervisors (Bartleet and Jordan 1868, p. 603). In fact a great number of evils were ascribed to the transforming power of factory labour: 'they [factory women] are supposed to be slatternly, coarse in speech, and gross in their amusements, without feeling, delicacy, or perception, irreligious, undomesticated, ill-mannered and "unfeminine"', lamented one contributor to the *Bradford Observer* on 15 June 1874. Feelings of paternalism fostered on patriarchal paradigms of care and protection were apparently mixed with certain ambiguities about the masculinization, and even brutalization, of the factory women by the industrial system in which they worked. It seems that factory reformers intended to reclaim for women a gendered character they had been stripped of at the factory gate. Nineteenth-century cultural expressions echoed these sentiments:

> The daughters too no moral precepts know, And from their hearts a train of evils flow.
>
> All noxious weeds spring up and grow apace, Shorn of their beauty, and each native grace,
>
> Far from the paths of virtue gone astray, Fair modesty's soft blush is fled away.
>
> *(The Factory Child, 1831)*

Conceptions of femininity of a type similar to those described above fuelled a justice system which punished women for immorality as much as criminality, and legitimated a system which made drunkenness and prostitution the most prevalent offences for women, since these offences against 'morality' were perceived to deserve legal sanctions. For example, on average, 20 per cent of the women appearing in Bradford courts between 1866 and 1871 and 31 per cent of the women tried summarily at Leeds between 1878 and 1883 were prosecuted for drunkenness (Chief Constable's Reports; Judicial statistics, 1866–83; *WYAB*, BBC1/2–5). Mill women, incidentally, were perceived by contemporaries as having a high regard for morality, and most mills turned away girls known to be prostitutes – see Doctor Hunter's evidence (*First Report of the Factory Commissioners*, 1833, C1, 20, 87, and C5, 15).

Does the low proportion of women prosecuted for workplace appropriation mean that it was viewed as less serious than offences which involved sexual impropriety? This is unlikely since appropriation was considered to involve major financial losses for worsted employers, and factory rule-books placed appropriation at the top of their list of circumscribed behaviour. However, if the offences for which women tended to be prosecuted not only infringed the law but also the moral construct of femininity in the nineteenth century, why was appropriation not seen as 'immoral' in the same way, especially when appropriation involved the breaking of two important nineteenth-century trusts: the first to God, as laid down by scripture, and the second to the master who gave her waged labour? Blackstone (1765–9, p. 410) stated that the 'three great relations in private life are: 1. That of Master and Servant. 2. That of Husband and Wife. 3. That of Parent and Child'. Appropriation of workplace materials, moreover, might have allowed women more freedom than was usually ascribed to them by a patriarchal society. The sale of appropriated goods could have contributed towards a woman's financial independence from her husband and family over and above the liberating possibilities of a weekly wage. The wages of male weavers between 1857 and 1863 were 4 to 6 shillings higher than those of female weavers (see *Reynold's Newspaper* 29 November 1857; Bairstow's Wage Books, *Bradford Records Office*168/47; 194/58). These shortfalls in the female wage could easily be made up with money made from selling purloined waste or piece ends. Independent women were another cause of concern to the anxious Mr. Baker-Smith. This concern caused him to undermine his portrayal of the factory girl as an innocent waiting to be corrupted by the malign influences of workmates and foremen by stating that factory life:

> leads a girl to a spirit of independence . . . Wages have become a greater power than natural affection. Then again, affected by the state of trade, by the seasons of the year, by fashions which chase each other through a thousand currants that ebb and flow according to circumstances over which they have no control, the factory girl is today rich, tomorrow poor. Today her labour is everything to be desired tomorrow it may be worthless.' (Baker-Smith 1868, p. 542)

His words seem to suggest that factory women would try and 'grab' what they could, whenever they could, as their employment could cease with a sudden downturn in the market. Pike also suggested that the independence of working women, together with the experience of living in industrializing areas, and competing freely with men in the labour market, led to a masculinization of women, and therefore a 'masculine' attitude towards achieving material gain through theft (Pike 1876, p. 527). Pike's opinions were in keeping with the dominant ideological construction of femininity as a quality to be treasured and protected from the contamination of working conditions. But there is another easily understood reason why some women had an incentive to appropriate, although they may not have acted upon it. Family responsibilities may have played a more prominent part in the minds of female workers than male workers, and the necessity of providing food and clothing for children may have driven some mothers to appropriate from probably the most immediate and obvious place – work. Indeed, some felt that the factory system inevitably threw the burden of responsibility for the family onto the women workers. As the *Bradford Observer* put it, 'the capability of the women to earn a considerable wage has in large classes actually inverted the usual relations which hold good for the family – making the woman the bread winner while the man is the luxurious being who only works two or three days a week and for the rest he drinks or lounges.'(*Bradford Observer* 26 September 1875).

More likely, however, is that for many women no incentive was great enough to overcome fear of the triple penalty: imprisonment, separation from children and loss of present and future employment (Johnston 1867). It must be remembered that the stigma attached to a woman after a period of imprisonment was even greater than that attached to a man, and it assumed real importance when it came to finding future employment since many mill owners operated an unofficial cartel whereby known appropriators, prostitutes or 'troublemakers' were not employed. As a local preacher opined 'Taking our Mills, generally . . . a female who has no value for reputation or character, is already a lost woman. So precious, remember, is the preservation of female purity, that a single error herein is a blemish for life.' (William Scoresby 1846). The 'game' may not have been worth the candle.

Engaging as these lines of reasoning are, we are still left with the fact that there is little contemporary discourse concerning female workplace appropriators, and their lives and motivations remain in the historical shadows. It is, of course, very difficult to gain a sense of offenders' lives as they are only glimpsed through criminal records. These records tend to portray offenders as people who have things done to them; they are rarely identified as people capable of making choices, altering their fate or even existing outside of the criminal justice system. Arguably, female workers are even less visible, since the diaries and journals of women do not survive as those of men occasionally do. Neither were the lives and experiences of workplace offenders examined nor even alluded to by moral reformers. There was considerable debate in their circles concerning the health and morality of female factory workers, but little explicit comment on the 'morality' of workplace criminality, or the attractions of appropriation for women. The risks the factory posed to the family, as identified by TNAPSS, were the removal of the woman from the domestic hearth, and not the possibility of imprisonment for taking home work materials. However, when that possibility neared reality, and women were tried in court, it appears that the magistrates' attitudes were mediated by the same ideological constructions of femininity shared by other elite social groups and moral commentators.

Methods of appropriation

Women and closely supervised workers may have had reduced opportunities for workplace theft than those workers who could legitimately move around the factory, or who could dispose of material without having to take it through the closely watched factory gates. Appropriated goods normally left the factory in one of two ways. They could be thrown over the mill walls and picked up either by accomplices or later by the appropriator themselves. Alternatively, they could be carried through the mill gate hidden in a basket or bundle carried by the offender when the factory whistle blew. '*Another Walking Wool Pack*' was how the *Bradford Observer* described a man employing the favourite method of appropriators. The newspaper recorded that 'he was not as stout a man as he appeared being thoroughly situated with jiggings and tops' (*Bradford Observer* 31 December 1840). Material was also secreted under petticoats, cloaks, pushed up trouser legs and stuffed down cleavages (see for example Bingley magistrates court, quarter sessions bundle, Bradford court; 7 March 1874, Bradford QS1/213/7).

Offenders caught with appropriated materials on their person often declared themselves innocent, but found it difficult to explain away their possession of the goods. John Pogson, a spinner, was one whose story was greeted with (understandable) disbelief. Pogson's basket was searched at the factory gate and some woollen waste and bobbins were found inside. His explanation for this was that some other persons must have placed it there without his knowledge. This was of course possible. However, when he removed his hat, some worsted waste fell out onto the table. It is a credit to his spirit that he then announced, 'Bloody hell, they've only put it in my hat an'all' (Deposition of John Pogson, 24 August 1841, QS1/180/10).

Offenders also hid the material inside the mill prior to removing it from the premises (22 July 1840 Leeds QS1/179/9; 7 March 1874 Bradford QS1/213/7). In one case tried at quarter sessions, for example, an employee found some cloth stored in a part of the mill where it did not belong. The foreman, assuming that it had been placed there ready to be removed at a convenient opportunity, had that part of the factory watched. When a stoker was seen near the same part of the mill, and the pieces were found to be missing, the police were called, the stoker's house was searched and he was arrested (*Bradford Observer* 29 January 1863; 15 September 1864; Pontefract QS, 6 April 1844, QS1/183/6). A favourite place to hide materials was outside the appropriator's work area, such as behind chimneys or in the mill privy (Bradford QS1/210/6), which again provided greater opportunities for those workers who had rights of mobility around the factory. The second reason for hiding goods was that break-times and dinner-times then provided opportunities for removing identification marks from the goods. One employee, for example, took 15lbs of soap, of which the ends, bearing the trade mark, had been removed and placed in a parcel elsewhere (*Bradford Observer* 11 October 1865). The removal of these marks could mean the difference between a prosecution under the Worsted Acts and one under the felony statutes (for which the penalties were even stiffer).

Higher-status workers were more easily able to exploit their relative freedom and autonomy to commit serious acts of appropriation. Foremen and warehousemen represented only 1.5 per cent of the mill workforce and made up a very similar proportion of the offenders prosecuted summarily by the Worsted Committee. Yet they constituted one in seven of those employees prosecuted at quarter sessions. This figure almost certainly reflects the fact that foremen were more likely than other types of employee to be prosecuted at the major courts.

Despite the fairly regular prosecutions of foremen, the newspapers always treated the cases as remarkable. For example, in 1855, a millowner suspected a foreman and his brother, a card nailer, so he and his son watched the mill all night, until they apprehended the accused men in the early hours of the morning. This is how the *Bradford Observer* recorded the trial:

> The excitement was still greater, from the fact that the parties suspected were considered to be men of sterling character, being always foremost in their denunciation of fraud and theft committed by anyone with whom they came into contact . . . From the cool deliberate and systematic manner in which they went to work on the morning when detected in the act, it is generally believed that the same system of plunder has been carried on for some length of time.' (*Bradford Observer* 3 February 1848; see also *Bradford Observer* 24 May 1855).

Similar language was used when reporting the trials of those warehousemen who were engaged on long-practised strategies to increase their wages. The warehouse offered appropriate opportunities, not just to the high-status warehousemen, but to all who worked in that environment. The simplest method was used by one lad employed to open up the warehouse at seven o'clock in the morning and to sweep the floor before men arrived at eight o'clock. With no one to watch over him, he simply took some cloth home with him when he left. After a routine checking of stock discovered the losses he was 'removed in tears to the lock up' by the police, as was the man to whom he had sold the pieces (*Bradford Observer* 21 August 1851).

Another apprentice, John Booth, had a more wholesale, business like and profitable arrangement. The young employee gave out cloth at the back door of the warehouse, and pocketed the money he received for it. The buyer then went to the front door of the warehouse and made a token payment for the cloth he had 'bought'. As both payments added up to less than the true value of the cloth, both the buyers and the apprentice were enriched by this arrangement.

However, higher grade warehousemen had more sophisticated methods of supplementing their wages, for example, accounting frauds – the sale of warehouse goods without recording the sale, and 'pocketing' the money. This was made easier for them because some companies allowed the sale of damaged material to the public as an unacknowledged supplement to their wages. In 1862, a group of textile manufacturers condemned any employer who allowed this practice which they thought was 'fraught with so much evil, and opened the door to fraud so difficult to detect and punish'. Damaged cloth with the tail and head markings removed was sometimes allowed to warehousemen as part of their wages, or sold to them, each transaction recorded in a cash book, and deducted from their weekly wages (see 11 November 1870, Bradford QS1/209/16). The manufacturers resolved 'not to allow one square inch of cloth to be removed from the premises without their permission' (*Bradford Observer* 13 March 1862). It was hoped that this would thwart the appropriations by warehousemen which were reportedly very common.

This objective seems to have failed. For example, one warehouseman was gaoled in 1866 for appropriating 25s.-worth of goods. The magistrate, in summing up the case, unconsciously indicated one reason why warehousemen and foremen escaped detection, stating that 'the prisoner occupied a position of status and trust, and had charge of valuable property' (*Bradford Observer* 4 January 1866). It was this position of status and trust which allowed the high grade workers not only the opportunity to appropriate but also the possibility of avoiding imprisonment.

Foremen not only had access to goods in all stages of their manufacture but also were in a position in which their conduct was rarely questioned. Moreover, as the main accuser, witness and apprehender, the foreman was able to falsely accuse workers under his charge when losses of stock were noticed, with little fear of his deceits being disbelieved. In addition, it must be remembered that supervisory scrutiny usually only worked in one direction. Under-foremen who suspected their immediate superior of malfeasance, for example, would have to be very confident of obtaining cast-iron proof, before risking an accusation. To make an accusation without sufficient proof, and see it subsequently rejected, would make an under-foreman's job untenable. For this reason, action usually followed only when an authority higher than the foreman became suspicious. Such was the case in 1840 for instance, when the millowner suspected that his foreman 'was not conducting his branch of the business in the proper manner'. His suspicions proved to be correct (*Bradford Observer* 31 December 1840).

In addition to their partial invulnerability to detection, the foremen's methods of appropriation were also influenced by the position of trust they held. The foremen were often responsible for either the weighing-out of raw materials, or the collection of work at the end of the day. This took place in rooms set aside for the purpose, and must have aided the suppression of appropriation since the weight of the raw material given out could be compared by the foreman to the amount received back from the worker, and the difference accounted for. Obviously, this 'checking' system relied on the honesty of the weighers-out, and this honesty could occasionally be tested. Thomas Walton's honesty was stretched beyond its endurance in 1841, for example. He was a weigher-out of Daniel Salt's who was approached by a waste dealer and one of Salt's woolcombers in a public house. The conversation they had was later repeated in court:

> I can mend your situation, if I could put trust in you. You're a weigher out aren't you? Do you know any man you can depend on? Can you depend on that man (pointing to the woolcomber)? You can weigh out to him two lathers, four lathers or six lathers and only put down two – can't you do that? (*Bradford Observer* 11 February 1841. See also the entry of 3 January 1881 WCMB, *WYAB*)

Walton decided he could when he was offered £2 a week to do so – it had already been pointed out to him that if he accepted the offer he could afford to buy his own business in a year. A variation of these 'counting and weighing' offences was the false accounting of wages rather than cloth. Since workers who left still had their wages issued until the foreman reported to the company accountants that they had left, and it was the foreman who collected each week's wages from the counting house, the opportunities for fraud are obvious. Moreover, foremen could also enter an employee as working longer hours than they had done, giving the worker the true amount, and keeping the difference. For example, a man employed for eight years as a department overlooker was imprisoned for fraud after he failed to inform the counting house that a hired man had left the firm's employment (*Bradford Observer* June 18 and 24 1874). The reason for the harsh punishment can be found in a newspaper report four years earlier, where five foremen acting in this way amassed over £1,000 between them over the time it had been practised (*Leeds Intelligencer and Yorkshire Post* 18 July 1870).

Other duties performed by foremen provided further opportunities for them to supplement their wages, for example the responsibility of maintaining the mill machinery. The overlookers of several firms sent unused fully covered rollers at the bottom of containers filled with rollers that needed recovering. The roller-coverer then charged the firms for covering rollers, which were simply returned in the same state [in which] they had been delivered to him. The overlookers, for their trouble, received a share of the profits of this scheme (7 April 1884 WCMB).

All of the foremen mentioned above may have considered themselves unlucky to end up in court. It must be understood that proficient overlookers could have a large influence on the profits of a mill. Israel Roberts described how his father, who was Hainsworth's foreman in the 1840s, tripled the profits of Providence Mill, from £180 to £540 a year (Roberts, I., *The Life of Israel Roberts, 1827–1881*, Yorkshire Archaeology Society, Ms.1079). Foremen who could cajole or coerce the workforce into greater profits, without forcing them into strike action, were a valuable and scarce resource, and employers strove to avoid prosecuting them. The manager of Victoria Mill explained to a Worsted Inspector how far he would go to keep good foremen. Their foreman, Barraclough, was suspected of taking home leather strapping worth thirty pounds. 'If the leather strapping was found in Barraclough's house, and he was taken into custody', the manager explained, 'very likely his two sons (who were overlookers) would at once leave work and he would be obliged to stop all looms until he could obtain overlookers to take their places'. Nevertheless, Barraclough was confronted, and his apology accepted. To the relief of all, both he and his sons continued to work at the mill (September 1916 WCMB). Rumours of a foreman's impropriety were unlikely to be transmitted to an employer, but if they were, they were unlikely to be believed. If, in addition, mill owners were loathe taking legal actions against fraudulent supervisors, the proportion of foremen prosecuted compared to other workers is likely to be an under-representation of the true picture. The benefits of rank, it appears, were helpful even to those suspected of appropriation.

In 1865, Messrs. Moore and Pollard believed that 'hangers-on' or casual labourers, paid by the hour, were sporadically stealing from their warehouse (April 1865 WCMB). Their suspicions may have been correct in this case, but appropriation was mainly carried out by experienced and established workers. Despite the occasional case involving newly employed workers taking goods home, and those who could be termed 'serial appropriators', such as the thrice convicted weaver who took weave patterns home after being employed for one week consecutively at three firms (*Bradford Observer* 12 August 1858), those coming before quarter sessions magistrates were mainly the long-term employed (58 per cent of defendants had been employed for over a year). Some like James Wood, who was indicted for appropriating rags, had been in service for thirty years (21 Sept 1843 Bradford QS1/182/4). These figures may reflect in part the fact that new employees were too keenly watched to attempt an appropriation, but the proportion of long serving employees prosecuted is too large to explain away in this manner. If established employees were less well supervised, how is it possible that so many of them were caught? It also seems clear that the rules of the factory would be well understood by someone employed for over a year, and that misunderstandings concerning customary practices were unlikely to occur at this stage. The fact remains that, whatever the disposition of more recently employed workers, a proportion of the 'old-timers' were perfectly willing to appropriate goods. This may be because of crises in the working life-cycle of male and female workers.

By linking age information in the indictment books to the depositions in which workplace appropriators can be identified, it is possible to conclude that those aged twenty-one and under constituted just 9 per cent of those tried for workplace theft at quarter sessions between 1840–5 and 1870–5. This is a little surprising because younger male workers were not only a large component of the factory workforce but were also the most mobile workers whose jobs involved picking up pieces of cloth or waste and carting it around to different areas of the mill which gave numerous opportunities for appropriation. It seems likely that many young workers were dealt with informally, and that only a few unlucky apprentices and young workers found themselves placed before the courts. The court narratives of those that did end up before the magistrates are very interesting. One apprentice, for example, was apprehended when taking some waste out of the factory in his dinner can. His father was called, who convinced that his son was not the real culprit and begged the boy to tell the policeman who had forced him into the act. No doubt he was dismayed to hear the lad say:

> My mother asked me to take it, she gave me 2d. or 3d. on Saturday nights . . . it's my mother that's brought me to this. If I had known I would have cut my throat. But when I get loose I shall [en]list for a soldier' (15 February 1845 Wakefield QS1/184/4).

A similar tale of vicarious appropriation and incitement to steal was heard by the Bradford magistrates in 1844:

> Mrs Mashiter, charged with having purchased of a person who had no right to dispose of it, a remnant of a damask piece. The principal witness was a boy of nine or ten years old . . . and giving satisfactory evidence that he was sensible of the doom that awaits all liars, he was duly sworn. The youngster is employed at the works of Messrs Smith and Brothers (dyers). The children of the prisoner, are his playmates, and on his being at the house on one occasion lately adorning himself and his companions as 'mummers' with some bits of cloth that he had procured at his employer's works, the prisoner enquired of the child whether he could obtain for her as much damask as would make a table cloth; promising to pay for it if he did so. The lad assented, and took her an end of cloth – she gave him 4d. for it. On the lad going home with some halfpenny pictures, which he had bought with the money, his mother questioned him; discovering the theft she hastened to the prisoner's, got the cloth, and next morning presented it with her son to his employers. A constable had at this time been sent for. These facts being proved, the prisoner was convicted in the penalty of £20 or in default three months.' (*Bradford Observer* 23 January 1844).

Young offenders may have been used to lead the authorities to the more important figures, such as receivers. This may have taken a proportion of young appropriators out of the prosecution figures. In contrast to young workers, thirty- to forty-year-olds, who represented a smaller proportion of property offenders generally, were strongly represented in the prosecution statistics for workplace appropriation. They were more likely to be dealt with formally, and less protected by notions of patriarchal care. Moreover, occupational groups which were over-represented in the statistics may have distorted the figures. Fraudulent foremen, for example, were often in their forties and fifties. The factory career structure which was closely linked to age may also have played a prominent part in determining the age profile of the appropriation statistics. For those workers who were becoming worn out by the relentless working pace of the factory, and perhaps taking home less piece-work wages each year, working children could sometimes provide a partial solution to the problems of family poverty. Aside from that source, there were only three ways out of this life crisis

– to carry on as best they could on ever reducing wages, to hope that they would to be made up to overlooker (Garrett 1988) or to supplement their wages from another financial source (such as illegal appropriation).

It is important to remember that the vast proportion of prosecuted factory appropriators were male. Women experienced a different life-cycle, and the incentives they might have had to appropriate were explored earlier. However, for the 94 per cent of workplace offenders who were male, age was a strong determinant in either encouraging or discouraging their involvement in workplace appropriation. Hardship engendered by age-related life conditions seems to have stimulated individual cases of appropriation, but it would be problematic to uncritically accept that workers made a conscious decision to appropriate solely based on career path frustrations, or because they anticipated (or had already entered) a difficult period in their life-cycle which had led to impoverishment. Their decisions to appropriate were also affected in a variety of ways by trade cycles and fluctuations in the availability of employment, as were the employers' decisions to prosecute such appropriations (modern studies of the links between trade cycles and crime include Box 1987 and Carlen 1988). Did appropriation offer an opportunity for lower paid workers to supplement their wage and avoid relative or absolute poverty?

What was taken?

The materials taken by workpeople can be ordered into four categories. The first category included all types of finished goods, such as fents and piece-ends cut from rolls of cloth, and these goods were mainly appropriated by the warehouse workers, whose activities have been previously described (7 February 1843 Wakefield QS1/212/4; 18 July 1873 Bradford QS1/212/4). The second group comprised the waste materials created by the processes of production. For example, workers took noils, jenny ends, small pieces of waste cloth which were used to clean the looms and the waste bits of fluff which were caught around the cogs of the combing and other machines (*Bradford Observer* 27 March 1848; 27 December and 11 October 1865; 15 February 1844; 13 July 1845 Wakefield 10 September 1860 QS1/183/5; Leeds QS1/184/12). Third, workpeople took home the raw materials which were used to process the wool, or facilitate production, for example, soap for washing the wool, charcoal used in the combing process and the oil used to lubricate the machines (*Bradford Observer* 21 September

1845; 24 May 1849; 15 February 1840 Pontefract QS1/179/4; 8 August 1840 Leeds QS1/179/9). Three pints of oil were taken by an engineman in 1854, for example. The accused man accounted for the oil saying that it was an accumulation of 'little drops' which he had over from the stock periodically given to him by his masters. He also stated he had no intention of appropriating it to his own use, but would have used it in the service of his master. His account was accepted and he was discharged by the magistrate with a warning (*Bradford Observer* 24 May 1854).

Last, there were many cases dealt with at quarter sessions concerning the taking of pieces of brass and of leather drive-bands from the mill machinery and steam engines (17 June 1840, Skipton QS1/175/9). Sometimes these goods were simply unscrewed or prised from the machines, or became 'misplaced' when the engine parts were replaced. All pieces of brass were supposed to be put into a waste bin so that it could then be sold to scrap dealers, thereby recouping some of the costs of the replacement part. However, some workers misconstrued the purpose of the waste bins. William Thackaray, for example, stated at his trial that he had taken some brass pieces because 'many pieces were thrown among the waste and I thought there was no harm in taking them' (Skipton QS1/180/617 June 1841). Whether such misconceptions were wilful or not is difficult to determine. For whatever reason, the journey from machine to waste bin could be hazardous for valuable pieces of old brass, as many mill foremen lamented. One foreman, for example, complained in court that old engine parts were being taken rather than going in the 'brass refuse bin'. He believed that this may have happened every quarter when the parts are changed (9 September 1847, Leeds QS1/183/10).

The variety of goods appropriated from mill machinery is illustrated in a case heard at Keighley magistrates' court. Richard Stell had long been employed as a mechanic at Clapham's Mill, and had the regular habit of selling brass nuts and bolts from the machines, spindles, leather belting and pulleys, all without the consent of his employer (*Bradford Observer* 3 September 1845). He was neither the first nor the last to be prosecuted at quarter sessions for that practice. Since petty sessions' magistrates may not have considered brass to come under the Worsted Acts, these cases were tried as felonies at quarter sessions, and consequently they are disproportionately represented in the quarter sessions courts. In the quarter sessions statistics of 1840 to 1855, for example, finished cloth goods constituted 6.6 per cent of all appropriated goods, unfinished cloth 21.3 per cent, waste 12.0 per cent, but 34.6 per cent of all appropriated materials were made of brass (a material much in demand with scrap dealers and pawnbrokers).

The agents of disposal

Secret appropriation was a means to an end. Spinners, woolcombers and weavers may have appropriated materials to supplement their meagre wages. Foremen and higher-graded employees may have appropriated for personal enrichment, but the act of appropriation would have been a largely barren and fruitless experience, had not pawnbrokers, waste dealers, hawkers, rag collectors and scrap dealers been available and willing to convert embezzled materials into shillings and pence. Philips (1977, p. 220) found that the most common way of selling on stolen goods in the Black Country was to pawnbrokers and other waste and scrap dealers.

Nearly half of the appropriated goods which were offered for sale were first shown to a scrap dealer. However, the quarter sessions dealt mainly with appropriations involving the taking of brass. Petty sessions punished the appropriation of cloth goods, or woollen and worsted waste. Since these types of goods were sold or pawned to waste dealers, rag collectors and pawnbrokers, all of these groups are under-represented in the quarter sessions statistics. Indeed, the impression gained from newspaper and Worsted Committee records is that they are under-represented to a great extent, for waste dealers, pawnbrokers and hawkers constituted nearly a third of those people prosecuted by the Committee for receiving or being in possession of embezzled goods.

Peripatetic waste- and rag-gatherers were commonly found visiting the textile districts of Yorkshire and Lancashire selling pots and bits of spice, and buying waste materials from weavers, spinners and other domestic workers in the eighteenth century (*Leeds Intelligencer and Yorkshire Post* 24 February 1784, 14 February 1791, 18 August 1796, quoted in Soderlund 1992). The deposition of John Burtop, manager at Holme Bolton Mill, reveals how factory workers and waste dealers continued their trade in the nineteenth century. Burtop told (the aptly named) Joseph Offended, a clothier, that he sold jenny-ends to a woman who came round the neighbourhood to buy them at night, as many women did, under the pretence of buying crockery. Indeed, embezzled weft was called 'bowl' weft in Lancashire because of its association with 'crockery' sellers, see Chapman (1904). Offended accompanied Burtop to the outside of a house at one o'clock in the morning. Burtop entered the house, and Offended brought in the goods when a light was shone in the window as a signal. The offender maintained in the deposition that he did not know the goods he took into the house were stolen (1 July 1843, Sheffield QS1/182/13). Signals, codes and other precautions were taken by dealers, not only when the sale was being made but also when storing the materials. The longer the materials remained on the dealer's premises, the more chance there was of them being discovered by a policeman or Worsted Inspector. This was especially true if the appropriated materials were not the type of goods one would expect to find in a waste dealer's warehouse, which is why one firm of waste dealers were suspected by the Worsted Inspector of cutting up tops to make waste (24 September 1888 WCMB). Goods were therefore quickly sold on by dealers to people at market stalls and/or to particular client manufacturers. (1 January 1841 Knaresborough QS1/180/1). Indeed, of all the 'receivers' prosecuted by the Worsted Committee between 1844 and 1876, the largest occupational group were the manufacturers. The Worsted Committee registers record that they made up 43.8 per cent of those receivers who were prosecuted (56D.88/1/3–4). Smaller mill owners bought goods from every kind of waste and scrap dealer, as well as from pawnbrokers, and directly from factory workers employed at other mills, often through a number of intermediaries (*Bradford Observer* 28 August 1845, 9 February 1854, 22 May 1854, 6 August 1863). Indeed the complexity of the route taken by appropriated goods may have protected many manufacturers from conviction. This complexity is well illustrated in this case from the *Bradford Observer*:

> The defendants said they bought warp from Thomas Craven, who said he got them from his brother John Craven, the overlooker at Messrs. Whitaker and Booker. Booker identified the warps and said that Craven had no authority to sell them . . . Shuttleworth (the Worsted Inspector) found Thomas Craven, a warp dresser of Whitaker and Booker, under the name of Henry Mitchell . . . For some time property was missed from Whitaker and Booker's Cannon Mill. (*Bradford Observer* 6 August 1863)

The larger manufacturers expressed the belief, articulated through the Worsted Committee, that the smaller manufacturers gained a competitive advantage over more honest rivals by buying appropriated raw materials at a cheaper price. Certainly the market in appropriated materials was stimulated by manufacturers, and it is arguable that the opportunities cheap embezzled goods provided for manufacturers in the first years of their business activities led to increased trade competition. It is therefore possible that the larger manufacturers directed the activities of the Worsted Committee towards controlling the flow of appropriated goods to smaller manufacturers. However, it should not be assumed that the only conduits for appropriated goods were manufacturers, waste dealers and pawnbrokers. Other non-professional agencies were also active and enthusiastic parties in this process. Beer housekeepers were perhaps best placed to buy, or even commission the taking of, appropriated goods. Publicans had frequent and close contact with workers of all occupations, and would probably know, through gossip, which of those workers were likely to be able to sell them the odd bit of waste, jiggings or nipping (17 November 1864; 6 November 1868 WCMB).

Certainly, the Worsted Inspectors were keen to extract, by payment or threat, any information from them concerning the activities of embezzlers. Any beer housekeepers that were found to be buying 'knocked-off' goods were prosecuted by the Committee, and where insufficient evidence could be gathered by the Inspectors, the Committee petitioned the police and magistrates to oppose the granting of a licence to sell alcohol. Seventy-nine beer housekeepers were prosecuted by the Committee between 1844 and 1876, which was a fifth of the total number of those prosecuted for receiving or being in possession of embezzled goods. As well as buying embezzled goods, many publicans exchanged beer and spirits (*Bradford Observer* 24 May 1849, 27 February 1862). This was part of the non-cash petty market-place culture which saw rags exchanged with salt dealers pound for pound, or with hawkers for pots and pans, or even exchanged for articles of household furniture. Six pounds of indigo card was exchanged with a druggist for a birdcage in 1840, for example (*Bradford Observer* 13 December 1849; 9 March 1854; 30 March 1840 Bradford QS QS1/179/6).

Local or visiting tailors also bought appropriated materials, or used them to mend the worker's clothes for a reduced fee. This was noted by William Cudworth, the renowned Bradford antiquarian who remarked in 1885 that:

> the clothing of people fifty years ago was rough, coarse, and ungainly. Sunday suits were no better nor as good in style as the week-day suits of to-day . . . The travelling tailor was an institution of those days . . . Generally, however, their work consisted in making up old garments, and cutting them down to suit the younger members of the family' (Cudworth 1885, p. 38).

Workers also converted materials to their own personal use, knitting stockings from appropriated yarn, for example, or mending boots with leather drive bands (April 1873 WCMB; 9 May 1873 Bradford QS1/212/6).

People also used appropriated silk and cotton to make poaching nets. By doing so, poachers who were arrested were liable to prosecution even if there was insufficient evidence to indict them for poaching, for if they could not provide an invoice which proved that they had purchased the silk or cotton legitimately, they could be prosecuted under the Worsted Acts for 'being in possession of goods suspected to have been embezzled' (April 1878; 11 April 1882; 4 January 1886; 19 April 1886, 20 September 1885 WCMB). It must also have been the case that poachers who had nets made of unappropriated material could similarly fail to prove the material's legal status. Appropriated materials could also provide the means to sustain small commercial activities, such as rug-making, or pillow-making (20 June 1870 Bradford QS1/209/8). In all kinds of ways appropriation thus provided an escape route from poverty and, perhaps in time, from the rigours of factory employment as well. Very occasionally, it could also provide a more direct avenue of escape. One apprentice, for example, used the £15 he made through appropriation to buy a ticket for a steamship to America. Unfortunately for him he was arrested on board SS Chester before he sailed (4 December 1844 Sheffield QS1/184/2).

The campaign against professional receivers

'No thief, however young or inexperienced, finds the least difficulty in disposing of stolen goods'. So said Edward Gibbon Wakefield in 1831, and his views were echoed by moral commentators, police agencies and the proto-criminologists of the nineteenth century. Their alarm at the ease with which thieves disposed of their ill-gotten gains stemmed from a frustration that unmarked and otherwise unidentifiable 'stolen' goods could sit in a pawnbroker's window without any possibility that the pawnbroker would be legally connected to their theft. T. C. S. Kynnersley, the stipendiary magistrate for Birmingham, offered a remedy for this situation. He suggested 'that what we want is the general adoption of a principle found in the 24, 26 and 27 sections of the Metropolitan Police Act, 2 & 3 Vict. c71' (Kynnersley 1858, pp. 362–3). The principle he referred to asserted that every person who could not account for any suspicious goods found in their possession would be liable to a five shillings' fine or two months' imprisonment (Philips 1977, p. 219). The 1839 Act to which he referred was a reaffirmation of the clauses of 7 & 8 Geo. VI, c.29 (1827), which made it a felony to receive stolen goods, regardless of whether the person who had delivered the goods had been convicted, or even apprehended. However, this principle, which made criminal the bare possession of unaccountable property, had already been enshrined in the Worsted Acts. These Acts, passed eighty years before Kynnersley's comments, formed the basis for the campaign against buyers of appropriated goods in the West Riding.

The *Leeds Mercury* in 1840 also reminded the authorities of another sanction which could be applied to buyers and sellers of suspicious goods:

> A correspondent informs us that numbers of individuals are in the habit of hawking woollen cloth for sale in Leeds and the neighbourhood, who, he presumes, are not manufacturers of the goods, but merely sell on commission, and he requests our opinion as to the legality of those hawkers offering to do business on such conditions, and without a licence. Answer, there is no doubt that parties hawking cloth in the manner referred to, are liable to severe penalties'. (*Leeds Mercury* 7 March 1840)

By both their refusal to grant licences to hawkers, and their conviction of buyers of appropriated materials under the Worsted Acts, the West Riding magistrates were determined to eradicate the market for appropriated goods, as the statements they made in court clearly show. Many of these judicial homilies concerned the 'misguided' workers who had been enticed into criminal activity by dealers: 'There is now no doubt existing that he (a rag dealer) has been the chief instrument in causing many poor woolcombers to become thieves . . . it is a long lane that has no turning, and honesty is eventually the best policy' (*Bradford Observer* 11 Oct 1855). Underlying such platitudes, however, was a genuine dislike of those who facilitated crime by providing access to a lucrative market. One magistrate wished scrap dealers could be 'put down', for example; another was gleeful that a scrap dealer was appearing before him, as he considered his kind as worse than the thieves themselves (*Bradford Observer* 16 March 1848, 11 October 1849, 1 December 1853). It is clear that magistrates had a 'determination to discourage the practice in every way within their power' (*Bradford Observer* 7 January 1868). However, judicial rhetoric remained impotent unless the receivers of appropriated goods were deposited in the Yorkshire court houses.

The policing of dealers of necessity took two forms. First, the Worsted Inspectors were pro-active in collecting information about the activities of waste dealers, and regularly searched the warehouses of cloth dealers, and the carts of hawkers as they passed through Bradford (23 June 1884 6 May 1852 WCMB). Second, both policemen and Worsted Inspectors reacted to the appropriation of (usually metal) goods by taking descriptions, or in the case of machine pieces, patterns, round to every local pawnbroker and scrap dealer (15 Oct 1840 Leeds QS1/179/9 and 12 February 1844 Wakefield QS1/183/5). As well as assisting in the finding of objects which had already been pawned, this strategy made pawnbrokers hesitant to accept a particular object if it was subsequently offered to them. Furthermore, it also provided the prosecution with convincing evidence that the dealer knew that the object had been stolen, if he was later found with the goods on his premises.

For example, one dealer was shown the pattern of a brass object by a policeman, but denied ever having seen it. Later, when the appropriator had confessed to selling the brass to the dealer, they were both arrested and convicted (16 November 1874 Leeds QS1/214/1). Generally, it was easier to gain the convictions of sellers, rather than receivers, of appropriated goods. A seller could not testify against the buyer of his appropriated goods without incriminating himself, and had no need to do so anyway. The unwary seller, however, had merely to misjudge the character of the pawnbroker or waste dealer to find himself in trouble. Moreover, honest dealers who wanted to avoid the risk of accepting suspicious goods, sometimes decided to 'turn in' the person who offered them the goods. In 27.5 per cent of quarter sessions trials, 1840–45, the pawnbroker or dealer who had been offered the goods had subsequently informed the police. Indeed, one or two dealers and pawnbrokers sometimes did more than just alert the authorities. Contrary to the impression of magistrates, it seems that some dealers actually apprehended those they suspected of offering them appropriated materials (*Bradford Observer* 6 October 1842).

Furthermore, quarter sessions records indicate that 57.1 per cent of pawnbrokers and 51.6 per cent of scrap dealers refused to accept the appropriated goods offered to them. If Tebbutt and Philips are correct, that pawnbrokers often refused to accept goods but did not call the police, then the proportion of pawnbrokers who refused appropriated goods could even be higher (Tebbutt 1983, p. 97, Philips 1977, p. 220). A few pawnbrokers even took precautionary steps to distance themselves from illegal practices, such as refusing to buy goods from apprentices unless they produced a note from the foreman stating they had permission to sell the goods they offered. However, it may be that the pawnbrokers' enthusiasm for keeping within the law is exaggerated by the quarter sessions depositions. These cases, after all, involved appropriators who had been caught, and pawnbrokers were wise to say that they always thought the goods suspicious, and 'now he came to think about it'.

It did not always take the direct intervention of a pawnbroker to lead to a seller's downfall. One man who always sent a woman into pawn goods seemed to have sufficiently distanced himself from the sale of goods he had appropriated to avoid arrest. However, he was searched at the mill and pawnbroker's tickets were found in his pockets. He was then taken to the pawnbrokers where the goods were matched to the ticket. He continued to deny the appropriation, stating, correctly, that the pawnbroker could not identify him, but he confessed immediately, however, when the policeman brought his female accomplice into the pawn shop, and she was identified by the pawnbroker (7 February 1843 Wakefield QS1/182/5). Tebbutt, may thus be right to state that 'The very existence of pledge tickets tended to assist the recovery of stolen goods and bring the pawnbroker to court as a witness' (Tebbutt 1983, pp. 95–6).

When pawnbrokers themselves were tried, they were anxious to persuade the magistrates and jury that they could not be expected to know the provenance of the goods they had accepted. 'I had received it [135 lbs waste] from a man and paid him,' stated one dealer, 'I do not know where they came from – they might come from America for all I know' (7 December 1872, Leeds QS1/211/6). Others, who seemed to be honest men, clearly did not pry too deeply about where goods had originated. Wilkinson was one such man. He regularly bought stuff pieces from Holmes, a waste dealer, who was often seen in the company of warehousemen. Invoices were provided for all transactions, but Wilkinson admitted that the identifying marks had been covered with daubs. The court heard that, after his warehouse had been destroyed by fire, Wilkinson was approached by a warehouseman who warned, 'If those sheets did not burn, then burn them now. If any one comes and asks for my name, don't know it.' Wilkinson then immediately informed the Worsted Inspector (16 June 1875 Bradford QS1/214/8). Whether through genuine regard for the law, or because of the success of the campaign against the buyers of appropriated goods, it does appear that for many dealers the risks of buying goods from factory employees were simply too great. Hence the comments of a broker, who refused to buy goods from workmen saying, 'I hardly dare do so, there are so many stolen' (10 May 1842 Sheffield QS/181/8).

Conclusion

It is impossible to develop a complete picture of the workplace offender, or any other offender. The motivations which prompt any group of property offenders to commit crimes, the way they lived their lives and the ways in which they committed their offences are only partially revealed, and often distorted and obscured by criminal records and trial reports. Fortunately, quarter sessions depositions, gaol records and Worsted Inspectorate records have allowed this study to cast some welcome light on at least one category of offenders.

In addition, these sources have shown that losses due to appropriation could, over time, become a serious danger to the financial security of worsted companies. Large losses were sustained not just because of the (well-reported) large-scale appropriations, but also by the mass of regular small weedings and perculations. Seen in this light, the employers' attempts to control appropriation were not meant solely to reinforce a symbolic managerial authority or prevent niggling losses, but were essential to ensure economic viability.

Small-scale appropriations have also been shown to have been a useful, if not crucial, 'alternative wage' to low-paid workers, which allowed them access to a standard of living unsupportable by legal means. By the exploration of the routes of disposal of embezzled goods, the chapter has also revealed something both about the operation of the 'non-cash' market place, where appropriated goods were exchanged for clothes, victuals or other goods, and also the opportunities for selling embezzled goods to small manufacturers. Appropriation was clearly endemic and routine to the worsted industry, involving quasi-criminal activity by manufacturers, foremen and all levels of the 'ordinary rank and file' workers, most of whom, it may be assumed, did not approve of, or indulge in, any other form of criminal activity.

4

The Construction of a Disciplined and Ordered World: Methods by which Employers Attempted to Combat Workplace Appropriation

In answer to the losses described in the previous chapter, the employers attempted to construct their own dominant factory culture which would compete with and attempt to overcome notions of customary entitlement, and prevent both small- and large-scale appropriation by imposing a framework of disciplinary norms. That framework was sometimes communicated through a list of factory rules or 'laws'. Mill regulations were pasted to the walls, or were printed in rule books. For example, in the Crowley Law Book, originally produced in the eighteenth century, Order Fifty-Three stated, 'In case any of this factory shall be guilty of . . . fellony [sic] or any heinous crimes which shall in justice oblige me to prevent or order their prosecution, they shall be prosecuted with the utmost severity of the law' (1952).

Authority structures within the factory

The control of labour was fundamental to keeping down production costs, but it also served both to symbolize and express the authority of the factory masters and their managerial staff (Dutton and King 1982). As Marx noted, work discipline could only be maintained by the Herculean efforts of employers, and employers used rules and regulations both to assert their authority, and to assist them in their control of workers' behaviour (Marx 1906, pp. 463–4).

The highest non-managerial positions within the supervisory structure were held by foremen. Historians have attempted to describe the position of foreman through labels and epithets such as 'the marginal man', 'the sergeant of an industrial army', 'the non-commissioned officer' and an industrial 'Emperor' (Wray 1949; Marx 1906; Melling 1980; Nelson 1975). These terms reflect the different interpretations both of the foreman's role and his position in the authority hierarchy of the factory. Usually few in number (unless the factory was extensive), they were responsible for the smooth-running and discipline of the entire factory. Under them lay the under-foremen or department foremen, who regulated the life of one particular department, sometimes with the aid of overseers or overlookers. If the mill was substantial, a large number of department foremen were engaged, and they answered either to the general foreman, the mill manager or (rarely) directly to the millowner. Lown (1990, p. 108) revealed that the owners of Courtaulds kept an equally vigilant eye on the overlookers as they did on the shop floor workers. The number of levels in the supervisory structure, and the distance between the workers and the mill owners, allowed the employer to present himself as the disinterested arbiter of discipline. In larger factories, this fiction was reinforced by having many departmental overseers, but also allowing employees to air their grievances directly to the master on rare occasions. Both department and mill foremen had the authority to discipline workers, impose fines and collect them and also to dismiss workers who did not do their duty to their satisfaction (Airedale Mill DMB 19 June 1862). At Hainsworths, for example, the overlooker reckoned up the fines and collected them every Monday morning (24 January 1842, Hainsworth DMBs, 1841–1850). The order to dismiss a foreman, by contrast, could only come from the mill manager or owner, or a full meeting of the company's directors (Airedale Mill DMB 19 June 1862).

The larger mills which had rooms (such as weaving-sheds) containing a great number of workers may also have used senior workers to look after a group of fellow employees in that department. Skilled workers, such as spinners, may have had responsibility for a group of piecers, for example (21 December 1871, Holly Mill, Directors' Minute Book; 1840 Report from the Assistant Hand Loom Weavers Commissioners, part III, 23, p. 542; Morris 1990, p. 86). In the cotton industry, this system was more formally organized. The leaders of family work groups which Davidoff and Hall (1987) believe were part of the authority structure had disappeared by the second half of the nineteenth century, however. Male mule operators were responsible for their attendant sets of piecers (generally children), and the mule master spinner paid the piecers from his wages. This system kept wages down, and ensured the proper supervision of young workers. The danger to the millowner was that it introduced another layer of supervision (and thus authority) which was not managerial in status, and not so easily controllable as the foreman (Thompson 1988, pp. 207–8). Perhaps for this reason this system was not adopted in the West Riding, where employers desired workplace authority to be invested only in themselves and the higher supervisory workers (11 October 1864, John Crossley DMB, WYAC, MIC: 22/1.

The supervisory hierarchy was stable but not static. Promotion for the unskilled and semi-skilled workers came not through qualification or training, but through serving one's time, keeping one's head down and catching the overlooker's eye (Thompson 1988, p. 210). Similarly, Morris explains how reliable men of a certain age, worn out by the arduous physical toil of factory work on the semi-automatic mules or the spinning jennies, could have their loyalty to the company rewarded by being 'made up' into overlookers and foremen (Garrett 1988; Morris 1990, p. 102). A contributor to the *Fortnightly Review* put it a little more strongly in 1868, stating that 'they are promoted from the ranks as a recompense for their subservience' (Abram 1868, p. 432). However, supervisors who fell from favour or failed in their duties could be demoted, and those who were found to have grossly misused their position could be dismissed and/or prosecuted despite their high position. For example, an under-foreman was demoted to willower, his former occupation, and his wages reduced 2s. a week accordingly (see 21 February 1842, Hainsworth DMB, 1841–50).

The authority of the foreman was wide and bounded only by the employer's infrequently expressed general policies and the worker's equally infrequent recourse to the law. In practice, apart from self-imposed limits the foreman's authority was mostly without boundaries and very formidable in the eyes of those under him. 'Each of these is a small centre of authority' said Abram (1868, p. 432). That is not to say that the workers did not devise strategies to undermine his power, or that those strategies were always unsuccessful, merely that the authority of the foreman, when he chose to exercise it, was almost unbreachable. As the semi-autonomous task-master who separated those who managed from those who were managed, he had a pivotal role in dealing with the detection and informal punishment of workplace offenders: those who appropriated materials or who 'stole' their employer's time.

The control of time

Labour was the greatest of all the production costs, and employers in the nineteenth century sought to maximize the potential of the labour they had hired by controlling workers' actions inside the factory. This rested on the belief that they had purchased both the labour and also the time of the worker for the period that they were employed. This relationship has been studied by Thompson, Hobsbawm and others, and has been the main focus for historians studying discipline in the factory. Hobsbawm explains how the 'Basic Principle' of nineteenth-century capitalism (to sell products for the highest amount while keeping production costs to a minimum) was better understood by the workers as the industrial system progressed, see Hobsbawm (1972, p. 344). Indeed, Edward Thompson's seminal work on the commodification of time saw this form of discipline as the defining characteristic of the factory system. As he explained in a much quoted passage:

> Those who are employed experience a distinction between their employer's time and their 'own' time. And if the employer must use the time of his labour, and see it is not wasted: not the task but the value of time when reduced to money is dominant. Time is now currency: it is not passed but spent. (Thompson 1967, p. 61).

Whipp has challenged the Thomsonian view, believing instead that time discipline was not the norm for most industries, and even in those that it was, the workers resisted the implications of time-thrift practices. His views do not alter the fact that in a factory-style production system, time-discipline was a necessary result of synchronized manufacturing processes, and was certainly in place in the larger Yorkshire textile mills by the mid-nineteenth century (see Whipp 1987, p. 218–9).

This ideology was codified into factory regulations and rule books such as the notorious Law Book of Crowley Iron Works (1952). Order 40 of that book, for example, noted incidentally, 'I have by sundry people working by the day with the connivance of the clerks been horribly cheated and paid for much more time than in good conscience I ought.' Similarly, the preamble for Order 103 complained that 'Some have pretended a sort of right to loiter, thinking by their readiness and ability to do sufficient in less time than others. Others have been so foolish to think bare attendance without being 'imployed' in business is sufficient'. Crowley employed a Monitor to detect any such 'sloth and villainy'. Later, in the more developed factory system, the role of the Monitor was performed by foremen. A century later, similar rules existed in the Yorkshire textile industries where production time lost due to this 'wasting' of time was recouped in fines and wage deductions. To quote the Stansfeld Mill rules:

> THE WORKPEOPLE are to observe the following RULES, and for every Neglect of each of them shall forfeit the Penalties annexed thereto; and if any of the Hands shall be found incorrigible by such Fines, the said Fine or Fines to be doubled and trebled according to the number of Offences committed. (Stansfeld Mill Rules, STA: 229)

Weavers found chatting or playing at their loom were fined two pence; those who left their loom without leave from the overlooker or master fined sixpence and any tarrying when handing in cloth to the taking-in room at the end of the day resulted in another two-penny deduction (Stanfeld Mill JM: 668). The Stansfeld woollen mill fined weavers one penny for every fifteen minutes they were late, and other factories locked their gates fifteen minutes after the mill engine had started, so that latecomers lost a morning's wages. At Moorcroft Mill in Bradford this practice continued until the 1960s, the only change being that the doors were closed after only five minutes if it was a rainy day, so the workers got soaked while they tried to persuade the doorkeeper to let them in.

Other rules in the nineteenth-century mills forbade talking between neighbouring machine minders (in fact this was usually impossible due to the deafening noise, and most minders quickly learnt to lip-read) and the playing of practical jokes. There were also rules which outlawed the drinking of alcohol either directly before, or during, work hours in case drunkenness caused inattention to duties. No ale was allowed within the Kellet and Brown or Hainsworth works, for example, with a five-shilling fine imposed on anyone found with drink in the mill (Kellet and Brown, Committee Book, 1847–73, Hainsworth DMB, 1841–50, Brotherton Library). At Bannermill, a female employee was fined 6d. because the glue on the end of the bobbin at which she attended loosened, and she was thus compelled to pay for the time which was required in replacing it (Duncan 1984, p. 43). Indeed, any time spent in non-production was subject to such fines. Again at Bannermill, 'About fifty persons . . . were compelled twice a day to pay a fine of 1d. for changing their clothes after going into the Mill, although only occupying them for five minutes at a time (Duncan 1984, p. 43). Some were fined a penny for turning their backs to a frame. Perhaps Crowley best summed up the time/wage relationship when he stated that he calculated wages, after all deductions for being at taverns, alehouses, coffee-houses, breakfast, dinner, playing, sleeping, smoaking, singing, reading of news history, quarrelling, contention, disputes or *anything forreign to my business*, any way loytering [our emphasis]' (Crowley Law Book, Law 103).

Although in some cases the control of time seems to have assumed a more fetishistic aspect, such as the overseeing of sporting leisure time outside of work, it was important to manufacturers primarily because it could affect production levels (Duncan 1984, p. 44). Increased profits by tightly controlling workers' time were not achieved without resistance from employees however. The amount of work completed by each worker during the hours they were employed was subject to contested rights of ownership, since time 'gained' by the workers involved a financial loss to their employers. This was a loss which may well have exceeded the costs of workplace embezzlement, but which is impossible to quantify. This loss of time, sometimes known as 'Corporation work' is discussed as an industrial crime by Samuel (1972) in discussion with other historians. Although the importance of time-management rules was reduced when work processes were mechanized (because steam-driven machinery set its own furious pace), large numbers of supervisory staff were still employed to watch that machine-minders did not 'waste' time or appropriate or damage their employer's property. As Pollard noted, 'When a mantua worker [embroiderer] chooses to rise from her seat and take the fresh air, her seam goes a little back, that is all, there are no hands waiting on her, but in . . . mills, all the machinery is going on, which must be attended to'(Pollard 1963, see also Ditton 1972; Lazonick 1978).

Tackling 'wilful' damage

Any damage to cloth or machinery, whether intentionally caused or not, was reported to the under-foremen, overlookers or managers, who then investigated how the damage had been caused (the term 'foreman' is used interchangeably with 'overlooker' and 'overseer'). In order to understand the status of the person or station they are referring to, it is necessary to know the size and organization of the supervisory hierarchy in the factory which is being described. In the smaller factories, for example, there may be only one supervisory worker, the foreman. In a larger factory, however, there may be a group of foremen who are primarily responsible for work discipline. Below them may be a series of under-foremen, and department overlookers, and above them, the mill manager or owner. Only in a few mills were cases of damage reported to the highest authority levels of the factory hierarchy:

> The Complaint book in which all complaints against workmen must be entered and signed by the complainant in case of bad workmanship such as slubbing,

> spinning or other kind of work done at this mill and in all cases, where practicable, samples of such bad workmanship to be deposited with the secretary for the inspection by the managers or for the inspection of the regular board meeting (19 June 1862 Airdale Directors' Minute Book, Brotherton Library).

After the investigation had ended, the foreman or manager then imposed the fine appropriate to the offence, as laid down in the rules. The spinners of Holly Bank Mill who were found guilty of damaging cloth were fortunate only to be fined five shillings (1 October 1869 Holly Bank Mill, DMB, 1868–77, *WYAL*). Workers in other factories were often required to pay compensation of double the cost of the damage, in addition to the fine. Moreover, workers could also find themselves in court for 'wilful' damage which was not only against factory rules but also contravened parliamentary legislation. For example, 12 Geo. I c.34, s.2 (1771) stated that any woolcomber or weaver who wilfully 'damnified, spoiled or destroyed any goods, was liable for double the cost of the damaged material, or three months' imprisonment in default' (Burn 1837, p. 516). Thirty-nine workers were prosecuted under this Act by the Worsted Committee between 1844 and 1876. The punishments of the twenty-four who were convicted ranged from their paying compensation to the victim to a number of months' imprisonment. Despite the provisions of the 1771 Act, which limited imprisonment to a maximum term of three months, two men received four months in Wakefield House of Correction, and one man was confined there for six months.

Judgements as to whether a piece of cloth had been damaged deliberately because of industrial sabotage, inattention to duties, or by faulty machinery, could obviously be marginal at times (21 June 1926 WCMB).The majority of wilful damage cases involved cloth damaged accidentally in the production process. The few cases of malicious damage done to cloth and machinery during, and in the immediate period before, strike action, were easy to distinguish from those of accidental damage. Industrial sabotage took the form of huge slashes in finished pieces, for example, or a deep cut through a number of sheets waiting to be dyed. It seems that foremen judged the existence of damage, however caused, as at least a fineable offence. Consideration of the quality of the raw material given to the worker or the efficiency of the loom (which varied greatly between looms in many factories) only mitigated the severity of the punishment. Moreover, financial losses caused by damage done to the piece, for whatever reason, had to be made up by the worker responsible. For these reasons, and because the wage deductions could be severe, the rules concerning bad workmanship were much resented by the workforce. In their efforts to conceal damaged goods they often caused themselves to come into contact with the Worsted Inspector. For example, a mill girl who feared that her poor work would be discovered and punished was found by the Worsted Inspector flushing the damaged bobbins down the mill water closet (June 1873 WCMB). Similar cases were also found in Oxfordshire (see Plummer and Early 1969, p. 22). In Lancashire, this problem was more serious, as the wage rate depended on the amount of cotton spun. Therefore, disposing of some cotton, whether worked up or not, would benefit the worker. Elliot describes how a great deal of cotton was thrown down the toilet, or out of the window, in order that a worker preserved her wages (see Elliot 1868, p. 330).

The Inspectors attempted to remedy problems of this kind by reminding the workers both of the penalty for wilfully damaging their work, and also that even if they had accidentally damaged their work, if they took it outside the factory to dispose of in order to avoid a fine, they were still guilty of embezzlement under the Worsted Acts. One-hundred-and-fifty notices, for example, were circulated in sixteen mills and among Ackroyd's millhands after several pieces of damaged goods had been found in the fields and streets around his mill (24 September 1866 WCMB). Although Inspectors and employers alike were unwilling to prosecute workers who smuggled out goods that had been accidentally damaged, the problem was a significant one and fines and prosecutions followed whenever it was decided that an example had to be made in order to discourage careless work.

The internal control of workplace theft

Both time 'wastage' and damage to raw and finished materials involved some reduction in profits for employers. The illegal appropriation of workplace materials, however, involved a more direct and potentially significant financial loss for the employer and gain for the employee. In the eighteenth century, the principal disadvantage of the putting-out system for the employers was the difficulty of supervising the labour force (Lipson 1921, p. 69). Concentration of the ownership of the raw materials, combined with the remoteness of the owner from the point of manufacture, made for special problems of supervision and provided particular opportunities for fraud (Styles 1983, pp. 173–74). Factory organization may have presented a chance to intensify employers' control through the imposition of a set of rules and regulations which could be enforced through an enhanced and centralized supervision of labour.

Warnings about appropriation were sometimes explicit. It would be difficult to misunderstand the nature of the rules which forbade cloth millers from taking soap out of the mill, or weavers from taking flocks home, for example (30 July 1838; 20 June 1842 Hainsworth DMB). Even clearer is the notice still hanging above a loom in a former worsted mill in Bradford (now a museum), which uncompromisingly warns that 'Persons repairing the machine must put all waste in the bin, persons removing waste will be prosecuted under the Act'. As previously discussed, the waste created in the production process, such as the pieces of wool left on the cogs of machines, was a frequent target for appropriation, and the management strove to reduce its vulnerability. Indeed, machine spinners, combers and weavers were not allowed to clean or repair their machines unless supervised by an overseer (those ignoring this rule were fined 6d. at Stansfield Mill (JM: 668). However, the most effective way by which the employers controlled the taking of waste was to prevent it being created in the first place. Since a good deal of waste was created in the combing and carding processes, machine makers sought to create a mechanical substitute for human labour. This they did in 1850, and the anti-appropriation uses of the condensing machine, which was the result of their efforts, were stressed in adverts, such as this one placed in the *Leeds Mercury*, in 1850:

> I calculate that under the present system there will come out of the cards about 10% of the best wool, which is as good as wasted, being mixed with the moats and knapps . . . now if only half of this fud could be saved and made into yarn, it would be a very material gain in the cost of cloth. It would also be the means of giving a check to the trading in fud or waste, which opens the door to all kinds of embezzlement of materials, which fudders are in the habit of receiving from any person without enquiring how he got them. The extent to which this is carried out would almost stagger belief, – a regular market is kept for the sale of it, and the manufacturing population of two or three townships are mainly employed in the making of clothes from this substance . . . It would be much better for the benefit of the trade if the makers, instead of selling the stuff, would burn it in their boilers, and never suffer a fudder to enter their gates (*Leeds Mercury* 23 February 1850).

The condenser reduced but did not eradicate the creation of waste, and since other processes also created waste products, control of the disposal of waste continued. Indeed, the efforts to control the appropriation of waste were redoubled when the 'recovered wool' industry began to use worsted waste as its raw material in the 1860s, giving a value to previously worthless dust and waste.

That decade therefore witnessed a proliferation of rules concerning waste and its disposal. Kellet and Browns 'Directors' Minute Books, to take one example, record that more attention had to be given to the sale of waste. They stored all of their waste in a secure shed until, after being cleaned, it was sold to the highest bidder (3 July 1866, Kellet and Brown DMB, 1847–73). Rule Eight at Stansfeld Mill stated that:

> All Weavers shall take proper care of their waste and put it in a bag provided for that purpose which bag shall be taken into the Warehouse at the time they go for the wages for their pieces, and those neglecting to do shall be fined Three pence (JM: 668).

Other companies employed foremen to see that all waste was cleared away and deposited in waste bins before the hands were allowed to leave the premises.

The rules mentioned above are unambiguous in their intent. However, other anti-appropriation rulings were more obscure. Measures which other commentators on work discipline have seen as only having symbolic meaning, specifically those relating to the control of movement around the factory, were in reality attempts to control appropriation. The principal disadvantage of the putting-out system for the employers was the difficulty of supervising the labour force (Lipson 1921, p. 69). Concentration of the ownership of the raw materials, combined with the remoteness of the owner from the point of manufacture, made for special problems of supervision and provided particular opportunities for fraud (Styles 1983, pp. 173–4). Factory organization offered a chance to intensify employers' control. The taking-in and weighing point where raw goods were picked up and finished work was deposited in the eighteenth century domestic system proved to be an imperfect system, but it did at least offer some protection, and therefore it was also incorporated into the design of the factories. The physical organization of the factory, with the importance of perimeter control in evidence, can be seen in the plans of Hunslett Linen Works (Calvert 1910); Whetley Mill (Anon 1893) and Bowling Dyeworks (Warehousemen and Draper 30September 1899) and in the laws of Crowley Iron Works; for example 'Law 45– Innkeeper's Entrance – clauses five and six . . . 5 'not to let any workman take any iron out of any door of the old iron workhouse except the lawful door going out at the office door and likewise the common door of the extra rod-iron warehouse; 6 not to lett (sic) any workman pass through my office with iron or otherwise take iron away out of my sight till I have first charged the same to the workman in my Iron Book for that purpose'. Workers picked up materials and took them back to their work areas and the 'weigher-in' checked the goods for 'lost weight' due to appropriation. Incidentally, however, this system increased the mobility of workers around the factory, and therefore increased the opportunities for appropriating goods while delivering one's own work. Rules were made to try and control unnecessary movement around the factory in an attempt to curb opportunities for theft.

One typical rule (in the Stansfeld mill Decalogue) stated that 'Workpeople of One Room are not to go into any Room or Rooms, unless they have a substantial reason for so doing, without forfeiting one penny for each offence.' Employers were aware that appropriated goods were hidden around the factory prior to removal, which may explain why even those workers with a good reason for leaving their own workrooms had restrictions placed on their actions. Similarly, the rule which stated, 'No Roving or Waste of any kind shall be carried out of the Room, and especially when going to the Necessaries, under three pence penalty for each offence' was an attempt to ensure that the mill privies were not the places where goods could be secreted on the person, stuffed down cleavages, trousers and so on. Obviously, leaving the room to visit the privy, or move materials around the factory, undermined the management's efforts to restrict employees to areas where they worked. However, many firms had prescribed routes of entry and exit to and from their interior work rooms. Kellet and Brown, for example, imposed a fine on anyone leaving the mill by going through a part of the mill where a lot of loose and unquantifiable wool was lying around (22 November 1872 Kellet and Brown).

These attempts to limit the movement of workers around the mill were aided by changes to the design of textile factories which took place around the mid-nineteenth century. Fully integrated mills, in which all of the processes of cloth production were carried out, began to be built with notions of internal and external security in mind from that date. Previously mills had been built next to open fields, or bordering streets and roads, with no physical barriers to separate them from the outside world (See, for example, James Wade's Mill, 1827; Walk Mill, 1839; D.W. Sharp's Mill, 1841. Marriner Invoices Brotherton Library 73/1), but in the 1840s and 1850s mills began to be more enclosed. Perimeter fences and walls were erected, and iron gates barred the way to those who tried to enter or leave the mill without permission (30 June 1848; 2 July 1852, Kellet and Brown; June 1868, Holly Bank Mill). These gates were put up at the single controlled point of entry and exit, which was next to what was sometimes called variously the gatehouse, the counting house or the time office. For example, Stubbing Mill, 1848; Horton Dye works, 1852; Dickinson Combing Mill, 1854; Cottingley Mill, 1855; Greengate Mills, 1860; Fleece Mill, 1860 (MM73/1 Invoices of Marriner and Co.).

The RCHM report also notes this change in mill design, for example in the plans of Saltaire Mill, Shipley, 1851; Spinkwell Mill, Dewsbury, 1851 and Alverthorpe, 1870. The RCHM plans are held in their London Offices, with copies available for view at Wakefield Archaeological Service headquarters. The external integrity of the mill was also preserved by other design features, such as the elevated gangway connecting Shed Mill to Victoria Mill, which meant that employees did not have to leave the mill enclosures when travelling between them (Sigsworth 1958). It seems that, as well as keeping employees in, such measures also preserved the physical integrity of the mill – and kept 'undesirables' out. However, only rarely do business or other records indicate the reasons why perimeter walls were erected, and it is therefore impossible to ascertain whether these external security measures were to stop appropriators taking materials out, or to stop thieves coming on to the premises to steal goods. The night-watchman's reports from Mark Oldroyd's mill mention, however, that the spikes put on top of the back yard walls were supposed to stop employees clambering over them (see reports of January 5 and 21, 1865, Complaints Book 1865–88, Mark Oldroyd and Son, Dewsbury Central Library, Ms. No. 361). The physical security measures which were internal to the mill, however, are clearly there only to control the behaviour of employees. Unfortunately, a comprehensive study of the interior layouts of mills is not possible. The RCHM 1992 survey found little information concerning the organization of rooms, and the numbers employed in each room, the number of internal doors and so on. Mill building plans or sale plans contain, in the main, little detail of mill interiors. Business records, however, do provide some information about the control of workers' movement around the factory by physical geography rather than rule books.

Workers who had to move around the factory because of the tasks they performed posed a problem to the foreman's attempt to control appropriation. Weavers and spinners, for example, could be kept constantly supervised in large rooms, and searched whenever they left the room, whereas wool porters and labourers were less easy to control (14 March 1865, Crossley DMB, Brotherton Library; *Bradford Observer* 3 July 1868). Accordingly, all rooms which contained valuable materials – pattern book rooms, or wool stores – were kept locked. Those employees who were allowed to enter them had to first obtain the key from the foreman (*Bradford Observer* 29 August 1865; Hainsworth, DMB, 12 February 1838, *WYAL*). Mill keys were jealously guarded because of the many robberies committed, not only in working hours, but also during the night. In April 1863, for example, the *Bradford Observer* recorded that two spinners were found breaking into the warehouse with a key; a month later a stolen key allowed entry to Illingworth's warehouse and in August a disgruntled ex-employee got into the mill with a key he had stolen while still employed (*Bradford Observer* 9 April, 7 May, 6 August 1863). In virtually all reports of robberies of this kind the newspaper stated that an employee or ex-employee had been arrested for the crime. The controls on movement around the factory, and the attempt to restrict access to valuable goods in the West Riding, seem like mere tinkering compared to the measures taken at Belper Mill in Derbyshire. This radial design mill, which allowed continuous supervision of the workforce, was modelled on Jeremy Bentham's Panopticon (an 'ideal' prison where inmates could be seen at all times by a warden in a centralized control centre). Indeed, it was the only building in England ever erected closely along Bentham's principles in the nineteenth century. However, the layout of Belper was not as efficient as those mills built in Yorkshire since the flow of production from raw materials to finished product was obstructed and this probably explains why the design never caught on.

Less than a quarter (23%) of the appropriations which were later prosecuted at quarter sessions were detected through random searches of employees, or other pro-active measures. Instead, news of the detection of an appropriation usually reached the attention of the foreman through other people. He could be informed by a policeman that someone had attempted to pawn appropriated goods, or sell them in the market place, for example. According to the quarter sessions evidence, however, most of the information that reached the foremen came from the workers under them (76%). The amount of attention which other employees paid to work-mates who were acting suspiciously was therefore crucial to the detection of appropriation.

Once the information had reached the foreman, his response was usually immediate. This is well illustrated in the testimony of these two witnesses heard in October 1840:

> Whilst I was waiting with my piece in the taking-in room, I saw a Tin Box without lid containing silk bobbins. Between 12 and 1 o'clock, the prisoner came in and sat down . . . in two or three minutes I heard a noise amongst the bobbins and I saw prisoner in a stooping attitude take something which she passed under her apron and put in her Pocket. When the Bell rang, we all went up Stairs – prisoner among our number. I communicated what I had seen. (George Lockwood, Fancy Weaver)
>
> In consequence of what Lockwood said, I pursued the Prisoner, overtook her 300 yards from the warehouse. I called out to her to stop. She turned round

> and said what's up. I said not much, but I want you to go back to the warehouse. When we had got into the first room I said what have you got belonging to us. She said 'Nothing'. I said she may as well give them up and she put her hand into her pocket and pulled out 3 silk bobbins . . . She said she had got them for her Tom – meaning her husband I suppose – so I said to Aaron Dalton in her presence 'Take care of this woman while I come back.' I went to Mr Norton (the owner then questioned her) then I called the Constable. (Thomas Eastwood, Foreman, 6 October 1840, Leeds QS1/179/9).

It was not unusual for the foreman to stop, search, accuse and question a suspected appropriator; approximately three in ten of those later prosecuted at quarter sessions were apprehended in this way. The foreman apprehended 27 per cent; other employees stopped 7 per cent and the police agencies apprehended 62 per cent of those prosecuted for embezzlement. In most of the remaining cases, the policeman or the Worsted Inspector was informed of the appropriation and then one or both police agencies stopped the worker, usually at the end of the working day.

Of course, those instances where the foreman decided that there was not enough evidence to warrant calling the lawful authorities, or when he decided to use informal sanctions against those he suspected, would not be recorded in the quarter sessions records. However, in those cases that were taken to court, the foremen seem to have been very successful in their questioning. 87 per cent of those apprehended and questioned inside the factory admitted their guilt to the foremen, and although these figures refer only to those cases of appropriation which were taken to quarter sessions, they sit easily with the impression gained of those cases prosecuted at petty sessions (if the newspapers, business records and Worsted Committee Minute Books are taken as indicative of how those cases were dealt with by magistrates).

Factory laws and the contract of employment

Within the factory walls, employers created a more ordered world through the use of sets of rules of behaviour. Managerial aspirations were transmitted to the workers vocally by the foremen, posted up on the walls of departments of the works, or painted on the factory walls as a visible and ever present reminder to the workers that employees who broke regulations harmed both themselves and the financial health of the mill. That message was reinforced of course by the fines imposed on each disciplinary indiscretion. The numbers of people punished by fines or dismissal for breaking factory rules undoubtedly ran into many thousands in the West Riding. Just one woollen manufacturer imposed 766 fines between March 1861 and October 1862 (Mark Oldroyd and Sons Complaints Book, 1861–88, Dewsbury Central Library, Ms. No.361). But to what extent were these punishments legally enforceable – were these rules contractually binding?

Employment contracts were concise documents which stated only what was needed for the company's administrative records – the number of hours to be worked, the rates of pay for the duties stated and the length of notice needed to terminate the contract, for example. In rare cases they also included the statement that the employee agreed to abide by the rules of the factory and consented to reasonable disciplinary measures if these rules were broken. At Stansfeld Mill, for example, the contract bound the worker to 'abide by all the Rules, Laws and Regulations, and Penalties of the said Mill or factory' (STA: 230). Statements such as these avoided the need to list every rule of the factory. Obviously there were problems in detailing all of the rules in the contract since they may have been lengthy and changed over time, but whether given in detail or in summary, an indication that factory rules would be accepted by the employee as part of his work contract would have allowed the employer to seek legal redress in the county or borough courts. In any case the opportunity to use legal force to reinforce the authority of factory rule books, by guaranteeing their adherence in an employment contract, was lost because of the reluctance of the textile manufacturers to use any form of written contract.

Anyone carrying out a survey of the textile business records of the West Riding cannot fail to be impressed by the almost complete lack of evidence of the contractual relationship between employer and employee. So much so, in fact, that Foster (1977) believed contracts to be largely mythical. Individual textile companies generated boxes and boxes of documents, including wage books, invoices, minute books of directors' decisions and so on, but few employment contracts can be found. The most comprehensive guide to Yorkshire business records is Hudson (1975); see also RCHM (1990). Given the fast turnover of staff in many factories, every large firm should have left hundreds if not thousands of surviving contracts. Simon's (1954) assertion that contracts were not used due to the illiteracy of the servant or even master cannot be correct. Although perhaps an unrepresentative sample of the working population, 43 per cent of those prosecuted at quarter sessions for appropriation in the 1840s, signed their name on voluntary deposition sheets, the rest made their mark. The prosecuting masters, as one would expect, had a higher literacy level (93%), as did the witnesses (with 78%), the majority of which were foremen. By the 1870s, the literacy level had risen to 78 per cent for the prosecuted workers, 76 per cent for the witnesses testifying against them and 100 per cent for masters. The majority of workers were therefore able to sign their names, and probably had at least a basic literacy. In any case, rules and regulations were read aloud to employees when they started work at some mills, and contracts, similarly could be read to the employee if need be. They could then signal their acceptance of terms by making their mark.

Having surveyed the records of thirty firms which yielded not a single contract, it seems incredible that written employment contracts were much used, let alone ubiquitous for the enforcement of employment duties in court. Not a single contract could be found in the documents of thirty companies held in the West Riding record repositories. Perhaps the fact that magistrates accepted evidence from foremen that factory rules had been broken indicates that oral contracts were more common, and that they were endowed with legal significance. The existence of oral contracts cannot be proved, of course, but if they did exist, master and servant legislation might have had an impact on appropriation.

The Master and Servant Act of 1823 only applied to servants, and not to agents, or those who were entrusted with their employer's property and therefore trusted with some autonomy (see Steinfeld 2001). However, later in the century, judges took a more expansive view, and included all those who were subject to their employer's authority as servants under the Act (Lobban 2012, p. 403). The 1867 Master and Servant Act (30 & 31 Vict. c.141) stated that direct imprisonment was to be reserved for aggravated cases of misconduct concerning 'injury to person and property, misconduct, misdemeanour, or ill treatment', but magistrates were still apt to give the clause a wide interpretation, and may have considered evidence of appropriation to be sufficient to convict under this clause (Burn 1837, p. 491). Under both master and servant and specifically anti-embezzlement legislation, the prosecution had to prove that the workers understood which materials were not allowed to them as perquisites. The courts pressed down on those who were 'failing to act in ways expected of those of their status' (Lobban 2012, p. 401). But how were those expectations expressed and reinforced?

How important were contracts and rules in establishing that this was the case? 'The servant', to quote Burn, 'implicitly contracts to obey the lawful and reasonable orders of his master' (Burn 1837, pp. 388–9), but were the courts willing to accept implicit contracts reinforced by the rules and regulations that were posted up in the factory as sufficient proof of contractual agreement? Reference to contracts was rarely made in trials for appropriation, and it appears that where the taking of customary perquisites was contested by both parties, the contract was seldom used to establish that the workers had agreed not to take certain goods. Rules and regulations, conversely, were usually sufficient to determine that certain appropriations were prohibited. For example, one set of magistrates decided that the rules of a factory were legally enforceable from the time they were originally communicated to the workforce, regardless of their being later defaced or even removed (*Bradford Observer* 8 December 1876, 4 December 1868).Workers may have defaced rules first, and most obviously, to demonstrate disapproval of the management and their laws, and secondly, so that they could plead ignorance of any rule they were accused of breaking. Accordingly, many of the rule notices posted up themselves contained warnings about defacement. Stansfeld Mill employees, for example, could be fined one shilling if they were caught damaging the rule notices (JM: 668). Similarly, in a case judged in 1873, it was proved that each employee had received a written copy of the rules seven years previously, and that those rules still legally bound the employees to act in certain approved ways. Similarly, Kellet and Brown required their workers to sign and swear that they had received a copy of the 'Factory Acts Simplified' (Kellet and Brown, DMB 1847–73). In yet another prosecution, this time against a striking female worker, it was asserted that she knew the rules of the mill as they were painted on the wall. Her reply that she could not read was ignored since the rules had been read to her on the day she started (*Bradford Observer* 4 December 1856).

Despite the general willingness of magistrates to 'recognize' factory law, there were occasions when they did not. Sometimes this was when the rules were found to support an employee's legal case. For example, the rules of one factory stated that those who neglected their work would forfeit their wages, and this several workers were prepared to do when they left the firm, but the magistrate still imprisoned them under the Worsted Acts. In this case the magistrate was willing to support the employers, despite both customs and rules. However, on other occasions, the prosecutors were unable to convince the magistrate that the transgression of work regulations was an illegal act. In 1873, for instance, a master and servant case was dismissed by the magistrates since the work regulations stated that fourteen days' notice was requested not required (*Bradford Observer* 3 January, 14 June 1873).

Simon also gives examples where the fact of the rules being posted up on the factory wall was insufficient to prove they had a legal validity. Simon suggests that in very many cases, the non-existence of a contract, or the lack of trade customs, was detrimental to the employee, especially in master and servant cases where the employer was being sued for not giving enough notice of dismissal. But this was not the situation with regard to appropriation, neglect or wilful damage cases. Mostly, it appears that the magistrates accepted that customs of the trade governed the internal life of the factory, with the foreman acting in court as the interpreter of these unspoken customs. Hobsbawm (1968) places the preservation of customs as central to the determination of wage levels. These also seem to have been accepted as valid by magistrates based on the customary rate for particular tasks. Why else would foremen turn up for court cases unprepared, with no documentary evidence to prove the existence of the factory rules which they alleged had been transgressed? Only on one occasion does the *Bradford Observer* record that the foreman produced a printed set of rules in court to prove that the regulations existed and were known to the employees (*Bradford Observer* 14 November 1849).

It was the lack of any contractual agreement which provided flexibility for the management. As long as magistrates were willing to accept the interpretations of the customs of the trade stated by management appointees as truthful and legitimate, contracts were unnecessary for the prosecution's case, and could only hinder the management's chances of gaining a conviction. Knowledge and adherence to 'the customs of the trade' was far more insidious, pervasive and successful in enforcing employer-dictated norms. But whenever employers perceived the customs of the trade to work against them, they were more likely to introduce factory rule books to eradicate, destabilize and undermine the existing value system. Whether through unspoken customs, or through printed rules, employers clearly wished to create a disciplinary world within the factory. When the workers entered their factory, they entered a largely private sphere of law and morality which overlapped with, and was bolstered by, civil and criminal legislation. Factory rules, the Worsted Acts and master and servant laws would therefore together have provided a textured layer of legitimacy for factory authority. So how far did employers actually rely on master and servant legislation as a disciplinary weapon?

The use of master and servant legislation in the West Riding textile districts

Between 1858 and 1867 in England and Wales there was an average of 9,000 prosecutions per year under master and servant laws, of which 5,800 resulted in convictions (Woods 1982, pp. 93–7). No wonder some historians have seen the master and servant legislation as the main weapon of discipline in the employers' armouries (Simon 1954, pp. 161–2). But the numbers of those prosecuted under master and servant laws between 1865 and 1869 in Bradford are small, compared to prosecutions in the similarly populated towns of Sheffield, Wolverhampton and Walsall. In Wolverhampton, master and servant prosecutions were taken out for 240 per 100,000 of the town's population. In Walsall, the rate was 145 per 100,000, and even Sheffield's low rate of 46 per 100,000 was higher than Bradford's 39 prosecutions per 100,000 (Bradford figures are compiled from the Chief Constable's Reports 1865–69. The figures for Walsall, Wolverhampton and Sheffield can be found in Woods 1982, p. 99). In other areas of the West Riding too, the master and servant laws were little used. In Wakefield, for example, between 1874 and 1880, only 24 per cent of those prosecuted at petty sessions for contractual offences were textile workers.

Woods and Simon agree that the master and servant laws were primarily used by smaller manufacturers. Support for this theory can be found in Sheffield, which was built on the small-scale cutlery trade, and in the Black Country workshop areas, which also had a greater number and rate of prosecutions than Bradford. Simon also stated that cotton manufacturers were slow to use the master and servant acts. However, there were one-hundred and ten prosecutions in Manchester in 1868, which equated to the same level of prosecution per capita as those in Bradford (Statistics of Crime, 1868, Manchester Central Library, 942.7389 M120, M122). Most of the Yorkshire court records and police statistics concerning master and servant are not sufficiently detailed to allow the identification of the prosecutor's occupation. The exceptions are the Wakefield Complaints Books, which reveal that textile manufacturers represented only a quarter of the plaintiffs in master and servant cases between 1874 and 1880. Since these records cover a short period of time, and a narrow geographic area which had a declining woollen industry, generalizations should be avoided. Are the low figures for Bradford due to textile manufacturers employing the Worsted Acts as an alternative to master and servant legislation? The Master and Servant Acts had their criminal claws clipped in 1875, when criminal jurisdiction was replaced with civil action under the 1875 Employers and Workmen Act. Subsequent legislation was more concerned with preventing strikes, or preventing the intimidation of blackleg labour by striking workers than ensuring that factory workers didn't take home waste materials. However, maybe the Master and Servant Acts were merely a distraction to those who could summon under the Worsted Acts.

Clause VII of the 1777 Worsted Acts was similar in tone to the master and servant legislation. Any worker who had not completed their work within eight days was to be proceeded against as if they had appropriated the goods. Originally aimed at the domestic worker to encourage the quick completion of work, the 'neglect' clause was equally applicable to factory workers who went on strike, or left to take a better paid job at another factory. Indeed, between 1844 and 1870, Inspectors took 322 workers to court for neglecting their work. Between 1844 and 1869, 11 per cent of the cases brought by the Committee were for neglect of work, and 26 per cent between 1870 and 1876 (WCR, *WYAB).*

The Worsted Acts were certainly more familiar to textile manufacturers than the master and servant laws. This, together with the easy availability of finding a person qualified to prosecute the abandonment of work, almost certainly meant that the employers may have favoured the use of the Worsted Acts over master and servant legislation. The critical difference between master and servant legislation and the Worsted Acts which may have influenced the manufacturers was the conviction rate. Whereas a low conviction rate was attained under master and servant legislation, 34 per cent in Wolverhampton, or 38 per cent in parts of Leeds, for example, the conviction rate for neglect under the Worsted Acts was 87 per cent (Woods 1982, p. 101; Bradford Chief Constable's reports, 1865–69; Batley petty sessions, 1874–80). The employers in Bradford faced a clear choice between using the master and servant acts, which had a conviction rate in Bradford courts of only 26 per cent, or the vastly more successful Worsted Acts. Indeed the high success rate of Worsted Committee prosecutions casts doubt over those commentators who have suggested that the employers wished only to 'frighten' workers by threat of legal action, which was then withdrawn when employees returned to work (Soderlund 1992).

Such a strategy may have been used to some extent. For example, in 11 per cent of the prosecutions prepared by the Worsted Inspectorate, against those 'neglecting' their work, the employer and employee settled their disagreement (in the employer's favour) before the case reached court. Notably this situation arose in the case of prosecutions aimed at breaking strikes. For example, only a handful of strikers, usually selected by the foreman, needed to be prosecuted to ensure the strike ended (14 April 1862 WCMB). It must be remembered, however, that this strategy worked best when the majority of those prosecutions ended in conviction. It seems clear from the Worsted Committee evidence that the employers wanted prosecutions to succeed whenever it was possible, since this was by far the best course for keeping work discipline. It is therefore likely that only a limited proportion of master and servant cases or Worsted Act cases were deliberately initiated by employers only to be later withdrawn.

Adding the number of prosecutions under the Worsted Acts to those under master and servant legislation does not seem to bring the figure up to the one that might be expected, given the size of the industrial population of Bradford. Possibly the deterrent effect of a very high conviction rate under the Worsted Acts was significant. Certainly the Worsted Acts struck hard at those who 'neglected' their work, and that may have deterred many workers from taking industrial action. It would seem that the high number of master and servant prosecutions in industrial regions other than the West Riding was due to the lack of protection afforded to employers in those regions by the Worsted Acts.

Detection and punishment

Where detected appropriations did not reach either petty or quarter sessions, the foreman must have been an even more crucial figure in the treatment of appropriation because the courts were only sometimes used as a theatre of punishment for appropriators and alternative punishment options were employed on other occasions.

The reactions of the mill authorities to the appropriation of materials were also often dependent on the gender of the accused. The physical geography of production in the factories particularly impinged on female workers' freedom of movement and actions within the working environment – a feature that non-industrialists were slow to grasp. In 1868, a contributor to the journal of TNAPSS suggested three ways of controlling female labour. First, women of 'staid character' should be placed in all rooms. Second, privacy must be made impossible, every spot being open to public view, so as to identify any misbehaviour. Third, each room must have, in addition to an overlooker, a general superintendent, a person whose duty is to visit each room regularly but without warning (Baker-Smith 1868). In fact, the author only outlined a situation which already existed in many of the large factories and a position which many smaller firms aspired to, if they could afford the necessary physical changes to the factory and the increased wage costs of more overseers (Half Yearly Report of Factory Inspectors, Saunders, 12 April 1842). Men were more likely to be prosecuted, because women, being unskilled labour, were easier to replace when dismissed (Half Yearly Report of Factory Inspectors, Report of James Stuart, 15 March 1837).

Overseers were much more likely to treat female offenders informally, as they were directly responsible for female weavers' behaviour. Nevertheless, despite the supervision, appropriation continued. Considering the relatively restricted amount of movement around the factory allowed to women, it is not surprising that their preferred way of taking materials from the factory (as with many other larcenies committed by women) was by hiding them on their person. Quarter sessions records reveal that all of the female offenders had secreted the goods on their person, whereas only 54.0 per cent of the men had done so. As previously stated, men had opportunities to leave goods appropriated from one area in another area for picking up at a better time, or could throw the goods over the factory walls to be picked up by accomplices, or by themselves, after work. Searchers at the factory gates being male – Constables, Worsted Inspectors and foremen – may not have been able to search women as thoroughly as they could men. However, since Esther Mitchell was found by a Worsted Inspector to have worsted waste hidden in her cleavage, some searches were clearly intimate in nature (July 1841 Wakefield QS). Moreover, since the searches in the weaving rooms were carried out by mature trusted women who performed more personal searches, most of the hidden goods must have been detected before the factory gates were even in sight. These women had no other function other than performing personal searches on workers, and they were never given overall responsibility for discipline (see *Half Yearly Report of Factory Inspectors*, Saunders, 12 April 1842). This was one of the first uses of women being used to search other women, and was later taken up by police forces for the searching of female suspects and prisoners.

Women did have some manoeuvrability within the factory authority structure when their misdemeanours were discovered since overlookers may have needed to tolerate a certain level of appropriation in order to maintain good labour relations with the spinners and weavers under them. Furthermore, women had ways of strengthening their negotiating positions which were not open to men. For example, sexual favours may have been offered by the women, or demanded by the foreman, in order to keep the offence from progressing further in the disciplinary process. Foremen may also have been sympathetic to women who pleaded poverty for themselves and their children. Therefore, female factory workers may well have employed various successful strategies to destabilize and rework the unofficial 'rules' which governed gender and class relations within the factory in a way which would enable them to negotiate a better position in the complex inter-relationship between the foreman and those under him. This was a relationship which formed a separate sub-culture within the dominant factory culture of time and work discipline. Nevertheless, the character and personal philosophy of individual foremen may still have been the most influential factor in the decision to prosecute female workplace offenders. Prosecution was more likely if the route from detection to prosecution did not involve the foreman. If foremen were involved, they mainly chose forms of punishment for workplace appropriation other than prosecution. The use of informal punishments for women may have been reinforced by the apparent difficulty in securing convictions over both married and/or young women. Coverture ensured that prosecutors were careful to proceed only with very good cases against women, or with cases involving unmarried women above the age of majority. With fewer and fewer women progressing through each stage of the journey from committing an offence to prosecution it is little wonder that the percentages of female to male appropriators were so disproportionate.

Indeed, recourse to physical punishment of varying harshness appears to have been the first and favourite punishment option of the foreman for women and children, with those who broke work disciplines subject to spontaneous and immediate physical sanctions. Overlookers used mild beatings to hurry-up slow workers as a matter of course. One foreman always gave the last boy to finish doffing a few kicks or knocks around the head with machine rollers which were of sufficient severity to leave bruises. On one occasion he caused internal abdominal bleeding which led to a nine-year-old-boy's death. The judge who sentenced him to a year's imprisonment said that, 'there was, in such factories as the prisoner was in the habit of working in, an amount of bullying and coarse treatment exercised by overseers and persons in the prisoner's position over little boys who happened to be under them' (*Bradford Observer* 2 December 1875). But this was an obvious remark to those who worked in the mills, for in the factory violence was casual and deeply ingrained in the working environment.

In a few cases the physical violence seems to have been more considered and pre-meditated. One such case was reported in detail by a Factory Inspector. In the mill he described, children who infringed factory laws in any way were made to stand on ladders holding a broom above their heads for up to twenty minutes. A young girl, Inspector Saunders related, had

> disobeyed an order which subjects every person going out of the room to a search, for the purposes of preventing the making away with the waste ends of worsted. She afterwards attacked, and beat the person charged with the duty of the search, for having reported the offence . . . She was ordered to ascend the steps and hold the brush. Booth (the overlooker), however, in addition to the usual punishment, now required the child to kneel down and beg his pardon before he would allow her to resume work' (Half Yearly Report of Factory Inspectors, Saunders' Report, 12 April 1842).

The child held the broom aloft for an hour and a quarter. The overlooker was reprimanded by the master when Saunders reported the incident to him, but he kept his job. As can be seen in Margaret Newbery's account of life at Drummond's mill in the pre-First World War period, these practices persisted well into the twentieth century:

> The overlooker would walk down the aisles waving his alley strap and cracking it on the floor. The alley-strap was a piece of leather about 27 inches long and 10 inches broad; it was fixed to a handle, and when swung round, hitting the floor with a violent whack, a most fearsome thing. I was always afraid of it. It cracked so often near me when I was least expecting it. I have seen George whang it round the boys when they misbehaved, he also used to get them round the ear and make them wriggle . . . if there were any arguments, the alley-strap would settle them (Newbery 1992, pp. 48–9).

Similarly, in the days before the World War II, the culture of the factory remained oppressive. The position and character of the foreman was more important than their gender. Vera Smith spoke of the first time she met the female overlooker at her mill:

> She asked to see my needles with which I mended the pieces. After taking one look at them she put them in her pocket and said they were no good as they were too long for this work and I would have to buy a packet of 'her' needles (then) I was told no-one sat down to burl, you had to stand up and if Miss Taylor saw you sat down she came up and shouted at you to stand. Miss Taylor's number one rule was no talking by anyone, anywhere in the room with the exception of herself. You could only speak during breakfast and dinner times. Her favourite pastime was walking up and down the aisles between the tables and then pouncing on some unsuspecting mender who was sat down mending a felt. 'I say, you' was the

> way she addressed everyone, she never ever spoke your name. 'Get on your feet where I can see you and stop wasting time.' She would take the felter the girl was working on, and pull out the threads saying 'This is no good, start over again.' This reduced most of the women to tears which was exactly what she liked and then she would come out with her favourite saying. 'The more you cry the less you'll pee' (consequently, less time would be wasted in visiting the mill privy, Smith 1990, pp. 106–7).

Prosecutions of over-physical or cruel foremen were rare, simply because workers had little to gain from a successful prosecution, save a few pounds compensation, unemployment and a reputation as a troublemaker. Moreover, just as the magistrates accepted factory rules as having legal force, the courts also accepted the foremen's assertions that they were entitled to physically discipline workers. Even those magistrates who eschewed this view, and made statements in court to that effect, were lenient in the sentencing of foremen. This may be because some magistrates lacked sufficient knowledge of the internal life of the factory to make appropriate judgements. For example, one foreman was tried for assaulting a lad under his charge, striking him twice in the face for neglecting his work. There was little doubt that this boy had been struck. However, the real nub of the case was that the boy had recently testified against a foreman in the same firm when he had been tried for the manslaughter of another young worker. The Mayor, who judged the assault case, said he was determined to teach the defendant and those occupying the same position that they were not allowed to strike those under their supervision. The foreman paid the £5-00 fine, and returned back to work (alongside the boy). So little appreciation of the conditions within the factory did the magistrate have, that he was unconcerned with the future working conditions the boy would endure: they cannot have been happy ones (*Bradford Observer* 5 December 1864).

Nor could the Mayor empathize with the position of female employees. Two female weavers accused of neglecting their work, declared that they had left the works to get away from the overlookers who, 'were in the habit of taking liberties, and, if not repulsed, using the workpeople improperly' (*Bradford Observer* 27 January 1853). As previously explained, this was not an uncommon occurrence, and many such cases were brought before the courts. The Mayor, however, merely stated that their complaints should have been taken to the masters, and he ordered them to return to work (*Bradford Observer* 27 January 1853). His assumption that the women would have access to the master, and that he would champion their cause over the foreman's was somewhat optimistic. The factory was, after all, to quote Morris, 'a world of dependence, violence, humiliation, paternalism, gratitude, degradation and decision' (Morris 1990, p. 116). Those women were unlikely to enlist the help of the master in challenging the authority of the guardians of this world, the foremen. As for the attitudes of the foremen themselves, only on those very rare occasions when workers took their foremen to court, were they made aware of the legal limits of their power. But perhaps the feeling most prevalent in the foreman's heart, after sentence and censure by magistrates for cruel and unnecessary discipline, was not contrition or regret, but surprise.

Decrying 'character' and constructing 'blacklists'

Subtle punishments were also dispensed which lacked the spectacle of immediate physical discipline but were detrimental to a worker's wage. For example, whenever foremen gave the better materials to women they favoured, or who had provided them with sexual services, and kept the poorer material for unpopular or ill-disciplined workers, they had an adverse proportional effect on the weekly wage (Smith 1993, pp. 137–9; anonymous letter from the warp dressers to Bairstow's, *WYAL*, 152: 42). Similarly when an awkward worker's loom was 'trapped' – i.e. jammed – the overlooker could be tardy in repairing it, so the weaver could not make good wages (*Bradford Observer* 22 March 1855). These sorts of punishments were difficult to avoid and hard to combat. When poor material continued to be given out to certain people, workers tried to find work in other factories, but were often hauled back by legal actions. For example, in 1848, two women left their factory because the warps given out were consistently poor, and three women left another factory because they waited long periods before receiving weft, which lowered their wages under the piecework system. In their trials under the Worsted Acts, all of these women were fortunate to receive sympathetic treatment from a magistrate known for his antipathy to mill owners. Colonel Pollard was a member of the landed classes, and coalfield owner. He and his sons George and Joshua were criticized by the Worsted Committee for their sympathy to the textile workers who appeared before them in petty sessions. He stated that 'he had never known either a master or overlooker in such cases acknowledge that the warp was a bad one!' before dismissing the cases (*Bradford Observer* 27 January 1848). However, although they had avoided the imposition of a legal penalty, they still had to return to a factory where they suffered lower wages than their peers. This was not the only informal punishment option.

Two subtle and long-lasting punishments were the blacklisting of 'miscreants' and the perhaps lesser sanction of not providing a reference. The *Bradford Observer* recorded the existence of a blacklisting system (23 February 1857), but the story (one almost might say parable) of Emily Johnston best describes the effects of the system: how the blacklist placed a *cordon sanitaire* around dismissed workers, and prevented them gaining employment at other works. In her autobiography she stated that:

> I was discharged by the foreman without any reason assigned or notice given, in accordance with the rules of work. Smarting under this treatment, I summoned the foreman into court for payment of a week's wages. . . . On account of that simple and just law suit I was persecuted beyond description – lies of the most vile and disgusting character were told upon me, till even my poor ignorant deluded sister sex went as far as to assault me on the streets, spit in my face, and even several times dragged the skirt from my dress. Anonymous letters were also sent out to all foremen and tenters not to employ me, so that for the period of four months after I wandered a famished and persecuted factory exile' (Johnston 1867, p. 24).

It can be surmised that this informal employment security network worked equally well with suspected appropriators, whether they had been prosecuted and convicted or not. The pleas of workers to ignore the blacklist was unlikely to be heeded by prospective employers. John Foster, for example, received a letter from an applicant which stated, 'I am aware you have heard certain statements about my character of an aggravated nature, but exaggerated, though some are true, but if I should have the honner to enter your service will never be repeated' (Foster, Private letters, Box 95, letter no. 135, Brotherton Library). The author was not hired. Another bar to gaining employment for workers who had been dismissed from another mill was the withholding of an employment reference. A good reference from a previous master or foreman could be crucial to securing employment. For an idea of the content of these references, see 'Testimonial to James Leach, 15 May 1860; and Testimonial to Thomas Lewthwaite, 14 May 1860; Holden Archives, Box 8/1 Brotherton Library. One employer, Barran, for example, kept every reference he received, and put a mark by those he engaged. If they were not taken on, a reason was stated: 'small'. . .'wears glasses'. . .'Catholic'. See Mr. Barran's Memorandum Book, *WYAL*. By doing this he could check who gave the reference for any worker who subsequently misbehaved.

Prospective employees turning up with a reference from that source were then treated more cautiously. Workers who could not gain a reference from their last master were sometimes driven to have references forged. However, any person who was found to be impersonating a master and giving false character statements could receive a fine of twenty pounds, or three months in prison in default – under the ubiquitous 1777 Worsted Acts. It hardly needs to be said that those dismissed for appropriation would not receive a reference, and the only occasion when their name was mentioned by one foreman to another would be to warn them off.

As Johnston's autobiography makes clear, once dismissed, a worker may have waited a long time before gaining another position. Possibly they would have had to move to another factory district before doing so. In the meantime, life could be hard. Unemployment was a constant fear of those in work, and a curse to those out of it. Dismissal from work could therefore be as harsh a punishment as a month's imprisonment. Those who ended up in gaol, however, still had to cope with unemployment when they were released. As previously discussed, the dismissal of workers was especially effective as a punishment when the economy was in crisis and jobs were scarce. When the situation was reversed, and dismissed workers were quickly employed by competitors who needed workers of any quality to complete orders, then the potency of this punishment may have been reduced.

In conclusion, it appears from the court, business and newspaper archives that physical punishments and fines were routinely visited on those who infringed any factory rule, except those dealing with the neglect of work or appropriation of materials. Appropriators were rarely allowed to remain at work after these offences had been discovered (24 September 1866 WCMB), and those employees who left work without notice were usually either dismissed or prosecuted. Those appropriators who did face dismissal or prosecution were left to develop limited options to deflect or mediate the foreman's discipline. If successful strategies were not developed, then workers were reliant on the protection and patronage of others.

Mediating discipline

Some historians believe a dynamic existed which placed boundaries around the foreman's actions. There was a close relationship between the activities and duties of the foreman, and the state of industrial relations within the factory (and indeed outside the factory in wider social contexts, see Smith 1993). The foreman's temperament, interpretation of his duties and general attitude towards shop-floor workers were all important factors in establishing a level of discipline within the factory. Several historians have suggested that the co-operation of workers was needed to maintain production times, and that the foreman could not risk being overly oppressive in case this co-operation was lost (Smith 1993, p. 144). 'Unless he could win the respect of his subordinates as well as the trust of his supervisors,' said Melling, 'the supervisor's position was untenable. At the same time, the position of a good foreman was not likely to be challenged even by his own employer, for fear of losing both a good workman and an able organizer' (Melling 1980, p. 129).

The last part of that statement is undeniable. Masters gave their foremen fulsome support both in the factory and in the courtrooms, not merely because the foreman shared in part the authority of the master, but also because masters relied on their foremen (*Bradford Observer* 8 March 1873). The foreman was not simply a shadow of the master, he was in a real sense the master's man. The co-operation of workers under him may have increased production rates, but so did the strict enforcement of the factory's laws. Moreover, the efficient performance of a foreman's duties, including disciplining the workers whenever rules were broken, would guarantee a foreman's job, unmolested by his superiors. However, Roethlisberger and others have noted that in modern times the foremen's freedom of action was reduced by the unionization of the workers under them (Roethlisberger 1944–5, p. 283, Wray 1949, p. 298). Could it be that workers turned to one of the numerous textile workers' organizations which sprung up in the 1870s to redress their real or imagined grievances?

Perhaps for this reason there was a vast increase in the number of assault prosecutions aimed against foremen in the 1870s. Textile workers may have challenged in court the right of the foremen to use violence as a chastisement, encouraged by moral and financial support from the newly formed trade associations. A strongly unionized factory would also be in a position to impose restrictions on the foremen with the warning of strike action (although strikes over the mistreatment of individual workers were rare). Collective resistance may have been facilitated by the strong communal identification engendered by unionization, but the form of action was still privatized, informal and covert. For example, an overlooker who worked through a strike, 'came to be looked upon with terrible hate by the union men who threatened him with violence'. In fact they solemnly swore that they would kill him, and the man's son, who later became first an overlooker and then a millowner himself, described how the family, 'durst not light a candle after dark for fear of being watched and injured' (I. Roberts, The Life of Israel Roberts, 1827–81, Yorkshire Archaeological Society, Ms.1079). Extra-legal measures taken within the opaque world of the workplace were perhaps more common and more successful than were courtroom outings.

Collusion, self-preservation and respectability

Some employees, for many possible reasons, informed on their fellow workers. This could be dangerous. Although the factory was generally an ordered environment, at certain times it could be an unruly place. For example, the many disputes between workers taking place at break times were not 'policed' by foremen since they did not usually interfere with production levels. There may have been numerous occasions – at dinner-breaks, at the end of shift and on the way home – when workers who had incurred the wrath of their colleagues could be confronted. Presumably informers would try to avoid such potentially violent confrontations, and an entry from the report of an Inspector in the early twentieth century illuminates the calculations 'honest' workers performed whenever goods disappeared. The mill manager told the Inspector that they were frequently missing things but that he could not get any information whatever out of his workmen. The Inspector spoke to a workman he knew, who admitted that fents did disappear, and that this was to be expected because:

> When a length is cut off a piece because it is damaged, or for any other reason, the short lengths are left in the finishing room where any of our workers can get to them, men of every department come in here and sometimes take a length' (31 December 1917 WCMB, 56D.88/1/7).

The Inspector suggested that if he took more interest and informed him who was taking the goods he would be rewarded. The man, however, dismissed his suggestion. 'If I did, and my workmates found out I had been peaching (informing)', he said, 'they would soon make the shop too hot for me' (31 December 1917 WCMB 56D.88/1/7). The Inspector had visited the factory a few times since this conversation, but the man he talked to could never be found. One imagines that informers could meet a similar fate as those who refused to join strikes. For example, one man reluctant to join a dispute in 1851 was strung up to a beam in the mill by his fellow workers and beaten with leather straps until he agreed to reconsider (*Bradford Observer* 12 June 1851). For this reason masters and Worsted Inspectors occasionally received anonymous notes informing them of the malfeasance of others. For example, an anonymous letter sent to Drummond, informing him that a man regularly took soft soap home in his breakfast can to sell to his neighbours (3 January 1881, WCMB).

Worsted Inspectors, after investigation, were able to judge whether these were useful underground or 'subterranean messages' (as one Inspector termed them), or malicious rumours without foundation (at least if the experience of twentieth-century Inspectors hold true for those in the nineteenth – see 23 June 1913 WCMB). However, the impression that no worker would inform on appropriators is erroneous. In fact, a majority of the witnesses that testified against the accused were her or his fellow employees, and the quarter sessions depositions relating to appropriation show that work-colleagues reported each other to the foreman, acted as witnesses against each other and also assisted the foreman to apprehend suspects.

There are a number of possible reasons why fellow employees of the accused would inform a supervisor of a workmate's appropriation, and speak against him in the courts. First, they may have felt compelled to testify under pressure from the foreman, despite broadly accepting the accused's right to appropriate customary perquisites. They may have only acted as a witness in cases which they considered to be 'theft' rather than issues of customary rights. They may have desired that someone in their factory be caught for offences which they also themselves carried out, as the appropriations of the person they informed on had become scandalous, and were causing unwanted attention from suspicious foremen. Last, most workers and supervisors may have shared the view that all appropriation was wrong, and should be punished. The foremen holding this view because it was their function to hold such views, and the employees sharing them because the domination of work over their lives 'consequently effected the acceptance of the authority that governed the routines of work' (Joyce 1980, p. 99). It is true that the proportion of fellow employees who testified against an appropriator declined as the century progressed (from 52 per cent in 1840 to 37 per cent in 1880). This may be because the beginning of collective organization in the 1870s strengthened the bonds of worker solidarity. More likely the agents of the factory supervisory system had become increasingly proficient at detecting appropriation. They then relied less on information provided by colleagues of the appropriator than they had in the 1840s. In the 1840–5 period, information about offenders had been received from fellow workers in 71.6 per cent of cases prosecuted at quarter sessions, by the 1870–5 period that had dropped to 42 per cent.

Unfortunately it is not easy to test any of the above hypotheses concerning witnesses. Nevertheless, from the depositions, and the autobiographies of millworkers, the dominant hegemonic ideology of the factory seems the most likely reason why so many workers informed on their workmates. The factory constituted so large a part of many workers' lives that it was 'perforce a source of pride and meaning' (Joyce 1980, p. 98). Appropriation by a few employees may have undermined the pride and feelings of respectability that many felt in their occupations, their factory and their class; see for example the discussion concerning labour solidarity and the reasons why fellow workers informed on one another, between Hobsbawm and Newens in *BSSLH*, 1976, pp. 5–8. Certainly this was the case at Preston in 1825. Chapman described how 'Weavers of the better sort felt keenly the disgrace into which the surrender to dishonesty was dragging their class' (Chapman 1904; see also Report of the Committee on the Petitions from Hand Loom Weavers, 1834, x Q5894–5). These weavers offered to combine with their masters to eradicate 'the monster' as they termed the appropriator (Chapman 1904). The majority of employees may have accepted the authority of factory supervisors and also shared their views on what they considered to be theft. If they did, they would have shared similar views to those workers praised by Gladstone in 1864 for their 'self-command, self-control, respect for order, patience under suffering, confidence in the law, and regard for superiors' (Thompson 1988, p. 206).

One has to be careful in advancing such views without a good deal of evidence to support them, and two factors must be remembered: first, that a considerable amount of appropriation continued to take place throughout the nineteenth century, and so the factory hegemony was not completely dominant; second, that the proportion of the workforce which shared the views of the witnesses cannot be determined. It is possible (although unlikely) that the people who testified were the only people willing to do so, in which case, the picture gained from the quarter sessions is skewed and biased. The depositions indicate real differences of opinion between the accused and the witnesses about the legitimacy of appropriation, but no sources exist which can say whether the views of the witnesses, or indeed the accused, represent those widely held by the whole of the factory workforce. The question of whether information about appropriation reached the ears of the foremen because some employees wished to ingratiate themselves with authority or because appropriation scandalized a respectable and respectful workforce therefore remains unresolved.

'Turning in' appropriating workmates, for whatever reason, could be useful in mitigating the foreman's discipline, since it bound workers and supervisors together in a spirit of co-operation and joint desires. But it was not the only means of creating associations between workers and supervisors. Other tactics included stressing old village loyalties to reinforce geographic identification (Smith 1993, p. 136). And there was also a degree of geographic loyalty demonstrated in local newspapers when a Worsted Inspector from another town or area prosecuted a popular local – see a case involving Yewdall in Chorley, reported in *Preston Guardian* 14 May 1853, for example. It is not likely that in Yorkshire this village patronage lasted well into the factory age, however. Most workers who joined factory workforces after 1840 were from the locale, rather than from other towns or villages some miles away. In any case it is doubtful that emphasizing the co-dependence of workers and supervisors in the production of finished goods, or the common features of their working and living conditions, benefited the shop-floor workers. The foremen regarded themselves, and were regarded by the workers, as the labour aristocracy, and did not view shop-floor workers as equals.

Nevertheless, the tactic, if it can be termed thus, which most benefited the worker was the development of a relationship based on daily contact, friendly chatter, good time-keeping and conscientious work methods. Modern studies of the foreman have all emphasized the consensual nature of relations between the supervisor and those under him. Joyce and F. M. L. Thompson have both suggested that this was also the case in the nineteenth century, while Price has described the conflictive model of industrial organization. The behaviour of the foreman can be taken as the barometer to measure the nature of industrial discipline. However, information about foremen's behaviour has mainly been obtained from the autobiographies of the supervisors themselves. Few autobiographies were written by the millworkers who experienced the effects of industrial discipline. Nevertheless, evidence can be found for the later nineteenth- and early twentieth-century from memoirs and oral history archives. They present mixed experiences of the factory, regarding both the disciplinary culture and the worker's ability to disable over-physical foremen.

All of these tactics may have been of some use in persuading a foreman to treat small infractions of the rules leniently. A foreman had to ensure, however, that the masters did not view the relationship between supervisor and supervisee as being too close, otherwise he could find himself accused of condoning or colluding in acts of appropriation. Such was the case in 1881, when a weigher-out in the combing department was suspected of appropriation. His house was searched, but nothing found, and it was decided that a prosecution was unsupportable. Nevertheless, the hint of impropriety was enough to have him dismissed (3 January 1881, Oct 18 1880 WCMB). He was luckier than the foreman who had been persuaded by his piecers that the previous foreman had allowed them to appropriate and sell worsted waste. He found himself appearing at quarter sessions (31 July 1843, Sheffield QS).

The concerns of the employers, with regard to the behaviour of the foreman, are perhaps best seen in this entry in the Worsted Committee Minute Books: 'It was thought that a spinning manager at Jos. Ackroyd was disposing of knitting material through one of his female hands, it however transpired only to be a case of undue familiarity' (18 June 1888, see also 23 June 1915 WCMB). Since the suspicion of collusion with employees could lead to dismissal or worse, foremen kept some distance between themselves and even the experienced and loyal skilled workers. Friendly work-relationships, developed over decades, might have stopped a foreman disciplining a reliable and skilled worker for a minor misdemeanour. Working friendships were less likely, however, to keep the foreman from reporting a suspected appropriator to his employer. Again, one must be careful, for if friendship stayed the foreman's disciplinary hand, then these cases would never have been recorded. What can be stated is that appropriation was considered a serious offence and in the majority of cases it was not tolerated.

There are numerous reports in the Bradford newspapers in the 1870s of foremen and some manufacturers being prosecuted for a range of physical abuses on female workers (Survey of the *Bradford Observer*, 1870–75). It may be that assaults on male workers did not offend sensibilities in the same way as assaults on women did, and that male victims did not seek redress through the courts. More likely is that they were less subject to violent informal punishments and more vulnerable to formal prosecution. To take two typical examples, a spinning manufacturer had recently hired an unpopular overlooker, and this man was regularly 'hooted' and jeered by the mill workers as he walked home. On one occasion the manufacturer came out to 'box the ears' of the culprits. He hit two passing mill girls so hard that one was made permanently deaf (*Bradford Observer* 7 November 1874). In another case, a foreman was accused of twice assaulting on separate occasions an eighteen-year-old described as being 'weak in mind' (*Bradford Observer* 20 August 1875). The assaults, probably of a sexual nature, were reported to the girl's father by another worker. The foreman offered the father £5 to 'square it', but he decided to prosecute instead, and the foreman was convicted. Possibly the irony of imposing a £5 fine was not lost on the magistrate.

The foremen who were accused of assault gave a variety of explanations for their behaviour. Aside from simple denial, they alleged that physical discipline was a part of working life, and implied that they enjoyed the same rights as parents in disciplining young workers. For example, one of Ripley Mill's foremen seized a woman employee by her hair and hit her on the head because she was not attending to her work. Previously she had been dismissed for inattendance, but her mother had pleaded for her reinstatement. The foreman thus contended that he had been given permission to discipline the girl by her mother, he was nevertheless fined five shillings (*Bradford Observer* 1 June 1878).

Some magistrates felt that it was their duty to protect female workers from physical abuse; others were more sympathetic towards the authority figures in the factory. For example, when an overlooker made improper remarks to a sixteen-year-old mill girl, his advocate asserted that 'there is no case to answer because if overlookers who had good characters were to be convicted on such evidence they would never be safe' (*Bradford Observer* 15 September 1873). The case fell. The general attitude of the magistracy in these cases can be summed up in this statement by a magistrate in 1874: 'Overlookers', he said, without irony, 'must always be protected from their hands' (*Bradford Observer* 27 June 1874). Even when assaults were proved, it was felt that female workers should be cautioned on their behaviour. For example, when a foreman was convicted of assault he pleaded for mitigation on the grounds that the victim had provoked him by swearing. The magistrate fined him 2s., but also chastised the woman for using foul language (*Bradford Observer* 19 November 1875).

Workers who felt they were unjustly treated (or in search of a successful strategy to undermine supervisors) may have attempted to skip a disciplinary level, or many levels, and appeal directly to the owner. Letters held in the archives of Holden, Bairstow and Foster contain personal requests for help of one sort or another, for example. However, most of the letters were attempts to keep employment or raise wages (letter to Bairstow from the employees of Oats Boyd Mills, WYAC, JM.670). In all of the letters the workers attempted to awaken the employer's sense of duty, and the fact that they are writing at all illustrates their belief that the master was the highest authority in the factory. Take, for example, this letter written in 1857:

> There is the duty of a man to his Master and also what is the duty of a Master to a man, and also there has been a honner in doing that duty, but you say I have not done my duty to you as a Master. Dear Sir and much Respected Friend. Friend I beg leve to say you have not a man in your imploy that ever did or ever can do you more honner that i have and will ever have reason to do so (Holden archives, Box 7, 8, August 20, 1857, Brotherton Library).

Other letters, too, assumed a belief both in the patriarchal care of employers, and also in their ability to right any wrong. A friend of a woman who had been assaulted (attempted rape) by an employee of Fosters, for example, wrote to Mr Foster asking him to dismiss the man, as he would then leave town (Foster, private letters, Box 95, letter no. 108, Brotherton Library). Presumably, workers felt that they would have a greater chance of having their requests granted by writing to the master, rather than approaching the foreman. Alternatively they may have written because the latter approach had failed. Unfortunately, there is no evidence available to determine whether any of these particular letters had an effect.

Letters of complaint also came from higher graded staff (Holden Archives, Box 7, 4, letter dated 5 April 1854, Brotherton Library), for example, the letter from the carding department overlooker who objected to the manager of the mill reinstating a female worker whom he had sacked. He objected on the grounds that this was exceptional behaviour for the manager to take and that his power had been usurped. Again, there is no evidence that these letters were heeded in any way. However, masters were not likely to disturb the supervisory hierarchy if they could avoid it, overturning neither the decisions of a foreman for the benefit of workers nor the decisions of a manager for the foreman.

Probably the least used of the worker's strategies for dealing with a foreman's abuse of power was physical retaliation. The memories of the millworker quoted below both reflect the intimidating conditions which women workers faced and also depict one rare occurrence when the behaviour of a foreman was challenged:

> There was one fellow we used to call 'Touchy' because every time he come on the box he used to be touching your behind . . . and on this day I didn't know he was on and I were doing something with the machine and he come and put his hand right across my bottom so I turned round, I picked a bobbin up and hit him with

> it, so that they had me in the office for it. I told this gentleman what [sic] were over the overlookers, 'When he stops touching my arse I'll stop hitting him with bobbins.' So he never touched us after that (Female Textile Worker, b.1927, Oral Archives A0058/02/28 Bradford Central Library).

The memories of millworkers were often incomplete, and contradictory. They themselves, in other parts of their memoirs, speak of good or kindly overlookers, as do many others. Even the people who received harsh summary justice at the hands of overlookers maintained that the foremen were only doing their job as best they could (Female Textile Worker, b.1911, Oral History Archive A0105/01/14 Bradford Central Library). This conflicting evidence reflects one of the inherent problems in evaluating conflictual/consensual models of factory organization. The same overlooker was either friendly or fierce depending on the pressure he was under to keep production going, his temper changing with the economic climate. When labour was scarce, and skilled workers were treasured, the foremen were more careful with their 'alleydashers' (hard, stiff leather straps used by some foremen to discipline workers). At the same time they were aware that production must be kept up to speed. The skill, experience and personal temperament of the foreman then determined whether he decided to encourage the employees by kindness and tolerance, or threat, fine and violence. The factory was therefore not arranged solely on either conflictual or confrontational lines, but by foremen applying any method of control that was felt to be the most successful. The ambivalent attitude of the workers towards the foremen also illustrates the acceptance employees had of casual workplace violence. Not only were harsh disciplinary measures up to a certain level accepted as unavoidable but also as legitimate, and a normal part of factory life. It was this attitude towards violent customary discipline that allowed the foremen to act in the manner they did. When workers did challenge foremen who were unusually intimidating, they did so with the knowledge that it may cost them their job, and all future employment in the district.

In conclusion, it appears that appropriation was viewed by employers in the most serious light, and they used a variety of legal and quasi-legal forms to attempt to control it. In this they were aided by the fact that many styles of informal control initiatives and punishment measures were endowed with legal significance by the West Riding magistrates. Second, the critical figure in the fight against appropriation inside the factory was the foreman. Like the ship's first mate or boatswain described by Rediker in his study of discipline at sea, the foreman was responsible for the work and behaviour of those under them.

Ships, like the factories, also had their own private laws which held sway within secure physical boundaries, and were administered by trusted appointees (Rediker 1989, pp. 84–5). The factory foreman was primarily responsible for the deterrence, detection and apprehension of all forms of worker indiscipline, but this was particularly the case when appropriation was involved. In these duties, individual foremen may have been very successful. However, generally the foremen's efforts to suppress appropriation were imperfect, and employers were forced to rely on a form of private policing instituted before the New Police were envisioned, but which continued to operate late into the twentieth century.

5

Private Policing in the Industrial Age

In recent years historians and social scientists have begun to emphasize the episodic nature of publicly funded policing, with the inference that the private organization of policing will prove more durable than publicly funded organization (South 1987; Johnston 1992; Reiner 2000). Indeed, the modern police are now viewed by some as merely a lengthy 'experiment' in public policing which is now returning to the 'traditional' organization of prosecution and apprehension forces which operated before the New Police. As South (1987, p. 72) noted, 'the modern police are indeed a 'new police' and in some important respects it is they and not the modern phenomena of agencies within the private security sector that are out of step with the historical lineage of policing forms'. By this he meant that the borough and county police forces created in the nineteenth century were only the most recent of a wide range of policing services which included the borough watches, parish constables and Poor Law officers, inspectors of nuisances and factories in the public sector and the many subscription-funded policing agencies in the private sector (Philips 1989; King 1989).

Thanks to studies by historians such as John Beattie, Alistair Dinsmor and others, it is now largely accepted among crime and police historians that modern policing in Britain did not begin with the creation of the Metropolitan Police in 1829 (see Beattie:2001, 2012; Cox 2010; Dinsmor 2000; Reynolds 1998). Recent research into pre-Metropolitan policing has revealed a wide range of both publicly and privately funded policing bodies, ranging from the creation of the first detective force in the Western world, the Bow Street 'Runners', founded in the winter of 1748/9 by Henry Fielding, the celebrated novelist and Chief Magistrate of Bow Street Court in Westminster, to the creation of full-time professional police forces in various Scottish cities in the last decades of the eighteenth century.

Bow Street Police Office operated a complex and hierarchical structure which included regular night and day patrols in the centre of London, horse-mounted patrols of the turnpike roads leading into the metropolis, and a small force of experienced plain-clothes detective Principal Officers, better known to us as the Bow Street 'Runners'. By the end of the eighteenth century Bow Street's model of policing had been adopted by several other London police courts and there were several hundred patrol constables pounding the streets of the capital.

However, despite the fact that the Principal Officers were used throughout Britain on the investigation of serious crimes such as murder, arson and bank robberies, they were small in number (never more than eleven officers served at any one time) and were also very expensive to employ. Often the only viable alternative was to utilize the age-old system of the parish constabulary.

Recent research has demonstrated that the parish constabulary system was not entirely peopled by individuals in the mould of Dogberry and Verges, Shakespeare's comic interpretation of constables in *Much Ado About Nothing*. Work by Sharpe has shown that the parish constabulary could occasionally prove effective in preventing and detecting crime (Sharpe 1984). Similarly, England's work on the investigation of murders in Northern England, which deals with four northern counties (Cumberland, Yorkshire, Westmoreland and Northumberland) in the period 1800–24, suggests that magistrates within the Northern Circuit often relied heavily on the investigative skill and prowess of their local constables (England 1985).

However, there undoubtedly remained much lacking in the general efficacy of the system, petty sessions' magistrates in 1839 summing up the perceived problems:

> As far as our experience extends, we are convinced of the incompetency and inefficiency of the old parish constable. He holds his office generally for a year; he enters upon its duties unwillingly; he knows little what is required of him; is scantily paid for some things, has no remuneration in many cases; he has local connections, is actuated by personal apprehension, and dreads making himself obnoxious (PP Police 8 Constabulary Force in England and Wales 1839 (169) vol. XIX 9–240, p. 146).

Therefore many wealthy individuals and organizations deemed it more advantageous to create or subscribe to a private system of law enforcement, responsible to them for the protection of a limited range of self-interests.

Such private subscription agencies and other forms of private detection and law enforcement have a long history. The employment of private, non-attested thief-takers began in the early seventeenth century; John Beattie has found that 'the term thief-taker dates back to at least 1609' (Beattie 2001, p. 229). Thief-takers were individuals who operated privately without any official status or power; they attempted to capture suspected criminals in order to claim any reward money on offer from either the State or private individuals. It was widely believed that many of them operated illegally by framing innocent people or enticing weak-willed persons to commit crimes for which they were then arrested, with the thief-taker claiming any reward that was on offer. By far the most famous (if somewhat atypical) thief-taker was the notorious Jonathan Wild (1683–1725), who was born in Wolverhampton but very quickly gravitated to London, where by 1712 he had developed an extensive network of thieves and informers operating throughout the Metropolis. He played the extremely dangerous but profitable double-game of acting both as a receiver for stolen goods, and as the taker of thieves in order to claim the often substantial rewards available for their successful prosecution. In 1725 he was finally hoist by his own petard, when he was accused of stealing and subsequently receiving a reward of £10 for the return of forty yards of lace valued at £50. He defended himself energetically and succeeded in being acquitted of the theft. However, he was found guilty of the receipt of a reward from the recovery of the lace under the provisions of an Act of 1717 (ironically informally known as Wild's Act, as he was perceived as being at least partly responsible for its creation), which prevented the receipt of rewards for the recovery of stolen goods.

Ruth Paley regards thief-takers as straddling 'the margins of the conventional and criminal worlds', who 'formed, in effect, a sort of entrepreneurial police force' (Paley, quoted in Beattie 2001, p. 417). However, their numbers were extremely limited, and those who operated in the provinces were largely confined to major towns and cities – for example, the *Staffordshire Advertiser* reported that in January 1801 the entrepreneurial industrialist, Matthew Boulton, after a series of robberies at his Soho Manufactory, 'procured some of the constables and thieftakers from Birmingham, to the number of twenty in the whole, who were well-armed, and concealed in the Manufactory' in order to arrest the offenders – but such thief-takers appear to have been localized in their operations (*Staffordshire Advertiser*, 3 January 1801).

Rural wealthy private individuals have long similarly attempted to keep a firm hold on their property. Peter King has argued that 'with their extensive rights to search labourers' cottages for game or poaching equipment [that] gamekeepers represented a powerful form of private policing'; these rights dated back to 1670, when they were 'given power to search houses for guns, bows or sporting dogs (in houses less than £100 freehold, £150 leasehold for 99 years or less, excepting houses of heirs apparent of squires and others of a 'higher degree' (King 2000, p. 64, and Stephen 1883, p. 280). Munsche goes further, arguing that the gamekeeper, in short, was a policeman. Indeed, aside from excise officers, he was the closest thing to a professional law-enforcement official to be found in rural England before the middle of the nineteenth century (Munsche 1981, p. 83).

A popular alternative in both rural and urban areas for those individuals who could afford to do so was to belong to a private prosecution society, funded by subscription. These were known as Associations for the Prosecution of Felons, and were usually comprised of members from either a single county or borough. The Associations were normally advertised in local newspapers, many giving the reason for their creation as 'Whereas several burglaries, felonies, grand and petit larcenies have frequently of late been committed . . . and the Offenders have escaped Justice with impunity, for want of proper Pursuit'. The first recorded Association for the Prosecution of Felons was created in Stoke-on-Trent in 1693 following a spate of horse thefts in the area, but by the end of the eighteenth century they had multiplied throughout the country. Eastwood regards the creation of such associations as 'the most significant components in a programme to deter crime in later Hanoverian England without abandoning traditional forms of communal policing', but in reality they had little effect on serious crime. Very few murders or other major crimes appear to have been prosecuted by such Associations, and because of the relatively high subscription costs, they were not seen as attractive or viable alternatives by many poorer members of the local community, who often suffered disproportionately from crime, but were largely unable to pursue suspects due to the prohibitive cost of private prosecution. Many of these Associations appear to have quickly degenerated into little more than an excuse for an annual social event in the form of a grand dinner, and by the middle of the nineteenth century most had disappeared altogether. The *Crewe Chronicle* of 20 October 1877 details the business of a rare active survivor: it reported on the activities of the Crewe and Church Coppenhall Association for the Prosecution of Felons for that year, stating that eighteen cases were brought before the Association. Of these, sixteen paid a small fine, and two were sent from the Association to the magistrates' court. Sutton's recent research into the Staffordshire Society for the Apprehension of Felons has found that in the years

1830–34, the Association brought just sixteen cases to the Assizes, with a further thirty appearing at Quarter Sessions (see Sutton 2002, p. 51).

Such Associations were also reactive in nature; the advantages of belonging to them were only brought into being after the crime had taken place. However, some Associations did occasionally provide their own privately funded police force, paid for by additional subscription. For example, the Dursley Association (founded in 1773) created a short-lived police force in 1814, consisting of thirty-six men on night patrols (Jerrard 1993, p. 231). It would seem, however, that most Associations or private businesses were unwilling or unable to meet the expense necessary for the creation of such forces; Philips remarks that 'a number of associations [did] establish their own private police forces or patrols, but the majority did not go to this extent, preferring to work through their relationship with the parish constables, or later, with the new police forces' (Philips 1977, p. 118).

In the early years of the Industrial Revolution, the advantages of providing a privately financed form of policing in order to control both one's employees and the activities of a nefarious public were often seen as outweighing the considerable effort and costs involved in maintaining an effectively operative force. Freshfields, the solicitors for the Bank of England, had employed their own team of men on at least a semi-permanent basis to investigate cases of forgery from the latter decades of the eighteenth century, one of the best known being Thomas Glover, who is referred to frequently in correspondence from West Country sources concerning widespread rumours of forgeries (see Bank of England Freshfields PapersF2/155 AB 91/12, various letters dated 6 April–21 April 1801). Such investigations often required a dedicated and resourceful individual, and both the stakes and costs involved could be high: the successful investigation of a forgery case at Cockermouth in 1812 carried out on behalf of Freshfields cost the Bank over £93 for the services of their investigators, Mr Christian and his deputy (Bank of England Freshfields Papers F22/8 AB64/2: Correspondence concerning forgery in Cockermouth 15 April – 8 July 1812).

Insurance companies have a similarly long history of employing 'in-house' surveyors, investigators and assessors, the first post of Fire Surveyor being created in 1696 by the Hand in Hand Fire Insurance Office (Hawkings 2003, p. 19) For a comprehensive account of the development of insurance companies (including the detection of insurance frauds), see Jenkins and Yoneyama (2000). Lloyds of London was particularly active in investigating fraudulent or suspicious claims, but many of their agents, being locally employed and therefore conscious of their vulnerability within their immediate community, often proved ineffectual when confronted with a situation in which the perpetrators were protected by many fellow inhabitants. A letter from a local magistrate and owner of Heysham Hall, near Lancaster, regarding the prevention of plundering on the Lancashire coast, sums up the situation:

> I feel that it is my duty as Magistrate to request that something may be done to check the practice of wrecking which prevails upon this coast. The agent for Lloyd's in this district has approached me and says 'I must be supported by those who are placed in situations to render me assistance'. The Parish Constable receives 2 shillings and 6d. per annum. I cannot expect him to be on the lookout for offenders in rough and stormy weather (HO 44/32 ff. 110–11).

However, in many situations, the existence of such private policing did provide benefits for the companies concerned. Newer institutions than the Bank of England or Lloyds of London therefore also soon perceived advantages in not having to rely on an increasingly outmoded parish constabulary system. Most prominent among these were several of the various companies that sprung up in the heady years of railway development in the late-Georgian and early-Victorian period, who by the accession of Queen Victoria in 1837 employed their own private police forces.

These were not always welcomed by the general public (or indeed by all the passengers); in 1839, the railway companies that had created their own police force were criticized in a Royal Commission Report: 'It has already been a subject of complaint that the railway police protect the companies against the passengers, without protecting the latter, and that they suppress and conceal information of accidents'(Crime and Punishment Police vol. VIII [IUP Reprints Series]: *First Report on the Constabulary Force in England and Wales* PP 1839 [169] vol. XIX, p. 69).

It was not just newly created organizations such as the various railway companies that created and employed their own private police forces; in 1825, An Act for the better Preservation of the Peace and good Order in the Universities of England (c.97 6 Geo 4) was passed, with the following preamble:

> Whereas it is expedient to add to the means anciently provided for maintaining peace and good order in the Universities of Oxford and Cambridge, the Chancellor and the Vice-Chancellor had the power to swear in constables

> . . . every man so sworn shall have full power to act as a constable within the precincts of the university for which he shall be appointed, and four miles of the same university.

This act was enthusiastically utilized by both Cambridge and Oxford universities. The work of the University Constables was to maintain the decorum and dignity of the universities, with one of their main duties being to prevent illicit liaisons between undergraduates and the less reputable type of woman who offered to provide perceived innocents with a less academic introduction to adult life. Cases involving University constables occasionally made the news:

> At the Oxford Vice-Chancellor's Court, yesterday, Reginald Haes Martin, undergraduate of Lincoln College, was charged with being drunk and with assaulting two constables. Accused, it was alleged, was very drunk, and, with others, was knocking at the doors in the public streets. The University constable's eye was blackened and a city constable's finger was bitten in making the arrest, and it required four persons to take the accused to the station. He was fined £20 and costs (*Birmingham Daily Post* 11 November 1891).

The arrest does not appear to have led to Martin being sent down. Born in 1872 to William Hill Martin, a member of the London Stock Exchange, he studied history at Lincoln College, Oxford, graduating in October 1893. He married in 1897, by which time he had embarked upon a successful career as a barrister at law, later becoming chairman of the Langham Hotel Co. Ltd. He clearly had fond memories of his time at Oxford, despite his brush with the law, as upon the death of his widow in 1961 the residue of their considerable estate was eventually to pass to his former college.

The Church of England also employed its own private police force; in fact, it can probably lay claim to the fact that it was the first body in England to employ such a force. Joseph Hobson states that York Minster employed its own constables, responsible for the Liberty of Saint Peter and Peter Prison (which enclosed the Minster Close) from 1285 until 1839. For further details of the York Minster police, together with several other 'Cathedral Constabularies', see Hobson (2011). From 1839 onwards, the responsibility for the Liberty passed to York Corporation, but the Minster continued with its private policing. Many other great English cathedrals, including Salisbury, Hereford and Liverpool, also employed their own private constables (who were attested with the power of arrest within the confines of the respective cathedrals). Several of these cathedrals, such as Liverpool, continue to employ Cathedral Constables. Despite having lost the power of arrest, such Constables continue to perform an invaluable security and preventative role.

The first half of the nineteenth century saw a blossoming of private police forces in the rapidly growing urban areas and the concomitant boom in trade. The following are just a few of the numerous forces with their establishment dates:

Grand Surrey Canal Police	1809
Commercial Docks Police	1810
Admiralty Constabulary	1834
Gloucester Docks Police	1836
Liverpool Markets Police	1837
Hull Docks Police	1840
Regents Canal & Docks Police	1840
River Tyne Police	1845

The status of the various docks police forces (with the exception of the Admiralty Constabulary) was consolidated under the Harbour, Docks and Piers Clauses Act 1847, which enabled two JPs to 'appoint such Persons as shall be nominated for that Purpose by the Undertakers to be special Constables within the Limits of the Harbour, Dock, Pier, and Premises of the Undertakers, and within One Mile of the same; and every Person so appointed shall be sworn in by any such Justices duly to execute the Office of a Constable within the Limits aforesaid, and when so sworn in shall have the same Powers, Protections, and Privileges within the Limits aforesaid, and shall be subject to the same Liabilities, as Constables have or are subject to by the Laws of the Realm'.

All of the private police forces shared one thing in common: they were only responsible to either essentially private committees or organizations. Unlike the public county and borough police forces in operation after the passing of the County and Borough Police Act of 1856, which effectively ceded a considerable amount of local control to the Home Office, private police forces remained essentially self-contained, both with regard to their constitutions and their affairs – they usually had neither jurisdiction or interest outside their own spheres of influence nor were they subject to external control. They were overwhelmingly concerned with internalized offending such as breaches of trust or internal larceny; they were never created for the good or benefit of the public at large, and remained largely unconcerned with external offences or influences.

However, the boundary between 'private' and 'public' policing has always been somewhat blurred, and it remains so. Early 'public' police forces such as the Bow Street 'Runners' and the Metropolitan Police were both allowed to charge for work carried out on behalf of private individuals (following the approval of their respective governing bodies), and both were allowed to receive any rewards offered by individuals or companies. The Metropolitan Police had a fixed-charge system for supplying officers to provincial forces such as those employed in the Midlands to assist with the Chartist uprisings in the 1840s. Discretionary rewards continued well into the twentieth century – for example, Crewe Borough Petty Sessions Register for 1918 contains numerous cases in which police officers (of various ranks ranging from Constable to Inspector) are noted as receiving rewards ranging from ten shillings to one pound for the capture of deserters from the Armed Forces (Chester Archives QPCr 3863/21). Similarly, Detective Inspector Richard Tanner (who achieved a degree of fame in 1864 for capturing Franz Muller, the first person to be found guilty of carrying out a murder on a railway train) recorded in his notebook which lists cases from 1856 to 1867 that he received numerous rewards ranging from 10s. to £50. Such rewards (although now from public funds) are still occasionally allowed; Section 31 of the 1996 Police Act states that: 'A police authority may, on the recommendation of the chief officer of police, grant out of the police fund to members of the police force maintained by that authority rewards for exceptional diligence or other especially meritorious conduct'.

Each of the current 43 police forces of England and Wales still provide a degree of 'private' policing most Saturdays; witness the thousands of police officers who watch over the behaviour of football fans. It has been estimated that the so-called 'consequential cost' of policing Premiership matches in 2011 cost the taxpayer £3.2 million (figure quoted by Aidan Burly MP, 18 May 2011–see *http://www.theyworkforyou.com/whall/?id=2011-05-18b.132.0*). Under current law, football clubs only pay for policing within the area of their 'footprint' – that is inside the stadium and any surrounding areas also owned by the club such as car-parks. Such costs do not cover policing for Tube or railway stations, or for the approach roads. In 2008, the Association of Chief Police Officers called for the introduction of 'full-cost' policing, which would include these concomitant figures. British Transport Police receive no extra funding for the policing of railways on days when large football matches are held.

In recent decades there has been a resurgence of interest in the provision of private policing, as public police resources are seen to being increasingly stretched. This has led to a significant growth in the number of private security firms, which are seen to provide a service to those who can afford to pay. For discussions about the recent resurgence in private policing, see Johnston (1992) and Jones and Newburn (1998). However, our focus now turns to the links between industrial capitalism and private policing, and the introduction of the most powerful body for the protection of employers' rights in the eighteenth and nineteenth century.

The Worsted Committee

Social scientists, such as Spitzer and Scull, have asserted that private policing was an entirely natural requirement of nineteenth-century industrial capitalism, which suggests that the activities of policing agencies, which operated in manufacturing districts at a time when industrial capitalism was well-established, would be an important area of historical research (Spitzer and Scull 1977). Little and Sheffield have begun to do this with an examination of the membership and operation of the Halifax Prosecution Association in their comparative history of private policing in England and vigilantism in America (Little and Sheffield 1983). In both countries they argue that it was the failure of the executive to implement the legislature that led to the respective creation of vigilante societies and Associations for the Prosecution of Felons; 'neither the concept of the law nor its content were in question – only problems surrounding the effectiveness of the law's enforcement' (Little and Sheffield 1983, p. 798). This agency existed in an industrial, if not factory, district, and continued until the end of the nineteenth century. However, research could usefully be undertaken to determine the level of activity of this agency in the latter stages of Halifax's industrialization in order to test Spitzer and Scull's assertions concerning the relationship between private policing and industrial organization. Alternatively, if adequate records could be found for the other employers' private policing and prosecution agencies which briefly flowered in the West Riding in the nineteenth century, then they too could be studied. For example, the Halifax woollen manufacturers sponsored a Woollen Inspector between 1802 and 1807; a Linen Inspector briefly patrolled Barnsley and there was a Woollen Inspector in Pudsey in the 1830s and also in Huddersfield between 1844 and 1851. See Soderlund (1992, p. 631). Unfortunately, no records of these private prosecution agencies survive in the West Riding archives. See also references to the activities of the

Silk Inspectors who operated in Macclesfield, Cheshire, between 1819 and the 1860s, in Barrett (1995). Fortunately, the most utilized prosecution association in the region dominated by factory production – the Worsted Committee – has left extensive records and can therefore be used to study the impact of private policing in this context.

The Worsted Committee was established by 17 Geo.III, c.11 (1777) to enforce the clauses of 17 Geo.III, c.27 (1777), and thereby to retain, intensify and strengthen the employers' supremacy over the production process by facilitating increased recourse to the criminal code. A committee such as this obviously needed to maximize its access to people with some expertise and knowledge of manufacturing – if not the workings of the legal system (although this knowledge increased over time). Additionally, they needed to construct and maintain a legitimacy to 'police' the industry, and to occasionally discipline wealthy and powerful manufacturers and merchants. Accordingly, the Committee was composed of twenty-seven members – eighteen from Yorkshire and nine from Cheshire and Lancashire – who represented the worsted industry in the North. Although all of the worsted producing regions and towns sent delegates to the Committee, in practice, from its inception till its demise, the Committee was dominated by, and largely run for the benefit of, the Bradford and Halifax manufacturers.

In the eighteenth century, the Committee had been composed of what one could term 'gentlemen-manufacturers' who were not only wealthy but also politically astute individuals wielding a good deal of local power. By 1840 the composition had altered in character, with large scale 'professional' manufacturers running the show. One aspect remained unchanged, however. The nineteenth-century members were still enveloped in a mass of overlapping matrices of elite connections: political, matrimonial, familial and social.

To run briefly through some of these connections, more than a third of the members of Bradford Chamber of Commerce were also Worsted Committee members, and the Committee supported the Chamber in a number of its campaigns (Bradford Chamber of Commerce, Minute Books, *WYAB*; *Bradford Observer* 7 June 1855, 28 September 1870). The Committee was also represented on the employers' other pressure group – the Bradford Mill-owners' Association – and other informal organizations which flowered periodically in the nineteenth century, for example, the 'Committee of the Unemployed' and the 'Wool-combers Distress Committee', both of which were born and died in the mid-1840s (*Bradford Observer* 23 February, 5 March 1846). Besides business and quasi-social connections, the manufacturers and the Worsted Committee shared regional political power. Two-thirds of Bradford's Watch Committee were Worsted Committee members. Moreover, three members: Samuel Smith, John Hill and William Rand achieved the office of Mayor of Bradford. No one political party seems to have colonized the Committee, however. Rather the Committee boasted the leading members of both parties who supported manufacturing interests: some 'Free Trade' Tories were members while other Committee members were prominent Liberals (*Bradford Observer* 29 April 1852). The political and social elite that sat round a table once a quarter to discuss trade, the detection and prosecution of appropriators, and presumably a host of other subjects, presided over the organization most determined to strike out appropriation and work-indiscipline from the worsted industry.

The Committee was able to wage war against appropriation because it could call not just on political and social capital, but also on a variety of financial sources. Primarily, however, (as we have seen in Chapter 2), the Committee was funded by a tax remittance on the soap duty paid by manufacturers. A considerable amount of soap was used in the preparatory processes of cloth production, and as a concession to manufacturers the government allowed them to drawback a third of all duty paid. The Worsted Committee was entitled to a proportion of this drawback. The percentage claimed from drawback was applicable to all manufacturers in the counties covered by the Worsted Acts. Accordingly, the Manchester Excise Office sent a cheque for £67-0-8 in 1847 which represents the payments of the few worsted establishments in Lancashire, thereafter there are entries for cheques from unnamed excise offices outside of Yorkshire ranging from £26 to £103 between 1849 and 1853. See the relevant entries in the WCAB 1835–85, *WYAB*. This percentage was changed periodically by petition to the Leeds quarter sessions, either in favour of the Committee or the manufacturers, but remained the financial mainstay of the Committee's finances until 1853. Three other sources of revenue existed: the share dividends from the Committee's investments in the Leeds to Liverpool Canal Company; money raised from the sale of seized goods which were believed to have been appropriated, but were unclaimed by the owner (although this never amounted to a significant sum) and the proportion of any fine imposed by the courts on convicted appropriators (up to ten pounds per conviction) which was given over to the Committee by the guilty. Heaton suggests these investments were ill advised. They did, however, provide an income of £70 p.a. between 1840 and 1856, and £134 p.a. between 1857 and 1862, before falling back to £48 p.a. after that date, and this money tided the Committee over some very straitened times. See Heaton (1965, p. 437). With regard to unclaimed material, the 1777 Worsted Act stated that any material found by the court to be embezzled must be returned to its rightful owners. If, however, the material remained unclaimed, or if the cloth had no identifiable markings, the material could be sold publicly for the benefit of the Committee. The Committee were the men who were heavily involved in the transition from cottage industry to the factory age (Soderlund 1992, p. 335).

The history of the Worsted Committee and their Inspectors in the mid- to late-nineteenth century falls into four distinct phases. Initially, the Committee and their Inspectors were brought into life by the 1777 Worsted Acts, and they were charged with suppressing fraud in the domestic cottage textile industry. Soderlund (1992) has described their operations, and their relative success until the development of a large-scale centralized textile production system arose in the 1830s (and which came to be the dominant mode of production by the 1840s). The second period was a short one, when the Committee was really 'initspomp' until the mid-century. In 1853, the Worsted Committee underwent substantial organizational changes in response to a financial crisis which ushered in a period when they operated at a reduced level. This third phase ended in 1870 when the Inspectorate were again animated by the employers' response to their self-perceived needs and fears, and this last phase stretched to the Committee's final denouement in 1968.

The operation of the Inspectorate in the mid- to late-nineteenth century 'in the field' remained unchanged in many respects from that of the late-eighteenth century. Since material was often temporarily stored in a worker's house or shed, before being sold, or used by the worker to decorate or repair his household furnishings, the homes of factory workers were searched as assiduously in this period as the houses and workshops of domestic workers had been. Inspectors merely had to obtain a warrant signed by two magistrates before searching the house of a suspect, often accompanied by police officers and/or the suspect's employer (made permissible by 17 Geo III c.56 1777). Rag and waste dealers too, as obvious receivers of appropriated goods, also continued to receive close attention, as they had done since the mid-eighteenth century.

The Committee were keen to preserve and expand all of their sources of income, and their services were advertised in the *Bradford Observer, Leeds Mercury, Manchester Guardian* and other newspapers in the textile areas. The Clerk of the Committee also sent court reports of successful prosecutions to be published, especially if the case established a precedent, illuminated the scale of appropriation or revealed a new method of appropriation which would worry employers into calling on an Inspector to investigate possible frauds. The wide reporting of successful prosecutions also helped to maintain a consensus that manufacturers should continue to fund the Committee's activities. This was vital since the Committee had difficulty in persuading manufacturers to pay over their drawback remission when profits were falling. Furthermore, any case which resulted in a severe penalty served as a warning to the workpeople, as is made explicit in the following entry from the Worsted Committee Minute Book:

> In the conviction which was for taking rovings from the Mill, I collected sufficient evidence to make a case of Felony against her and she having several former convictions proved against her the court ordered her to be kept in penal servitude for seven years. I then consulted as to the desirability of giving publicity to this case in the newspapers in order to deter others from doing the same (17 January 1870 WCMB).

These advertisements served to make the Inspectorate well-known to workers and employers alike, and the range and extent of their activities made them an obvious choice for those who wished to control appropriation.

The Committee encouraged this view by delineating clearly their area of jurisdiction and expertise. By concentrating their operations within well-defined geographical and legal areas, they established a moral authority in pressing their right to police the industry, and were able to dissuade other agencies from 'interfering'. For example, when the Silk Trade Protection Society wrote to the Committee in 1852 offering to co-operate in prosecutions where the Worsted Inspector found silk mixed with other purloined materials, the expenses of the cases being shared, they received a courteous but dismissive reply (Memorial from the Silk Manufacturers to Disraeli, Manchester Central Library MSC 677.4). This compact with a fellow trade prosecution society would have been profitable, especially in the western regions where cotton and silk production existed alongside that of worsted, but the Committee resented the lesé-majesty of the Lancastrian society, and this led them to reject the proposed plan.

The Inspectors continued to have little involvement with the direct supervision of the production process once factories had replaced domestic forms of production, although they occasionally placed agents inside the works in order to gain information. In January 1888, an Inspector placed an agent inside the works in order to find the man who had been stealing patterns from the mill. After identifying the man, the Inspector placed an advert in the *Bradford Observer* stating that he was a new manufacturer looking for patterns. The unsuspecting culprit sent the patterns along with a request for a job.

The undercover nature of much of the Worsted Inspector (and Yewdall's in particular) tended to engender opprobrium in the columns of Liberal-leaning newspapers such as the *Bradford Observer*. In an editorial concerning a large number of Worsted Act cases that involved woolcombers' waste, the newspaper contained detailed criticism by several inhabitants of Yewdall's 'espionage'. The editor of the newspaper regretted the fact that subterfuge must be of necessity involved in the work of Worsted Inspectors, but then goes on to state that if the complainants 'would only tell our detectives how to discover offenders without using vulgar espionage, they would no doubt be duly grateful (*Bradford Observer* 28 April 1864). Only Yewdall went on to say that Mr Lister 'ought to know as a magistrate that detectives must use various means to discover the tricks of thieves, both wholesale and retail, and he knows that I got most of my information from his own men' (*Bradford Observer* 12 May 1864). However, for the main part, the work of a Worsted Inspector was almost reactive rather than preventative in nature, and often included a considerable detective element. For example, on 1 February 1858, following receipt of information concerning large-scale theft by fraud of wool from Varleys' of Stanningley, Jesse Yewdall 'concealed himself in a wool bin in the warehouse, near to the scale where the wool is weighed, and where he could hear and see everything which went forward' (*Leeds Mercury* 4 February 1858).

If much of the Inspectors' operational methods remained largely unchanged across the nineteenth century, the rise of the factory system did engender one major change in their *modus operandi*. The organization of the factory introduced a physical point at which searches could be conducted, and offenders apprehended – the factory gate. Surprisingly perhaps, only a seventh of the searches conducted by the Worsted Inspector and/or a Constable which led to prosecution took place at the factory gate (although this would seem to be the most beneficial place in terms of the prosecution proving an intent to steal in any subsequent court case). Nevertheless, the proportion of people apprehended at the gate, together with those apprehended inside the premises (49.8%), makes it clear that the factory authority structure and physical organization contributed to the successful apprehension of appropriators. The authority of the foreman's testimony in court was apparently sufficient to over-ride the problem of whether the appropriated property could be said to have been 'stolen' if it had not left the premises.

The factory system, with its physical control on the entry and exit of personnel, altered both the physical point and the place on the route to court, at which the policing agencies were introduced. The Inspectorate adopted a more and more reactive stance. The speculative searching of houses and the regular checks on the wares of waste dealers continued, and yielded good results, but in many cases the initiation of action now came at the request of the foreman, who was the head of the internal supervisory structure. As the quarter sessions records show, the workers suspected of appropriation who were arrested inside or just outside their workplace were usually first questioned by the foreman, and only later questioned and arrested by a police officer. The suspect could be released through lack of evidence on the advice of the constable or Worsted Inspector. This did not prohibit the foreman from initiating informal disciplinary sanctions as the previous chapter has shown. These records may be misleading, and under-represent the involvement of Worsted Inspectors in the process of arrest. Depositions tend to overemphasize the role of the police officers, since the arresting constables always provided a witness statement, and were not shy of outlining their involvement to the exclusion of other interested parties. Even so, witnesses' depositions mentioned that the Inspector was present at the arrest of the suspect in 20 per cent of cases, and involved in the questioning of the suspect after his/her arrest in 29 per cent of the cases between 1840 and 1845 and, although in the 1870 to 1875 period, the Worsted Inspector is recorded as only apprehending the suspect in 4 per cent of cases, in 45 per cent of cases a Worsted Inspector and a police officer worked in tandem to apprehend an offender.

If the Inspector was not involved either in the detection process or the arrest of the suspect, he was still integral to the decision to prosecute. By using his specialist knowledge and experience of the legal system, and through interviewing the suspect, the Inspector assessed the likelihood of conviction, and advised the employer as to whether a prosecution should be prepared. Such advice was welcome. The laws which could be applied to appropriation were numerous, and intricate in their detail, as has been shown earlier. Thus legal opinion was sometimes sought even by the Committee to clarify points of law, or in order to prepare test cases to establish a legal precedent. For example, they sought the opinion of the Solicitor General in 1843, and dropped a case on his advice (10 April 1843 WCMB, *WYAB).* A year later the Committee were prepared to take the advice of defending counsel in ending a complicated case which had already been periodically taking up the court's time for nine months.

Two years later the Committee sought the opinion of legal experts when the Secretary of State for the Home Department, at the request of Mr Busfield Ferrand, Knaresbrough's Member of Parliament, liberated Mary Dawson (who had been convicted of neglect of work under 17 Geo.III cap.56). The Home Secretary insisted that 17 Geo.III cap.56 had been superseded by 6 & 7 Vict. cap.40. However, as legal counsel confirmed, the original conviction had been correct, and 'the proceedings regular' (29 March 1847 WCMB). Inspectors too, mindful of their conviction rates, sometimes decided that cases which were too complicated could be abandoned. For example, one employee who was found with 260 bobbins in his house declared he was keeping them until he received his wages. His employer, who had already had the man in court once and was now being counter-sued for false imprisonment, admitted owing him wages, but wished him locked up regardless. The Inspector clearly did not relish this intricate and confused case, and he gladly entered in his ledger that he had withdrawn from the case (3 April 1882 WCMB).

Although they occasionally withdrew from cases, they were anxious to create the impression that all of those they apprehended would be prosecuted as a matter of course. Indeed the prosecution process was initiated even if the evidence against the accused was inconclusive. By uniformly prosecuting those they suspected, the Inspectors hoped to avoid accusations of corruption.Turning a blind eye in return for small bribes must have been both an ever-present temptation for Inspectors, and a constant concern of the Committee.

The quality of the service

> Wanted by the Committee of Worsted Manufacturers for the Counties of York, Lancaster, and Chester, a diligent, steady and active Person to serve as INSPECTOR OF WORSTED YARN, and to put into execution, under the Direction of the said Committee, and their General Inspector, the several Acts of Parliament relating to the Worsted and Woollen Manufacture. (*Leeds Mercury* 23 March 1823)

Who were these 'diligent, steady and active persons' who became Inspectors of Worsted in the Yorkshire, Lancashire and Cheshire area? Thanks to a combination of Victorian bureaucracy and the increasing availability of digitized online sources, it is possible to trace the lives and careers of at least some of the men who answered the call to become Worsted Inspectors. Jesse Yewdall's work as a Worsted Inspector is well documented in the two main local newspapers of the time: the *Bradford Observer* and the *Leeds Mercury*. He makes frequent appearances in the column-inches of both newspapers as the prosecuting agency in a number of petty (and occasionally large-scale) thefts from the worsted mills.

Jesse was born 13 December 1820 in Horton, Bradford, to non-conformist parents Abraham and Elizabeth. By the time Jesse was 18, his father Abraham was Deputy Constable of Horton, sworn in by the Manor Court (and remaining so for at least three years). This appears to have been quite a dangerous public office, as Abraham is reported as having been seriously assaulted on several occasions (*Bradford Observer* 8 February 1838, 22 June 1839). In 1841, Jesse is recorded as being employed as a woolcomber, still living with his parents and three of his younger siblings at Horton. His father is still recorded as a constable, but by the following year he had become a bailiff of the Court of Requests in Bradford. This seems to have been a similarly dangerous occupation; a collier was charged with making a 'murderous attack' on Abraham, who had his jaw broken in two places and some of his teeth knocked out (Bradford Observer 24 October 1844). However, such assaults do not seem to have unduly deterred Abraham, who continued as Deputy Bailiff for the Bradford County Court until at least 1859. In that year Jesse married Ann Brear on Christmas Day at Horton Lane Chapel, Bradford. For the next seven years Jesse seems to have remained a woolcomber, becoming a father to three children, Elizabeth, Henry and Charles. However, by late 1852 Jesse had changed occupation and is first recorded as an Inspector of Worsted. By 1861 he was father to four children (having lost at least two children in infancy) and was firmly established in the ranks of the emergent middle-class, living in a reasonably affluent area of Bradford at 3 Peel Park Villas (named after the public park named in honour of Sir Robert Peel which was opened in 1853), next door to his brother Henry, who was practising as a solicitor. Jesse was elected a Committee Member of the Friends of Peel Park in March 1861 (*Bradford Observer* 21 March 1861).

By 1865 he and his family had moved to 111 North Parade, Manningham, and were now prosperous enough to employ a live-in domestic servant. After losing another child in infancy during 1868, Jesse suffered a further loss when his wife Ann died in early summer 1874. Jesse remarried on 20 February 1875 to Esther Firth, another native of Bradford. Jesse was not to enjoy his second marriage for long, as he died at North Parade on 23 February 1879, leaving under £200 in his personal estate (National Probate Calendar Index of Wills and Administrations, 1879). This relatively low amount of personal estate seems surprising, although he may have put his affairs in order well before his death and transferred monies to his surviving relatives at an earlier date. He seems to have escaped the fate of his brother Henry, who was declared bankrupt in 1890, owing several thousands of pounds to creditors, and who died the following year leaving a personal estate of just over £76. He appears to have worked as Worsted Inspector up to his time of death, as the last case in which he is reported as acting in this capacity is reported in the *Leeds Mercury* of 14 July 1877. Circumstantial evidence suggests that his failing health had begun to affect his ability to carry out his duties; an entry dated 23 June 1879 in the Bradford WCMB records that an attempt by Yewdall's widow Esther to receive backdated payment for her husband's work up to the time of his death was unsuccessful, the Committee being of the opinion that this was not warranted as they had paid him when he was ill and incapable of doing his job properly. The same entry records that on advertising for his successor, the Worsted Committee received forty-three applications for the vacancy; despite the likelihood of the nature of the post not making a Worsted Inspector the most popular of individuals among the worsted workers, there was clearly no shortage of applicants for the position. The majority of Worsted Inspectors appear to have been involved in the worsted industry for a considerable period prior to their engagement as Inspectors. Edwin Wadsworth, Worsted Inspector in Halifax from 1892 to at least 1901, had been a linen draper, while John William Burgoyne, who served as an Inspector in Bradford from 1892 to at least 1911, had previously been an overlooker (*Leeds Mercury* 13 October 1892; *Huddersfield Chronicle* 21 July 1900).

Yewdall served as Worsted Inspector for over a quarter of a century and this, together with his previous experience as a woolcomber, must have enabled him to amass a considerable amount of knowledge as to the myriad of ways in which some workers in the worsted trade tried (often unsuccessfully) to supplement their wages by misappropriation and theft. This knowledge and experience was clearly appreciated by the Worsted Committee; we have seen that Yewdall continued to receive payment for his services while ill, and similarly the widow of Joseph Redmaine, who served as Inspector at Keighley from 1831 to 1848, was sent 30 guineas by the Worsted Committee upon his death as a 'mark of approbation of his good conduct and efficient service'.

However, not all those appointed as Worsted Inspectors proved up to the job; indeed Redmaine himself had been implicated in a conspiracy to defraud in January 1841. The *Northern Star* (a Chartist-supporting newspaper) reported that Redmaine and another man, described in the newspaper as 'two notorious characters from Keighley. . . a sort of bailiffs and bastard inspectors [sic]', had allegedly conspired with another individual in order to implicate an innocent man in the theft of worsted weft by hiding the material in his public house, and that this practice had been going on for at least three years (Northern Star 16 January 1841). However, although the newspaper stated that investigations into the matter were ongoing, nothing further seems to have happened, and Redmaine continued in his post. A more definite case of incompetence/criminality can be seen in 1879, when a Mr Sutcliffe was appointed as a Worsted Inspector, but after being described rather witheringly in a report of a case in which he was involved as 'a man having been appointed to an office for which he appeared not to have the slightest personal ability or qualification', he was sacked in September 1879 and sent to gaol for 2 months for embezzling £11 subscriptions (*Bradford Observer* 14 May 1879).

Yewdall himself was not afraid to criticize his colleagues if he considered their work to be substandard. On 18 June, 1877, Bradford WCMB records that he accused a newly appointed Inspector, Mr Parker, with four counts of incompetence: 1) that he was not up at 10.00 am when Yewdall called for him; 2) He does not consult with Yewdall; 3) He made false entries of work when he was locked up at Huddersfield; 4) That he had gained not a single conviction. Parker vehemently denied these charges and Yewdall was instructed to show Parker his duties and to work pleasantly with him. This was not the end of the matter however, as on 21 September 1877 Parker reports to the Worsted Committee that he has no cases, 'which I think is due to me visiting the factory more frequently than Mr Yewdall'. Parker also accuses Yewdall of not answering his letters and 'cutting him' in the street. There was clearly no love lost between these two individuals.

Although the Worsted Acts covered Lancashire and Cheshire as well as Yorkshire, the Inspectorate were mainly active in Keighley, Leeds, Bradford and Halifax, the worsted producing regions of the Pennines, such as Newchurch, Colne and Blackburn (as well as Morley and Chorley for a brief period). These districts covered the main areas of production, and main living areas of industrial workers, for example, the Bradford district included Manningham, Heaton, Calverley, Bowling, Thornton, Handsworth, Pudsey, Adwalton, Shipley, Horsforth, Eccleshill, Horton, Clayton, Birkenshaw, Leeds borough, Idle, Rawden, Bolton, Allerton, North Brierley, Tong and Wakefield Parish. As the century progressed, the district shrank to only include the factory districts. Each of these districts was patrolled by an Inspector who reported his actions at every quarterly meeting of the Committee, which also checked the accuracy of the Inspector's recording of prosecutions and convictions. The caution shown towards the entries in the Inspectors' books was due to the persistence of eighteenth- and early nineteenth-century Inspectors, who had invented convictions, and made false entries to boost their conviction rates (see Styles 1983; Soderlund 1992). Indeed, 40 per cent of Worsted Inspectors were dismissed between 1777 and 1828 for some kind of misconduct (Soderlund 1992, p. 646).

By 1840, however, there had been a conscious effort to raise the standards of behaviour in, and the standards of entry to, the Inspectorate, and Inspectors who made false entries or were slack in their duties could be immediately suspended by the Committee member responsible for his district. The internal discipline of the Committee stretched to its upper echelons too; three members of the Committee were fined half a crown each for being absent longer than the Chairman had allowed them. This effort to increase the internal discipline of the organization was apparently largely successful in all areas apart from the Colne District where the Inspectors were repeatedly cautioned and dismissed. The Colne Inspector was given a month to improve his behaviour, on 28 September 1846 and dismissed in January 1847 after failing to do so. However, the new Inspector was being warned about his behaviour only nine months later, and discharged a year later. The Committee felt it best to have the Keighley Inspector look after the Colne District, but due to the continued growth of worsted production in Blackburn, a new Inspector was appointed at the end of 1849 (27 September 1847; 25 September 1848; 31 December 1849 WCMB). Along with more scrutiny and increasing professionalism came financial reward. Only two Inspectors were found to be embezzling conviction money in the second half of the century, which was a small number in comparison to those disciplined in the eighteenth century (see entries for 5 January 1852 and July 24 1879 WCMB, *WYAB*).

The Worsted Inspectors were under the supervision of a General Inspector, who was salaried at £130 per annum in 1852, and who also received £1 for every conviction their Inspectors secured (5 April 1852 WCMB). The original wage of the Inspectors under him had been set at £50 per annum in 1777 but had risen to an annual salary of £210 by the mid-nineteenth century. Between 1847 and 1867, the Worsted Inspectors' salaries (which included rewards for successful prosecutions) approached that of Bradford's Chief Constable (£235), and left Bradford's detectives on £65 a year far behind (WCAB, 1847–76, 56D.88/3/3;

Borough Watch Committee records, Bradford, 1847–65, *WYAB*, BBC1/2–5). This level of remuneration left only senior police officers earning more than the 'Assistant Inspectors', who were hired on an *ad hoc* basis to assist with the searching of houses and arrest of suspects, but who were not given an annual salary.

Notwithstanding the high salaries, some Inspectors in this period did leave to join the higher echelons of the borough and county police forces since they offered a more secure and pensioned occupation, but a few higher-ranked policemen journeyed in the opposite direction to join the Inspectorate. John Cheeseborough was a Worsted Inspector (appointed in 1847) who left to become an Inspector (later Superintendent) in the Bradford Police (*Huddersfield Chronicle* 2 July 1853). Similarly, John Ingham, a Worsted Inspector, became one of the two constables of Bradford in 1827, while Benjamin Sutcliffe, who served briefly as a Worsted Inspector in the mid-1840s, was previously a special constable. Sutcliffe is described as such in a worsted theft case in the *Bradford Observer* 13 February 1842. By 1846 he had been appointed as a Worsted Inspector, but was soon in trouble; he was given a month to improve his behaviour, and was dismissed as unsuitable a year later. Bradford parish constabulary annually appointed a Constable for East Bradford and another for West Bradford.

Several Worsted Inspectors later took up similar posts in local authorities. Joseph Seed (who served as a Worsted Inspector from 1839 to 1853) took up the post of Inspector of Nuisances and Encroachments for Calder and Hebble rivers within Halifax in September 1854, and four years later was appointed Inspector of Weights and Measures, Halifax (*Leeds Mercury* 23 September 1854; *Bradford Observer* 30 September 1858). Similarly, Richard Henry Kaye, a Worsted Inspector at Huddersfield from the mid-1840s, was appointed Inspector for Weights and Measures in June 1853 after being recommended for the post by Huddersfield Magistrates (*Bradford Observer* 30 June 1853). He may have held both posts simultaneously, as he is referred to as a 'Woollen Inspector' in a report in the *Huddersfield Chronicle* 22 January 1859. Both types of police agencies recruited from the same pool of labour and appointed similar types of men. Indeed, prior to the creation of the Bradford Police in 1848, at least one man, George Ingham, appears to have been both a member of the parish constabulary and an 'Inspector of Worsted' (*Bradford Observer* 15 March 1838). Ingham's father William had been a Worsted Inspector, and George briefly followed in his footsteps, dying after a short illness at the age of 40 in October 1838.

Conclusion

It is clear that throughout the period the Worsted Committee attracted men who were able to perform detective duties in the field, as well as being able to act as prosecutors on behalf of victims in court. Aspects of this part of their role were sometimes challenged. For example, the legitimacy of an Inspector acting as both witness and prosecutor in the same case was challenged by a defendant's advocate in 1844. The advocate stated that the Bench would never consent to an attorney's clerk conducting a case, and similarly, they should not allow the prosecutor's servant to act as witness, prosecutor and advocate for the prosecution case. The magistrates discounted this view and directed the case to proceed, but were further interrupted by a senior lawyer who was in the courtroom at that time. He asserted his opinion that the defending advocate was correct in the first instance, and the magistrate reluctantly ordered the Inspector to leave the court. Extraordinarily, it appears from the press report that the Bench then acted as surrogate prosecuting advocates (*Bradford Observer* 6 June 1844). These criticisms were brushed aside, however, and the Inspectors continued their practice of acting as both witness and prosecutor unabated until the second half of the nineteenth century when professional counsel was employed by the Committee. Indeed the financial crisis that hit the Worsted Committee in 1853 created a great deal of change for the Committee and the Inspectors they employed.

6

Policing without the Inspectorate? The Changing Role of the Worsted Committee 1853–1968

Until 1853, the Worsted Inspectorate was indisputably the main force for combating illegal appropriation within the worsted industry, and the figure below demonstrates the level of their activity; they achieved hundreds of prosecutions in the years up to 1853. This period had seen the Inspectorate successfully adapt their operational methods to control appropriation in the factory, and, aside from relying on the police to arrest offenders, they remained the supreme external agency for the control of appropriation.

In 1853, however, the number of General Inspectors was reduced from eight to three. This reduction did not come about because the factory had eradicated fraud, or because the practice of illegal appropriation had ended, 'on which distant day', Heaton speculated, 'lawyers, magistrates and worsted inspectors may find their occupations gone' (Heaton 1965, p. 437). The Committee was forced to cut back on its activities, not because the need for their services had disappeared, but due to a financial crisis. The Committee had used its influence with Parliament to maintain, and periodically increase, the allowance for drawback on the soap tax, which was its life-blood. That life-blood was drained away by the Chancellor of the Exchequer, William Gladstone. Out of the money due to the manufacturers as a rebate on their soap duty, the Treasury kept back the proportion due to the Committee, which was then sent directly to them. Heaton explained the utility of a policing system funded in this manner:

> All masters who prepared their wool for weaving were affected by this drawback, but at the same time all were to benefit by the activities of the worsted inspectors. Therefore let the cost of the police system be defrayed out of the drawback which the clothiers received. This was the arrangement established by the Worsted Act (Heaton 1965, pp. 423–4).

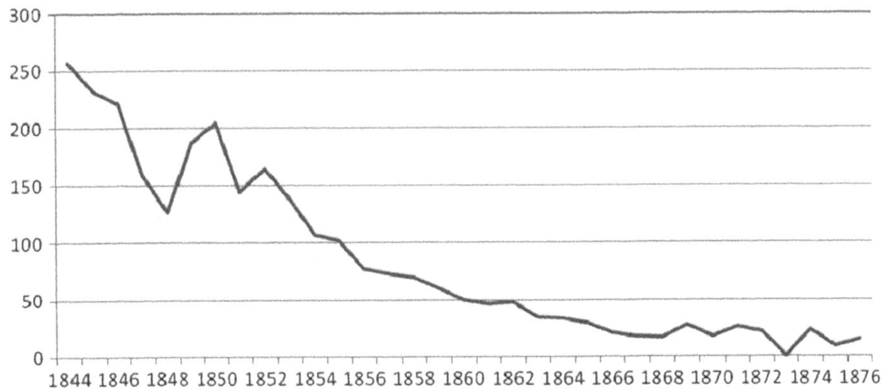

Figure 6.1 Cases proceeded by the Worsted Committee, 1844–76.

The Government in which Gladstone served had pledged to repeal the tax drawback on soap and this they duly did in July 1853.The Cabinet debated budgetary considerations over a number of days in April 1853. From Gladstone's rough notes it appears that some members, such as Lord Lansdowne and Sir Charles Wood, advocated a reduction in soap duty by half, but in the end the Cabinet decided to completely remove duty on soap (see British Library Add. MS. 44778 ff 84–7; 98–105). The consequences of Gladstone's budget appeared to have been seen as catastrophic, and prompted the Committee to wonder if they could continue their work. The decision to go on primarily turned on the fact that they considered 'the new improved system of Police insufficient for enforcing the Worsted Acts', and eventually they decided that rationalization and cost-cutting could ensure the Committee's survival if at a more circumspect level (26 September 1853 WCMB). Indeed, once the Committee's funds had dwindled after the 1853 crisis, the fall in the number of prosecutions which had resulted from the Committee's reduced operations, paralleled the financial health of the organization (see Figure 6.1). The Committee's bank balance continued to grow after 1853 because of the effective cutting of costs. For example, the dismissal of all but two Inspectors saved hundreds of pounds in wage bills. They also rationalized their assets by selling some shares, and collecting debts owed to them from manufacturers who had not fully paid over their drawback fees by 1853. Rather belatedly the Committee had foreseen the possibility of the withdrawal of soap drawback and had hastily attempted to pre-empt the revenue crisis by raising funds through subscription. Five thousand handbills were distributed, and Inspectors visited manufacturers to advertise their services and attract new patrons. The recruitment of subscribers was slow work, however, and the

Committee were never again fully able to police the districts as they had in the 1840s and early 1850s.

Relations between the police and the Worsted Inspectors

In the 1830s and 1840s, the relationship on the ground between Worsted Inspectors (who, despite having the power of entry and search within the homes of suspects, did not have any arresting powers) and the attested officers of the local police seem in the main to have been cordial and co-operative. There also seems to have been considerable crossover with regard as to who investigated cases of misappropriation and theft until at least the mid-century: several cases are reported in both the *Bradford Observer* and the *Leeds Mercury* in which the investigation was instigated by the police and then passed onto a Worsted Inspector. Yewdall in particular seems to have worked closely with at least two of his counterparts in the Bradford police: Inspectors (later Superintendents) John Shuttleworth and William Burniston. There are numerous reports of these individuals working closely together in order to investigate cases of workplace misappropriation (see for example *Bradford Observer* 9 February 1854, 15 June 1854; *Leeds Mercury* 10 October 1857).

But, if anything, the move to factory production encouraged the police to pass workplace appropriation cases over to the Worsted Inspectors. The 1838 guidelines issued to the Leeds borough police spoke of patrolling streets, thoroughfares and houses. The factory was not suggested as an area which needed supervision. In fact, the Metropolitan Police ordered their officers not to obstruct people from going to work, nor were workpeople to be arbitrarily searched, so that relations between police and the working-class could improve (Police Orders, 4 March 1840, Metropolitan Police Orders – General regulations and Orders for the Government and Guidance of the Metropolitan Police Force A136/158). It remained the duty of a constable to arrest anyone he saw committing (or suspected of having committed) a felony. Appropriation of workplace materials, however, mostly occurred within the workplace, and while inside the factory an offender was unlikely to be caught red-handed by a passing bobby. Indeed, the constable was unlikely to have been allowed by factory owners to freely patrol inside the perimeter fence. A number of Chief Constable's reports, for example, make it clear that the police felt no responsibility for stopping the numerous thefts taking place in the warehouses and manufactories, since they had no right of access.

Bradford's Chief Constable blamed the robberies on the inattention of factory supervisory staff, and suggested that the responsibility for catching the perpetrators lay with private security forces and not his men (see, for example, the Bradford Chief Constable's Reports of 1863, 1869 and 1873 BBC/1/2). It is true that the security of material left outside as part of the production process, such as drying cloth on tenter racks was a police responsibility, but tentering was increasingly being carried out inside the factory (Huddersfield Borough Police Force Occurrence Books, 1873–5 *WYAW* A90/136). Therefore, although the arrest of appropriators was legally the responsibility of the police officer, in practice he was unlikely to be involved in the detection of 'theft' within the factory, and was only called upon to exercise the power of arrest at the instigation of the foreman or the Worsted Inspector. The Bradford policeman, then, had the authority, but perhaps lacked the time, resources and inclination to intervene within the factory walls. They saw their duties beginning at the factory gate and out into public space, regulating only public space (1873 Huddersfield Police Occurrence books, *WYAW* A90/136; 4 October 1864 John Crossley and Co. DMB 1864–66, WYAC MIC:21/1).

In reality, the Worsted Inspectors were more capable of pursuing workers for these offences than were the police. In addition to lacking expertise and legal knowledge in this area, the police were seen as intruders into workers' lives (Storch 1976, 1981). Using Colne as an example, he discussed the bitter feuding that sometimes occurred between police and the occupants of the Northern industrial districts. How much more bitter might this war of attrition have been for the Worsted Inspectors as they stopped workers in the streets, searched their houses with no warning for scraps of cloth, searched their lofts, dustbins and outhouses and questioned their families – and yet there is little evidence of such resistance. Even in Colne, which Storch takes as an example of the intransigent opposition of industrial workers towards the police, the Worsted Inspector was never physically prevented from going about his work. The attitude of the textile workers is summed up in one case recounted by Reverend Room. He described the scene after an old widow had been acquitted at petty sessions for the possession of appropriated worsted waste:

> The tender lamb of the flock had been delivered out of the teeth of the spoiler, and I was prayed for and against as a Phayroh, a Senna Cherrib, a Nebby Chad Nayzer, a Phillistian, an Amlakite . . . Satan transformed into an angel of light . . . They were the heroes of the night, the champions of the poor combers, the victors of the battle for the working man's rights. The worsted manufacturers were

> anathematized as tyrants, bloodsuckers, who wished to rob the working man of his just rights, and hired a bloodhound to hunt him down (Room 1882, p. 110).

The defendant was vigorous in her condemnation of the Inspector's activities, and let him know what she thought of him in uncompromising terms:

> 'Tha'r a blood-sucking varmint; Thah lives like a lord o' the fat o' the land, An wod giv nowt but skilly to a poor fact'ry 'and;– Nowt but skilly an bran, and t'ahse o' correction; An that comes o' thee an thi wark ov inspection – Poor kimmers and weyvers – tha'd starve 'em to death An if thah could help it, they muddent ev breeath. Ah knaw thee ov old. Ah sal allus hate thee, For t'troubles tha's browt on mi naybors an me.'(Room 1882, pp. 129–38).

The outcome of the case was obviously of some irritation to the Inspector, but the widow's supporters' party was the most serious challenge to the Inspector's authority that he could remember, and yet there was no physical attack, or even threat of violence issued against him. Indeed, there were only a few recorded cases of assaults against any Inspector or their families, and these tended to be fairly minor. There was, for example, a revenge attack on Inspector James Wilcock's horse and cart by the brother of an individual whom Inspector Wilcock had previously taken into custody for throwing stones at special constables during the investigation of a case (*Bradford Observer* 2 March 1843). Similarly, in 1839, a suspect addressed a memorial to the Committee 'praying not to be prosecuted for obstructing J. Whitworth in the execution of his duty' (25 March 1839 WCMB). His donation of £1-00 to the Ladies Charity at Baccup as a sign of his good faith failed to save him from a conviction for assault, however (17 June 1839 WYMB). In the same year, 'a large assault[was]made upon Joseph Seed and the constables assisting him' while they were searching a suspect's house. Again the assailant was convicted of assault. The Committee was obviously keen to prosecute in all cases of assault, both to protect their Inspectors and to defend the legitimacy of their methods. 'The Committee takes proceedings to make a proper example of such offenders' (5 April 1819 WCMB). One way of doing this was to run newspaper adverts in which a prospective defendant in an assault upon a Worsted Inspector issued a very public apology in exchange for the dropping of a prosecution for assault:

> 'PARDON ASKED – WHEREAS I, LEVI WARD, of Clayton, in the County of York, Weaver, did, on the 31st Day of July last, assault and ill-treat Mr Benjamin Wood, of Bowling, Inspector of Worsted Yarn, for which Offence he has commenced a Prosecution; but on my agreeing to ask his Pardon and pay Expenses, he has consented to stop the Prosecution. I do, therefore, most

humbly ASK his PARDON, and thank him for his Lenity, and promise never to be guilty of the like Offence again' (*Leeds Mercury* 20 October 1821).

Such adverts fulfilled a duplicity of purpose; not only did they ensure that the individual avoided prosecution but also publicly reinforced the authority of the Inspectorate and warned prospective offenders of the consequences of their actions.

All in all, however, Worsted Inspectors appeared to go about their work with only occasional hindrance or opposition, let alone fear of attack. Compare this to the hostility shown to policemen in Colne, or Bradford, where there were well over a thousand cases of assaults on policemen recorded between 1869 and 1879 (Bradford Chief Constable's Reports, BCC1/2). Policemen, of course, had to deal with disorderly drunks and vagrants, but even so there seems to be a vast difference in the number of assaults on the officers of these two enforcement agencies. So real was the threat of violence that, until 1856, the police did not dare venture into some industrial parts of Leeds, yet Worsted Inspectors patrolled these areas apparently without fear. It may be assumed that they were disliked, even hated, but they were not seen as alien to the working class districts in the same way as police constables were.

The reduction of the Inspectorate to a single member and the withdrawal of the Inspectors from various areas in 1853 had left something of a vacuum. Able to step into the space were the borough, and later county, police forces. However, they were only willing to partially fill the void.

Both Bradford and Leeds borough forces grew rapidly after the mid-century. Bradford's police force grew by 60 per cent between 1848 and 1858, and by 70 per cent between 1859 and 1870 (Bradford Watch Committee Minute Books, 1848–58 *WYAB*; Chief Constables reports, 1859–70 *WYAB*, BBC1/2–5). As Elliot (1976) stated, the Bradford force was 'superior in numbers, training, equipment and discipline to the previous law enforcement officers'. Its reputation for efficiency grew alongside its numbers, and by the late 1850s, it was confident enough in its field of operations to launch an offence against 'every species of ruffianism', dog-fighters, prize fights, street games, prostitution and pawnbrokers. For example, Bradford Police first patrolled visiting fairs and circuses in 1852, and started to attend cricket matches in 1853 (see Borough Watch Committee Minute Book, 1852–56, *WYAB* BBC1/5/2). Policemen were also encouraged in this period to replace Factory Inspectors, which would have brought them physically into the workplace (see Johnston 1992, p. 5). The pursuit of workplace appropriators would not have been out of keeping with this moral crusade.

The arrest and formal charging of suspected appropriators had always been the responsibility of the police, but henceforth the police had the staff to test their investigative skills on factory appropriation. Three plain-clothes detective officers were employed in 1843, a progressive development which was a rare and early experiment in detective policing, with an Inspector appointed to head up a Detective Department in 1846. This they effectively failed to do, however. If the Worsted Inspectors had left the field, the police forces were disinclined to pick up their swords. Nor were the West Riding county force, which was formed in 1856 (Emsley 1983, 1991). Neither borough nor county policemen involved themselves with workplace appropriators while they remained within the factory, unless they were called in by the foreman or Worsted Inspector to exercise the power of arrest. The police simply lacked the expertise and inclination to usurp the Worsted Inspectorate's specialist policing functions. There still seemed to be a place for the Worsted Committee and their Inspectors if only they could animate their former supporters to give them the resources to carry on.

The fracturing of collective security and the emergence of selective security

Why did the worsted manufacturers not make financial provision for the Worsted Inspectors to continue their work after the drawback remission was withdrawn? If the Worsted Committee were so influential in protecting their interests, why did the manufacturers not pay voluntarily what had previously been involuntary – a levy which would ensure their interests continued to be protected? The answer lies in the principle of collective security.

After 1853, manufacturers were unwilling to fund a policing system which was provided for the benefit of all, but not funded by all that benefited. Many of the larger employers believed that smaller sized competitors were able to undercut them by buying cheaper (appropriated) raw materials. For the smaller manufacturer, this may have been the only advantage they had over their large specialized and mechanized neighbours. It was therefore not in the interests of the smaller manufacturers to subscribe to the Committee. Perhaps this reason more than any other explains why the Committee could not quickly re-animate itself, and why an attempt to appeal to sectional interests within the textile community failed. This attempt, made in the 1860s, was designed to demonstrate to manufacturers that the Committee could prevent severe losses which they had sustained due to the 'customs of the trade' adhered to by commission combing firms, thereby persuading manufacturers that collective security for just this one section of trade was possible.

Fraudulent hand-combers had long been a target of the Inspectors. The waste worsted material left on the combs was perceived by the domestic combers to be a customary perquisite. In many cases, the employers concurred with this view in order to maintain good labour relations, and by allowing waste to be considered as a part of the comber's wage they reduced labour costs. Worsted Inspectors therefore had a difficult time persuading employers to outlaw the combers' practice of keeping waste, especially since it was almost valueless, and there appeared to be no advantage to the employers in pressing home the law. Similarly, in the mechanized combing process a certain amount of 'waste' was created, although it may have been of better quality. Worsted strands were caught on the iron combs of the machines, and this waste was removed by the machine combers who were asked to distinguish between waste which could be re-used and that which was worthless. This was a difficult task, and one which relied on the same interpretation and definition of which waste was 're-usable' being held by the employer, foreman and combers. The *Bradford Observer* illustrated the inherent difficulties in this practice:

> Machine woolcombers, as much as the hand comber, were liable to return to their employers all the material they received, of whatever character it might be. Wool was made into tops, noils, waste, and fluff, but whatever was worth returning must be returned – not dust of course. Waste allowed to a spinner and waste claimed by a woolcomber were very different things. A spinner might agree to spin tops and have a certain allowance for waste, which could not possibly be collected, but waste with a woolcomber was very different. The waste made by a woolcomber could be collected and was of great value and ought to be returned to the party from whom the wool had been obtained. (undated clipping, *Bradford Observer*, Mariner records, Brotherton Library, PH II 23).

Combing machine minders were prosecuted by the Committee, as described in Chapter 3, and it is clear that shop-floor workers appropriated combing waste, but it was the retention of waste by commission combing companies which the Committee chose as a site of legal conflict in the 1860s. The question they posed was simple: to whom did reclaimed combing waste belong – the combing shop owner who had been sub-contracted to comb the wool, or the client manufacturer who had deposited his wool for combing?

The Committee became determined to answer this question in 1864, and answer it in a way that would meet the approval of the client weaving and spinning manufacturers. The campaign launched by the Committee was unusual in two respects. First, the defenders of customary practice in this case were manufacturers, and not employees. Second, the campaign was designed not only to curb appropriation, but also to re-launch the Committee's fortunes.

The campaign started well with one combing manufacturer convicted in January of selling 1,000lbs of appropriated Mohair noils valued at £120–230 (*Bradford Observer* January 1864). This conviction prompted other commission combers to return waste, and the Inspectors believed that in time all commission combers could be persuaded to adopt this practice (*Bradford Observer* March 1864). Emboldened by their success against one combing manufacturer, and coming to realize that the attack on this form of appropriation could be used to persuade one section of the worsted trade that subscriptions should be raised to fund the Committee, the Committee targeted another commission combing company. The foreman of Lister and Co., the largest combing company in Yorkshire, was prosecuted in April 1864. Both the defence and the prosecution paraded witnesses in front of the magistrates in an attempt to prove that waste was a legitimate perquisite belonging to the combing manufacturers, but there was no uniform view given by the managers and owners of combing shops that were selected to testify. It became clear that the customs of the trade varied in different regions, and in different companies. Holden's manager, for example, insisted that the 'sliver' from combed tops was always returned after combing since it constituted between 8 and 25 per cent of the wool that had been combed. In reality, however, the case was less about the old customs of the trade, than the new ones, as the *Bradford Observer* intimated:

> It strikes at the foundation of trading morality by making the comber the judge of what is wool and what is waste . . . We believe that wool combing by machinery has considerably reduced the waste allowance made by employers in the old days of hand combing . . . As long as his customers did not grumble, nothing was more natural than that Mr Lister should look upon waste as a comber's perquisite. (However) Has it not been shown that in the hands of honourable men, the waste of a large concern may produce revenue of several thousand a year, and therefore, Good Heavens! What a handsome return the waste of a small combing establishment might yield in competent hands! (*Bradford Observer* 23 April 1864).

The editor of the *Bradford Observer* missed the point however; it was not the small combing establishment that posed a problem. The smaller commission combers returned all waste as a matter of course in order to drum up business. 'Well and Good; but Mr Lister was not to be ruled by them.' (*Bradford Observer* March 1864). Lister had never returned waste in the fifteen years he had been a commission comber, and he derided the case as a rebellious conspiracy by men whom he had raised from the 'dunghill', but who were now ungrateful sniping competitors. In the end the case was dismissed and Lister carried on his business as normal, continuing to retain all of the waste. The other commission combers had followed the case closely, and the magistrates' decision was seen to both vindicate past behaviour and legitimize future practice (*Bradford Observer* 19 May 1864). The court case having such a high profile also reflected badly on the Committee. They had suffered a very public defeat and, in attempting to demonstrate their vigour and endeavour, they had demonstrated the reverse. The attempt to gain the funds for new Inspectors had failed, and the single Inspector continued his work alone.

The re-birth of policing by committee

On 23 June 1870, the leading manufacturers in the West Riding met to discuss the possibility of re-establishing the Worsted Committee by raising regular subscriptions from manufacturers and employing two more Inspectors, one in Halifax, the other in Keighley. The Inspectors were installed in Halifax and Keighley two days later (*Bradford Observer* 23 June 1870; *Leeds Intelligencer and Yorkshire Post* 25 June 1870). This section explores two possible reasons why the employers breathed new life into the Worsted Committee at this time. The first possibility is that the manufacturing elite perceived there to be a general and relative decline in the level of policing in the West Riding, and that they took steps to bolster the agents of order in the manufacturing districts.

Were there reasons why the employers felt bereft of protection in the late 1860s and early 1870s? In this period, many new mill chimneys were seen on the West Riding skyline, and the new factories brought thousands of new workers into the industrial townships. Were the police facing a crime wave resulting from the increase in population which prevented them from patrolling the manufacturing districts effectively?

The Bradford police statistics indicate that the numbers of those prosecuted summarily escalated from 2,000 in 1867 to 3,400 in 1870, mainly due to rising prosecutions for vagrancy and drunkenness (Chief Constables Reports, Bradford BBC/1/2–5). This is a prodigious rise of 70 per cent over three years, especially given that the numbers of policemen employed in Bradford rose by only 16.4 per cent in the two years before 1870, and similarly the Leeds force only increased by 16 per cent over the same period. Thereafter, the pace of recruitment slowed in Leeds but not Bradford. The Leeds borough force had swelled by only two more men in 1874, while the Bradford police service had employed another sixty-six in that time (see Chief Constable's reports, Bradford, BBC1/2). The police had a limited role in the control of appropriation, and the manufacturers agitated for more Worsted Inspectors, not policemen, so it appears that the elite industrial class of Bradford had no *extraordinary* fears about lawlessness in the borough at this time. Manufacturers may have been concerned about vagrancy, burglary and drunkenness, but their concern did not translate into agitation for reform of the police, increased men on the beat or a call for police to patrol inside factory perimeters. They seem to have been responding to a different need in calling the Worsted Committee again to arms.

The second reason why employers may have wished to re-animate the Worsted Committee is that economic conditions in the 1870s prompted the manufacturers to take action, both to preserve profits and minimize losses. This was a natural enough reaction to a period of trade depression, but was there also an intent to defeat labour militancy in the boom years?

As Ittmann noted:

> From 1850 to 1872, the number of powerlooms in the Bradford district increased by almost 120% and the number of spindles by over 140% and entrepreneurs constructed more than 1000 mills and warehouses in the borough. The mid-Victorian era was a golden one for textile manufacturers. Between 1856 and 1867, the level of assessed profits in Bradford shot up 250% (Ittmann 1995, pp. 14–15).

The good times did not end there, with the period between 1868 and 1873 being particularly rosy. This made the following slump seem both unexpected and severe. From 1873 through to the early 1880s, the worsted trade experienced a deep and profound depression due to the increased competition from woollen manufacturers. A fall in the price of wool had made woollen products affordable to more people, and the demand for worsted products dried up. Manufacturers, as they had always done under the 'Bradford system', attempted to minimalize losses by shedding labour, reducing wages, using cheaper materials and promoting tighter work discipline among the workforce.

Worsted Inspectors had always had the power to prosecute those accused of breaching their contract, slackening off or striking for better conditions (especially in times of slump, when conditions and wages fell). Nevertheless, Inspectors saw little profit in enforcing work discipline within the factory, and neither did the Committee. The Committee did not see the enforcement of contractual law as a part of the rationale for their existence. Nevertheless, by performing the useful task of prosecuting 'idle or unprincipled' employees who left their work, they were able to ensure that the manufacturers witnessed the efficiency of the Committee in bringing employees back to their work. The manufacturers were then more likely to subscribe to their services. The success of the Committee in these cases, where a conviction rate of 87 per cent was achieved, naturally led to calls for them to encompass this kind of work. The proportion of those convicted in Bradford under Master and Servant is not discernable; however, in Manchester the conviction rate in these cases was 63.6 per cent (*Lancashire Opinion*, 1868). For example, in the same year as the new Master and Servant Acts was passed, a memorial was received by an Inspector signed by 'the largest and most important Worsted Spinners, Manufacturers . . . Wool Merchants and Wool Staplers in Bradford, Halifax and Keighley' (June 1867 WCMB, *WYAB*). However, their request for a public prosecutor who would deal with breaches of contract, as well as fraud and misconduct, fell on deaf ears. The Committee still preferred to leave master and servant law to the employers, as one Inspector made clear:

> There has been some convictions under the Master and Servant Act, and I have had application for me to pay the expenses of the prosecutions, but I have declined to do so, the employers having money to buy their own informations, and if there is any benefits from doing so, they themselves receive it. (30 December 1867 WCMB, *WYAB*)

The Worsted Inspectors preferred to concentrate their attentions on the control of appropriation, sending out circulars to all worsted manufacturers to enquire if they would raise money for the Committee to take on more Inspectors to eradicate appropriation (30 March 1863 WCMB). Inspector Yewdall had reported in 1863 that the manufacturers had cast aside the circular, and optimistically suggested that a personal visit to each of them might be more successful (28 September 1863 WCMB). It was not. However, the opportunity to improve their appeal to potential and existing subscribers by broadening their activities beyond the detection and prosecution of appropriators only slipped by for a few years. The poor judgement and management, which combined to ensure that this avenue for renewal and expansion lay undiscovered, was pushed aside in the 1870s when the matter was taken out of their hands.

Relations between capital and labour, 1870–80

The extreme periods of rapid economic growth (1868–73) and contraction (1873–80) had many implications for the relationship between capital and labour. In the boom period, workers were better able to negotiate wage increases. If wage demands were not met, employees were easily able to find employment at another mill. Accordingly, the manufacturers' attempts to use the master and servant laws, and threat and persuasion, to keep their employees from being tempted away by other mill owners were unsuccessful, and many workers left to take better paid jobs with rival manufacturers. At the same time, the manufacturers were faced with wage claims by those workers who remained. These claims were increasingly being articulated through trade society mouthpieces, for, despite the fact that the West Riding textile workers had been slow to collectively organize themselves, several societies had come into existence in the 1860s and 1870s, representing skilled and supervisory workers. There were seven woollen and worsted workers' societies created before 1860. Between 1860 and 1875, the following were created – Huddersfield and Dewsbury Power Loom Society; Managers and Overlookers Society; Yorkshire Twisters and Drawers-In, Leeds Cloth Pressers; Leeds and District Power Loom Overlookers Society; Halifax and District Power Loom Overlookers Society; Huddersfield and District Cloth Pressers and the Huddersfield Warehousemen.

The hegemonic control over employees which had long been exercised by the Bradford manufacturers was therefore being challenged by intra-industry competition for labour, rising prices and the challenge of organized labour. The employers' reaction was twofold. First, they formed employers' societies which would oppose by common cause the demands of the nascent trade unions, and second they turned again to the Worsted Committee as an effective power for the enforcement of contractual obligation. As Magrath stated, it was only when the employees began to organize that the employers felt the urge to join together collectively to oppose their workers (see Magrath 1988, p. 44–64). It was to this end that the owners met in 1870 to re-animate the 'sleepy' if not yet 'sleeping' giant. These men were anxious to have Inspectors installed in their districts, and by virtue of the fact that they contributed 75 per cent of the Committee's income, the Inspectors became very much the servants of the subscribers. The Worsted Inspectorate was a 'ready made' employers' union *par excellence*, and was now re-orientated by the new Committee members to enforce work discipline as well as prosecute fraud. This change in emphasis is evidenced by the statistics; after 1870 the number of neglect cases prosecuted by the Committee tripled.

In the period after 1870 the Committee re-established their authority over the detection and prosecution of suspected appropriators, not that this authority had been seriously challenged by the police force. They were also able to return to old campaigns, sending circulars to all commission combers informing them that they would be prosecuted if they did not return all combing waste to their clients (January 1881 and 11 April 1881 WCMB). The borough police forces and the Committee consciously redefined their roles, confirming that felony cases and workplace appropriation cases were dealt with separately by the respective forces. This separation of duties was strictly enforced on the Committee's side, and even the suggestion that Inspectors were involved in cases where the Worsted Acts could not be applied was quickly pounced upon. Jesse Yewdall, for instance, was censured for saying in his report that he had not convicted anyone of 'felony'. The decision as to which cases could be handled by the Inspector, and which should be referred to the police officer, was taken either by the Inspector when the theft was detected or later by the Committee in the time between the suspect's arrest and his/her appearance in court. As previously stated, the Worsted Acts could be interpreted in a variety of ways, and the Inspector's judgement was not infallible. Yewdall quickly explained that 'whenever I get any such information I at once report such cases to the Chief Constable or Superintendent of Police where they properly belong' (26 March 1877 WCMB). By so assiduously moving such cases over to the police, the Inspectors were able to regain their moral authority to root out appropriation. This system seems to have been reciprocated by the police, and when Detectives realized that an offence came under the Worsted Acts, the arrested person was handed over to an Inspector (3 April 1882 WCMB).

The new Inspectors hired by the Committee, however, were not necessarily of the same quality as those of the earlier period, and lower salaries re-introduced the temptation of corruption: embezzling subscription money or accepting bribes from apprehended suspects, for example (June 1879 WCMB). As the older Inspectors left or died off, the Inspectorate became a deprofessionalized force, much to the exasperation of longer time servers. The difference in quality between the old and new Inspectorate became evident in their work. As previously stated, the Inspectors had always been responsible for presenting the prosecution case in the courts. This situation, which in itself had been barely tolerated by the legal profession, was now made almost impossible by the low calibre of the new Inspectors. The defending solicitor who described a new Worsted Inspector as 'a man having been appointed to an office for which he appeared not to have the slightest personal ability or qualification' (*Bradford Observer* 14 May 1879) was wrong, however. The Inspector was qualified to bring suspects to trial but not to conduct the prosecution with all the intricate legal knowledge which required. Evaluating the 'quality' of Inspectors is problematic. One measure that can be employed, however, is length of service. Both Inspector Whitworth and Inspector Yewdall worked for the Committee for over fifteen years, avoiding any charge of corruption or inefficiency for that time.

If the Inspectors were of less use in the court room, they became more useful as enforcers of work discipline within the factory. As part of their role as a general 'employers' protection service', they performed several types of duty. First, they prevented the free movement of labour, and attempted to dissuade employees from initiating industrial action, as one Inspector made clear: 'Many petty disputes between Employed and Employer most especially between weavers in most of which my explanation of the Laws and gentle persuasion have had the desired effect' (5 January 1880 WCMB). Where gentle persuasion or intimidation did not work, and industrial action could not be avoided, the Inspectors would summon the strikers for neglecting their work. Notices were first sent out by the Committee to the workers who had made themselves absent, informing them of the penalties of infringing the Worsted Act clause regarding 'neglect'. When they did not return to the factory, prosecutions followed (April 1871 WCMB). In the case of walk-outs or strikes, only the spokesmen needed to be threatened with legal proceedings, for the point to be made to the mass of the strikers. 'I put an end to a strike at Shaws', boasted one Inspector, 'by serving twenty of the leaders with notices to complete work, consequently 350 returned to work' (June 1887 WCMB). When faced with such evidence, it is easy to understand the huge impact the Worsted Acts and their enforcers could have on industrial relations in the textile areas.

A second duty performed on behalf of the employers was the defence of their subscribers in court actions. One of the first cases fought by Inspector Yewdall after the Committee was reborn involved the successful defence of a manufacturer in a claim against him for wages he owed to a worker (21June 1870, *BDT* 21 June 1870 WCMB). Further entries in the minute books for the 1870s-1880s detail the Inspectorate's role in defending employers from claims of owed wages, wrongful dismissal and other claims under master and servant actions initiated by the employees. 'We have to defend our Manufacturers for refusing to pay wages', stridently asserted an Inspector in January 1875. Only those who subscribed to the Committee were defended in these cases, but occasionally it seems that manufacturers were able to subscribe after they had been summoned to court for non-payment of wages (28 September 1885 WCMB). The Inspectors also protected their subscribers from factory safety legislation, such as the Employers Liability Act. The Inspector in self-congratulatory mood described the circumstances of a case in 1883: 'A boy having been killed while engaged in repairing a belt. The Father sued for about £100 compensation, when on the case being heard the lad's father unfortunately, through me, missed his way – the case being dismissed' (1 January 1883 WCMB).

It is an indication of how far the Worsted Committee and its Inspectorate had moved along the road from controlling appropriation to being a general employers' aide that they were sometimes involved in negotiating wage agreements on the employer's behalf. The 'painstaking care, tact and delicacy' exhibited by an Inspector negotiating a new wage agreement at Temperance Mill was commended in a letter written by the millowner to the Committee (letter dated 29 October 1884, Correspondence to the Committee, *WYAB*, 56D.88/1/6). Tact and tactical use of the threat of litigation could achieve much for the employers on these occasions as can be seen from this Inspector's report:

> I got six of them (the striking workers) in the office and told them that the masters had taken the order at such a price that they (the masters) could not possibly give any more, therefore I should take proceedings if they did not return and work up the warps . . . they said they would come back for 3d. per piece advance, Mr Sichel and the Manager consulted and agreed the advance (3 April 1882 WCMB).

It must be remembered when studying the new duties of the Inspectors that they may not have imbibed completely the new philosophy of the Committee and may have continued to view the prosecution of appropriators as their primary function, rather than preventing strikes or other duties. However, it is evident that the enforcement of work discipline, and the new subscribers that work attracted to the Committee, brought in funds which were essential for the continuation of the struggle to control illegal appropriation. Cases of appropriation therefore continued to be regularly brought before the courts by the Inspectors throughout this period and beyond. Eighty-nine persons were charged for offences other than neglect of work between 1870 and 1876. A printed sheet in 1934 gave accounts of thirty-eight people recently charged under the Worsted Acts, and the Inspectorate was still active in 1951, Inspector Batty charging William Brook with embezzlement on 3 January (Printed Circular of the Worsted Committee, *WYAB*, 56D.88/5/7 and Deposition of Worsted Inspector, *WYAB*, 56D.88/5/9).

The Worsted Committee changed not only its operational methods and organizational structure during the late-eighteenth and nineteenth centuries but also its relationship with industrial capital. In the last decades of the eighteenth century, the Worsted Committee had been the engine behind prosecutions, indeed the 1777 Act was partly envisaged as a means of compelling recalcitrant employers to prosecute their workers for short-reeling and other domestic appropriations. By the 1840s, however, many more employers were willing to establish industry-wide standards of behaviour and working practices for their employees, and by 1870 the factory owners perceived themselves to be in need of the protection of the Worsted Inspectorate in order to maximize their profits and minimize their losses. Composed of the most important factory owners in the county, and powered by over a hundred subscribers, the Committee in 1870 worked solely for the benefit of the subscribing mill owners. The Committee therefore became a manufacturer-led force for the protection of property during production, and the control of labour.

As labour became more organized in the nineteenth and early twentieth centuries, the Yorkshire manufacturers had to cope first with barriers to their considerable power (Frank 2010; Curthoys 2004). If not a new lease of life from the declining utility of Master and Servant legislation after 1875 (Hay 2004), the Worsted Committee certainly continued with a *raison d'être*. However, the unionization of millworkers meant that the Worsted employers faced difficulties in simply carrying on as they had previously. Like many other industrial workers, the Yorkshire textile workers also went on strike in the periods before and after the World War I. Relations between labour and employers were tense and heavily contested. Not surprisingly, prosecutions by the Committee seem to have been undertaken in cases where the context of the theft was unambiguous – neglect of work cases fell away – and so, apparently, did any case where customary right could be defended by unionized labour (where before it was weakly defended by individual defendants). Although still periodically prosecuting workplace appropriation (especially in the 1920s and 1930s when the mills suffered a slump), the number of cases dwindled rapidly. Where once there were hundreds of cases, by the World War II, there were only tens per year – less than ten some years. By the time the Worsted Acts were finally repealed and replaced by the 1968 Theft Act, the activities of the

Inspectors and the running of the Worsted Committee organization was being carried out by a firm of Bradford solicitors. The considerable records of the Worsted Committee then found their way to what is now the West Yorkshire Archive Service in Bradford: a somewhat mediocre and dusty end for this most active of policing agencies.

Effects of the Worsted Committee on public policing

A private policing agency as dynamic and regionally important as the Worsted Committee must have had an impact on the development of policing in Yorkshire, if not England. Since the existence of private police forces controlled by manufacturers has been relatively under-researched by historians, it is worth briefly reviewing three questions raised by this study. First, how well supported were the New Police by the manufacturers? Second, what effect did models of private policing have on public policing in the West Riding? Last, is the classification of policing agencies into 'public' and 'private' sound?

As is well known, the relationship between industrialization, urbanization and the development of formal policing agencies in the nineteenth century is usually represented as a causal one. The theory that the threat to public order posed by the increasing numbers of workers crowding into the manufacturing districts, together with the rise of industrial and political 'militancy', 'provoked' the middle and upper-classes to call for uniformed and disciplined bodies of men to act as locally controlled police services, is well known and does not need to be rehearsed here (Silver 1967); Chartist agitation, for example, which was rife in Bradford in the 1840s. Although in most of the industrial areas of the West Riding, military, not civil, forces were used to contain the disquiet.

However, this theory relies on the assertion that the northern borough forces were supported politically and financially (through local taxation) by the industrial elite, and that the police in turn provided services for the manufacturers. These duties included the protection of the millowner and his property in the street, in his house and in his factory, but also the protection of his commercial interests when threatened. Thus, for example, the legal and operational requirement to preserve the public peace necessitated police governance of strikers' actions in times of labour disputes. Living in the towns and cities as they did, 'the new manufacturing and merchant urban bourgeoisie lacked certain protection against crime which the rural gentry enjoyed. They did not have the ecological safeguards of large estates and lack of proximity to the 'dangerous classes' according to Brogden (1981, p. 49–50). It was therefore necessary, Storch (1981, p. 93) asserted, to create a force which would protect the factories, and also the homes of factory owners, to turn the police into a weapon of the employers. It has been suggested that, for this reason, the working classes resisted the introduction of the police, while the urban and industrial elites welcomed them with open arms (Storch 1976, 1981).

These assertions can be challenged, however, notably on the question of policing industrial disputes. The first problem is that of 'class sympathy'. Most members of the borough forces previously held agricultural or industrial labouring occupations (Emsley 1991, p. 180). The sympathies of a police force drawn from the same social background and living in the same communities as those people on strike may have undermined the loyalty they held to the law (Reiner 1985, p. 22; Foster 1977, pp. 56–61; Storch 1976, pp. 89, 92–3). Conversely, policemen drawn from a higher social class may have 'exacerbated rather than mollified class violence' (Silver 1967, p. 10). It appears that the use of policemen drawn either from within or outside the local community may have handicapped the control of striking workers. This, however, was not the opinion of those northern mill owners who testified to the Constabulary Force Commissioners in 1836 (Emsley 1983, Storch 1981, pp. 92–3). This is not surprising; the Commission was after all designed by Chadwick to find evidence that a national police force would be beneficial to many sectors of society. With this in mind, they concluded that for 'the want of an efficient preventative force, the peace and manufacturing prosperity of the country are exposed to considerable danger' (1836 Constabulary Commission Report). Those manufacturers who testified were not from the West Riding, however.

Was this because the mill owners in that region already had control over a preventative force which acted directly to protect mill owners' property? The borough force were charged with controlling labour disputes when they reached the streets, but the truly effective work of dissuading employees from leaving their employment had already been achieved by the Worsted Inspectorate. Naturally, manufacturers were loath to contribute financially for policing services they did not need, or for a duplication of services (Hay 1975, p. 59).The Bradford Watch Committee were always seeking to reduce the costs of policing the borough, and many entries record their resistance to increases in policemen's wages. They went so far as to regularly commission surveys of other comparative forces to ensure that they paid the very lowest rates of pay (Borough Watch Committee Minute

Book, 1862, *WYAB*). Similarly the 1871 survey revealed that the Chief Constable of Bradford received the lowest salary of all Chief Constables controlling forces of over a hundred men. Witness their reluctance to financially support the Worsted Committee between 1853 and 1870 when many manufacturers believed that their internal supervisory structures were sufficient to cope with the appropriation 'problem'. It must also be remembered that prominent manufacturers were in a dominant position to affect the development of the borough forces. A quarter of the Watch Committee which oversaw the introduction of Bradford's borough police were Worsted Committee members, and two-thirds were manufacturers eligible to subscribe to their services (Borough Watch Committee Membership lists, Bradford, 1847, *WYAB* BBC/1/2).

Rather than acting as a positive model for the new police, the Worsted Committee and their Inspectorate impeded the development of both the Bradford borough force and the West Riding county force. The latter was opposed by manufacturers and the West Riding urban elites before its compulsory adoption in 1856 when all counties and boroughs were required to establish police forces under the 1856 County and Borough Police Act, long after the permissive 1839 and 1840 County police acts (Emsley 1983). As Emsley (1982, p. 76) states, criticism of county forces was evident in rural as well as industrial areas, and the reasons why the West Riding failed to quickly adopt a county force are not the concern of this book. Nevertheless, it may be that the existence of the Worsted Committee was a contributory factor. Jones believes that the stationing of the military in Bradford's Belle Vue Barracks, who could deal with industrial disorder, also hindered the adoption of domestic police agencies in the industrial West Riding (Jones 1983:157). The Worsted Inspectors were an efficient and competent force, as one police historian admitted; Smith believes that the Inspectors helped the burghers of Bradford to decide to establish a professional force of policemen, but offers no evidence for his theory (Smith, G., *Bradford's Police*, Bradford, undated). However, their example had not led to agitation for borough forces, and certainly not for a county force, but rather acted as a constant reminder that privatized police agencies were efficient, cheaper and easier to control than official police agencies. Manufacturers in areas patrolled by Worsted Inspectors did not gleefully welcome ever increasing legions of blue-coated workers; rather they saw the police as a necessary evil to be tolerated. No doubt, even in areas where private police agencies existed, manufacturers desired a strong police presence when industrial strife spilled over onto the public streets. However, in the districts patrolled by the Worsted Inspectors, there was clearly an ambivalent attitude towards the police forces. For example, at a meeting of Halifax ratepayers, Inspector Seed (the Halifax Worsted Inspector), together with prominent businessmen, formed a Committee to express local discontent with the Halifax borough force. They declared that, 'all policemen are evil; but they were a necessary evil, and the dire anarchy that would reign if they were done away with would be infinitely worse than having to pay for the police out of the rates'(*Bradford Observer* 22 July 1876). This can hardly be taken as a ringing endorsement. Clearly, police historians should at least recognize the differences in attitude towards the police in those industrial areas which had established private police forces, and those that had not.

Conclusion

The employers' most faithful servants – the Worsted Committee – survived the 1853 crisis and a couple after that, to continue their work until their final dénouement in the second half of the twentieth century. In the length of their service they were an atypical prosecution service. While many of the private police forces described earlier continued throughout the remainder of the nineteenth century, they were increasingly seen as anachronistic in an ever-more centralizing system of policing that was seen as more integral to communities as a whole, rather than representing vested interests. The cathedral constables lost their powers of arrest, no longer being attested, while others such as the Admiralty police were absorbed into larger organizations, or simply faded away. Many other private prosecution agencies morphed into private security forces, responsible for the day-to-day smooth running of, for example, cathedrals or Oxbridge universities, but ultimately dependent on the local police authority to deal with more serious crimes that occurred on their premises. The Worsted Committee, by contrast, lasted for nearly two hundred years as a viable concern, continuing to act in the interests of their employers until well after World War II. Unusual too was the range of their duties, pursuing the suspect from the point of crime until the final judgement of guilt or innocence was delivered in court. Even in its depressed period between 1853 and 1870, the Committee made an impact, prosecuting over 800 cases. It must be concluded that this employers' police, empowered by law to coerce and intimidate the workforce, may have been the most dynamic private policing agency seen in England in the last three centuries.

7

Sentencing and Punishment in Worstedopolis

We Justices are all Worstedopolis bred,
And we know all the tracks and tricks of our trade;
So the hearing went on, and poor Mike was convicted;
And to Prison he went; for his funds were restricted.
And justice was satisfied: each got his own,
And the Worsted Inspector a leaf to his crown.

This extract from Reverend Room's poem (Room 1882, pp. 129–38) infers that only those magistrates who understood the nature of the worsted industry could fairly judge workplace theft. This chapter will examine to what extent conviction rates, and the sentences that were imposed on appropriators, were affected by the occupations of the magistrates who judged the cases, and what chances there were for justice in 'Worstedopolis'.

As with most offences, there was a statutorily determined punishment framework for appropriation which, in practice, was unevenly applied.

The table below portrays the penalties imposed at petty sessions, while outlining the punishments that were dispensed at both petty and quarter sessions.

The majority of offenders sentenced at petty sessions were required to pay a fine of twenty pounds, or in default spend a month in Wakefield House of Correction. (see Figures 7.1 and 7.2)

The sentences awarded by the quarter sessions magistrates were more severe than those imposed at petty sessions, reflecting the relative severity the offences with which they dealt. At the summary courts only 6.5 per cent of convicted appropriators were given sentences of four months or over, whereas half of those sentenced at quarter sessions received sentences of four months or over. The 1827 and 1861 Acts, with minimum tariffs of two and four years' gaol, respectively, do not appear to have ever been applied to West Riding workplace appropriators.

Year	Act	Offence	1st offence	2nd offence	3rd offence
1777	56 Geo.III c.56	Embezzlement/ unexplained possession	£20 fine/1 month gaol	£30 fine/2 months gaol	£40 fine/3 months gaol
		Buying embezzled goods	£20–£40/3–6 months	£50-£100/3–6 months	same
		Selling embezzled goods	£20–£40/3–6 months	£50-£100/3–6 months	same
1823	4 Geo.IV c.9	Breaking contract	Damages/1 month gaol	same	same
1827	7 & 8 Geo.IV c.29	Larceny of wool in process of manufacture	4 years gaol/7 years transportation	same	same
1861	24 & 25 Vict c.96 s.62	Larceny of wool in process of manufacture	penal serv. 3–7 years/2 years gaol	same	same
1867	30 & 31 Vict c.141	Breaking contract	Damages/3 months gaol	same	same
1875	38 & 39 Vict c.86	Breaking contract	£20 fine/3months gaol	same	same

Figure 7.1 The punishment structure for appropriation, 1777–1880.

Offence		Less than 1 month	1 month/£20	2 months/£30	3 months/£40	4 months	over 4 months
Unexplained possession/ embezzlement	No.	23	337	35	55	4	2
	%	5	74	8	12	1	0.4
Buying embezzled goods	No.	0	10	0	5	2	0
	%	0	59	0	29	12	0
Selling embezzled goods	No.	1	0	1	22	0	22
	%	2	0	2	48	0	48

Figure 7.2 Punishments imposed for appropriation-related offences prosecuted by the Worsted Committee, 1844–1876.

Were extra-legal sentences imposed at petty sessions? Some defendants received sentences of four months' imprisonment, which not even fourth-time offenders were supposed to serve. In addition, nearly 60 per cent of those convicted of buying appropriated goods received just one month and not the three to six months required by 27 Geo. III c.56. Moreover, many people convicted across a range of offences received less than the minimum £20 fine/ one month's imprisonment, while pawnbrokers and waste dealers received far heavier penalties than the offence seemed to warrant. The magistrates may not have had the chance to punish all the dealers they wished to, but seemed to make sure that the ones that they could reach received stiff penalties.

Given the discretionary and flexible ways in which offenders were sentenced, it is perhaps surprising that the penalty structure remained relatively unchanged by economic conditions. The periods of boom and slump described earlier left little mark on either the severity of the penalty or the proportions of defendants convicted. The apparent tendency for harsher punishments in the 1844 to 1853 period, when the Committee was at the peak of its activity, probably results from the greater numbers of prosecutions in this period, and therefore the larger number of repeat offenders rather than a rise in levels of punitiveness.

The conviction rate for workplace appropriation was higher than that for comparable property offences. For example, the conviction rate for the offence of simple larceny at Bradford petty sessions between 1865 and 1870 was 64 per cent, while for the larceny of goods valued at less than five shillings it was 62 per cent (Chief Constable's Reports, 1865–70, BBC1/1/2). Conviction rates cannot be viewed as either 'too high' or as 'too low', for modern historians cannot know whether those the court pronounced guilty had really broken the law. Nevertheless, it is clear that the Worsted Acts had a higher success rate than other comparable acts. Was this due to appropriation cases being judged by magistrates who made their money by manufacturing, and was the occupation of the magistrate a predictor of the trial result?

The principle of judicial impartiality

There exists today a judicial principle that magistrates should not judge a case with any motivation other than the execution of justice. Self-interest on behalf of the magistrate is therefore in theory precluded from the judicial process (Paley 1818, pp. 15–19). However, it was not until the last quarter of the nineteenth century that these principles became enshrined in statute law. In 1872, the *Bradford Observer* reported that:

> Under the new Trade Union Act, the Bench were disqualified by the clause relating to jurisdiction, in so much as they were themselves engaged or interested in the cotton trade, out of which the dispute arose. The prosecution at Leigh was withdrawn as every magistrate in the division was covered by the clause (*Bradford Observer* 20 September 1872).

However, the boundaries of a magistrate's moral and legal jurisdiction were established in the main by case law, not by statutes. It was ruled in 1851, for example, that magistrates who held shares in a company should not try cases involving that company (R. v. Glamorganshire JJ, 1857, *Justice of the Peace*, 21, p. 773; R. v. Hammond, 1863, *Justice of the Peace* 27, p. 793). Neither should magistrates try cases where they had a direct pecuniary interest, however small (per Blackburn, J., R. v. Rand; R. v. Justices of Bradford, 1866, *Justice of the Peace* 30, p. 293). Further, it was held that there was a danger of 'substantial bias' when members of committees, boards or members of prosecution associations, acted as JPs in trials of certain offenders, where they might have an interest (R. v. Henley, 1892, *Justice of the Peace*, 56, p.391. See 28 & 29 Vict. c121.,s.61; R. v Allan 4 B & S. 915).

As these examples show, case law ruled only over specific circumstances, but together these rulings and the reasoning which underlay them collectively established a more general code of conduct. This code was summed up in one case ruling: 'it is highly desirable that justice should be administered by persons who cannot be suspected of improper motives' (Per Mellor, J., in R. v. Allan, 1864). Magistrates should not place themselves in a position where they are interested in promoting one particular verdict out of self-interest, 'since no man may be a judge in his own case' (R. v. Hoseason, 1811, 14 east p. 605; see Harris 1969, p. 273–4). These rulings and legal opinions often presumed they defended justice from an individual magistrate's greed, envy or prejudice, but they did not preclude magistrates from acting collectively from class interest, or with views based on shared perceptions of offenders. To what extent were magistrates making judgements in workplace appropriation cases where they had an interest, whether personal or collective? To answer this question we have to examine the social and occupational structure of the West Riding magistrates.

The social and occupational structure of West Riding magistrates, 1840–80

In the early years of the nineteenth century, the gentry still dominated the West Riding magistracy. F. M. L.Thompson stated that the Lords Lieutenant constructed a gate-keeping system for new admissions to the bench: 'This sieve was designed to ensure a bench . . . which until after the middle of the nineteenth century was taken to evince those with any close connexions with trade or business' (Thompson 1963, p. 110). Swift's study of Staffordshire illustrates the difficulties industrialists experienced in entering the magistracy, stating that 'persons connected with industry and commerce . . . were not considered to be socially equipped for appointment to the bench' (Swift 1992, p. 77). Aside from respect for the niceties of social hierarchy, the Lord Lieutenant was concerned that industrialists were incapable of administrating the law impartially.

However, by approximately 1830, under the pressure of rapid population growth and an expansion of judicial business, the Lord Lieutenant of Yorkshire had been compelled, despite his own grave personal reservations, to appoint men engaged in commerce and manufacturing to the Bench (Harewood Estate, Lord Lieutenant's Papers, Box Two, Harewood to Lord Cottenham, Lord Chancellor, 3 December 1837 *WYAL*; see also Zangerl 1971). Knipe suggests that he resisted this administrative imperative long into the nineteenth century not because of his own prejudice against merchants and industrialists, but because such people were not thought to be able to act impartially in cases involving workpeople (Knipe 1970, p. 28; Harewood to Lord Cottenham, 3 December 1837, *WYAL*). However, despite the Lord Lieutenant's fears that the aristocratic and landed elements on the county benches would be swamped by industrialists, only 12.5 per cent of those eligible to sit on the West Riding Bench came from the manufacturing and trade sections of Yorkshire society in the 1840 to 1880 period (Knipe 1970). Similarly, in industrialized Lancashire, less than 5 per cent of the county bench were manufacturers at the mid-point of the century (Foster 1971, appendix 1, also see Johnston 2005, pp. 43–64). Zangerl's (1971) examination of the returns of Justices of the Peace from 1831 to 1887 found that the magistracy in 1842 overwhelmingly comprised of the gentry, with the next largest group being the clergy, with the emergent mercantile/middle classes not yet being represented. Indeed, even if the manufacturers were disproportionately likely to convict workplace offenders, their influence could only have been slight at quarter sessions. Statistically, in those courts, there was only a one-in-eight likelihood that an appropriation trial would be attended by a manufacturer. However, appropriation cases were mainly tried at the petty sessions in the worsted-producing districts. Only if sufficient evidence was available to prove a felony had taken place, would employers hazard the quarter sessions. Even if such evidence existed, they may still have preferred summary justice, since jury trial was unreliable (Sweeney 1985, p. 83). In the petty sessions of West Yorkshire, the chance of a manufacturer hearing an appropriation case was one-in-three in the 1840 to 1875 period. In reality, approximately six hundred cases initiated by the Worsted Committee were heard by at least one manufacturer, usually at Halifax, Bradford or East Morley petty sessions.

East Morley division dealt with an area stretching nearly to Leeds, Halifax and Colne, excluding the borough of Bradford, which was under a separate jurisdiction from 1847 (West Riding quarter sessions magistrates had concurrent jurisdiction over both of these, and indeed all, petty sessions courts within the Riding). The membership of these two minor courts overlapped, but essentially the two sets of magistrates were drawn from the same social backgrounds. For example, Bradford's mayor and aldermen were all entitled to sit on the borough bench, and since 84 per cent of the aldermen between 1847 and 1860 and all but one of the mayors in that period were textile manufacturers, just as in East Morley, the textile interest predominated (Elliot 1982). At Bradford borough court, magistrates did not sit on a bench, preferring to sit at a table placed on a platform between the bench and desk. At or near this table were the magistrate's clerk and his assistant, the superintendent of police, the attorneys and their clerks and representatives of the press, which made for a very crowded and intimidating arena of justice (*Bradford* Observer 7 February 1870). Less crowded, but inevitably more oppressive for the accused, were the summary hearings held in the magistrate's own houses (Cudworth 1887, pp. 36–7). E. C. Lister, for example, regularly held summary hearings in an extension of his home (Firth 1990, pp. 185–6). He was one of the eighty manufacturers who judged appropriation cases in West Yorkshire between 1840 and 1880. At least one other manufacturer held sessions in his factory. Holdsworth, a member of the Worsted Committee, bailed a woman suspected of embezzlement at his works in January 1860 (Lower Agbrigg petty sessions 1839–1880, *WYAW* P7/9). Fortunately, trade directories sometimes indicate the status of manufacturers within their industry and the local community, and by matching Worsted Committee membership lists to entries in these directories a picture can be formed of manufacturers who, like Holdsworth, were both Committee members and JPs.

The impression formed is that, as in other regions, magistrates were drawn from the local elites, and in the West Riding that meant the largest and most powerful manufacturers acted as magistrates. It may be useful here to list some of the West Riding magistrates who belonged to the Committee: John Foster employed 2,500 people in Black Dyke Mills in 1843; James and William Garnett employed six hundred in the 'very extensive' Valley and Greenside Mills, Joseph Wade, whose firm was 'among the first in Bradford to introduce the power loom, the combing machine and the general application of steam power to the textile industries', was also a large employer, as were the Peel brothers, who had eight hundred on their books. Other large employers were William Busfield and Swithin Anderton, prominent Committee members and eminent Bradfordians. It is little wonder that these men were concerned with the control of appropriation, their membership of the Worsted Committee proved as much. But were such men blinded to justice inside the courthouse by their own interests? Before undertaking any detailed statistical work which may be the best way of answering this question, can a public discourse be found which would reveal how 'manufacturing magistrates' were perceived by the wider working community?

Perceptions of judicial partiality in West Riding in the nineteenth century

Periodically the Yorkshire newspapers reflected the 'tensions' which existed between the magistrates and some sections of the local populace. For example, a Leeds magistrate received this letter in 1870:

> Sir I have to inform you the Poor Working Man Wants Justice and Justice he must have in this Part of the country – therefore for the time to come Inquire into more than you have done Scince you have come to Site on the Bench. take a friend advice in time for there is mor Ways for to get at them than you think of try for once in your Time you have Rouges and likewise Whoer for to look after. But the Working man must have What he requires for the good it is by the Working man that you ar Paid therefore get him Justice I do not intent to Say that you may be Shot Some Fine Day if you do not like yur Work Lieve the Bench and let Some other man hav the Work for to do that will give Justice to the Pour Workingman. By a Citisenn (*Bradford Observer* 31 May 1870).

The Leeds stipendiary magistrate to whom the letter was addressed had judged a master and servant case the previous day:

> But he wished to say that . . . he didn't believe there was a working man in Leeds who would write such a letter. He believes, from the style of the letter and the handwriting, that it had come from someone with a better education (*Bradford Observer* 31 May 1870)

He seems to have taken the letter lightly given that there had previously been attacks on law officials during major industrial disturbances. For example, one magistrate had been assassinated by Luddites, and the Governor of Wakefield House of Correction had been shot at within yards of the prison during the Chartist uprising. The bullet passed through his hat (*Bradford Observer* 22 January 1846). Later, in 1879, there was also an attempt to blow up the Leeds courthouse, when gunpowder had been placed under the justices' bench (*Bradford Observer* 17 May 1879). Can this be taken as proof of working class dissatisfaction? One letter reprinted in a newspaper and a few assaults on law administrators is slim evidence to base general theories on, even if their sentiments find resonance in comments made by middle class commentators, such as the anonymous parson who said that:

> As far as my own experience of county magistrates enables me to form an opinion, I believe no conscious partiality against them could be sustained (yet) in questions between masters and servants, there would obviously be especial danger at the local bench unconscious feeling of class privilege (*Bradford Observer* 2 February 1865).

As the tone of this letter exemplifies, the criticism of local justices was rather slight and tentative, and members of the middle-classes showered approbation upon their local bench. One solicitor said about the Bradford magistrates at the Licensed Victuallers Association Dinner:

> He had at all times seen a determination in their part to administer justice equally to all men, with becoming fairness, but at the same time tempered with mercy. Without claiming for the Borough Magistrates the attributes of infallibility, he thought their decisions had given satisfaction to the public (*Bradford Observer* 19 January 1854).

Since he practised his art before these magistrates, the tone of his speech is unsurprising. More authoritative words came from the Leeds Corporate Commission which stated that 'the great respectability of the present members of the corporation and their impartial conduct as justices were universally acknowledged'. The Commissioners also reported that 'the magistracy appointed . . . had performed its duties fearlessly and independently to the satisfaction of the inhabitants at large' (Fraser 1980, p. 53). The 'middling sort' were clearly well satisfied, even smug, about their justices. However, criticism, opposition and bitter complaint may have been covertly expressed by working people, but in private since they had no public voice with which to speak.

Fortunately, an insight into the attitudes of both factory workers towards magistrates and magistrates towards workplace appropriators can be gained through the study of sources not normally available to historians. In addition to the recording of magistrates' remarks made during the trial or when announcing the sentence of the court, there are commentaries on the efficiency and ideological stances of magistrates in the Worsted Committee records. Furthermore, because the Committee's minute books recorded the names of the petty sessions' magistrates who convicted or dismissed appropriators, a quantitative analysis of the occupational bias of magistrates can be constructed.

The impact of judicial bias

Judicial principles notwithstanding, there is a historical consensus that justices from particular occupational groups had a direct or indirect interest in some of the cases they judged. Moreover, it has been asserted that their interest precluded any hope of a fair trial for the accused. In the East Midlands, for example, Chapman asserts that the factory owners used the summary courts simply as an extension of their private powers (Chapman 1904, pp. 185–7). Similarly, in the West Midlands Hay states that local magistracy and the great manufacturers shared a common outlook. He described how this close relationship worked in practice:

> So that lessons would not be lost, the firm could also rely on at least some occasions on the willingness of the bench to order punishment where it would do most good: in 1789 a thief they successfully prosecuted was then publicly whipped at the factory over a distance of 150 yards at noon hour, before being sent to the House of Correction for three months' hard labour (Hay 1983, p. 48).

Trainor agreed, that in Staffordshire, 'although the JPs sometimes dismissed cases brought by masters, the magistrates frequently betrayed their own self-interested bias . . . and magistrates only showed sympathy to working-class defendants when neither industrial discipline nor public order was at risk' (Trainor 1993, pp. 142, 170). Did West Riding magistrates similarly reinforce the authority of the manufacturers, and did the West Riding magistrates and police act together as a weapon of the employers, as scholars such as Storch have suggested (Storch 1981, p. 93)?

A notable historian of Yorkshire, Herbert Heaton's assessment of the relationship between the magistrates and the manufacturers includes a curious paragraph. He asserts that the Worsted Committee had to contend with the

> ignorance, apathy, or actual hostility of the magistrates . . . Many cases which were brought forward by the inspectors were dismissed by magistrates who did not know the nature of the Worsted Acts, and the committee was constantly printing digests of the law, handbills &c., or sending deputations to explain to these benighted justices the wonders of the statutes. But knowledge when it came, did not convince the local authorities of the error of their ways. Doubtless they objected to being taught their duty by an upstart industrial organization (Heaton 1965, p. 428).

Heaton had previously made a strong case for the potency of manufacturing interest in judicial affairs. Clearly, however, there were a number of schisms within the 'strange alliance' (Heaton 1965, pp. 428–31). Both the Worsted Inspectors and the Factory Inspectors complained that magistrates were obstructive of prosecution cases that they brought against employers for buying embezzled mate from dealers, either through ignorance or complicity (Field 1990). In his exasperation one complainant conflated two possible reasons for their truculence. 'The conduct of some of the magistrates is simply abominable,' he said:

> The magistrates either will not or cannot understand the Worsted Acts. I frequently find them making mistakes in their interpretation of the clauses. Judging by their decisions I should infer that they regard the Worsted Acts as devised and passed for the oppression of the poor working man – not for the protection of the manufacturers (Room 1882, p. 8).

Worsted Inspectors occasionally expressed wonder or incomprehension at the magistrates' decisions. Two typical entries to the Minute Books stated, for example 'I beg to state that I never had a better case for conviction, and never failed before with such materials and respectable witnesses as I should before the court at Otley' (April 1873 WCMB) and at Leeds, a case was dismissed 'contrary to all expectations of the Public in the court which consisted of many highly respectable manufacturers from Bradford who heard the evidence' (30 March 1863 WCMB). With the majority of failed cases, however, the Inspectors strove to find reasons to explain their failure, and the ignorance of magistrates was as good a reason as any. It was an excuse also much used in the eighteenth century (Soderlund 1992, pp. 425–7). It seems unlikely that, as an Inspector alleged in one case, neither the clerk of the court, the defending advocate nor any of the magistrates understood the provisions of the Worsted Acts since they all witnessed so many cases brought under those Acts (2 January 1888 WCMB). However, this reason was possibly more palatable to the Committee than accepting that magistrates opposed the Worsted Acts *per se*. Nevertheless, magistrates did make statements which revealed a clear understanding of, and contempt for, the provisions of the 1777 Acts. It is therefore worthwhile examining these statements in order to understand why some magistrates held the Worsted Acts to be morally repugnant.

First, it must be understood that the statements made by magistrates in court and occasionally rehearsed in the *Bradford Observer* were not part of a coherent attack on the Worsted Committee and their works. Nor was there ever a co-ordinated attack made on the Worsted Acts by the whole, or a significant section of the magistrates. The focus of the magistrates' criticism was dispersed, and reflected concern over the plight of the poor working people, as much as an anti-manufacturing rhetoric or a desire to reform the laws regulating workplace appropriation.

Nevertheless, an individual magistrate's sympathy for the accused, for whatever reason, had real effects. A number of workers were allowed to leave the dock because the magistrates seemed determined to excuse their behaviour. One case against a man who had 'neglected' his work was dismissed, for example, since the defendant had left his loom because it was 'so near the privvy in the mill that the stench was intolerable' (*Bradford Observer* 16 August 1849). Another man was released when the accused produced some invoices for the cloth alleged to have been appropriated. He had not been able to produce the invoices at the time of his arrest, but had subsequently managed to lay hands on some. Nevertheless, the magistrates dismissed the case (*Bradford Observer* 11 March 1847). More simply a weaver who had been in court five times for embezzlement was released since 'there was some doubt on the minds of the Bench, and they were inclined to give the defendant the benefit of it' (*Bradford Observer* 8 September 1853). It would be impossible and indeed unwise to attempt to re-try the accused men even with over a hundred years of hindsight. Who may now say whether these men were rightly or wrongly released, or what motivations prompted the magistrates? What may be stated is that the magistrates in some cases did not apply the Worsted Acts in as strict a manner as their colleagues did, while at other times magistrates applied the letter but not the spirit of the Acts in order to favour the accused. 'Under the Worsted Act', stated one magistrate, who was not named in the *Bradford Observer*, 'the bench would have nothing on presumption, but only where a case could be clearly made out; for it was sometimes difficult enough for a man who might be honest to show that he came honestly by his wool' (*Bradford Observer* 23 November 1842).

Further statements made by magistrates were also unequivocally antagonistic, not least those made by Joshua Pollard. This prominent magistrate, ironmaster and coalmine owner continued a campaign of scepticism, hostility and distrust against the Worsted Inspectors. Having carped at Inspectors' actions, and criticized their investigative techniques, the *Bradford Observer* reported that 'Previous to the case being gone into, Mr Pollard asked the Inspectors if they or the constable had taken the goods to the prisoner's house, and that in future he would invariably ask that question' (*Bradford Observer* 23 November 1848). Pollard's reputation as an enemy of the Committee may have been strong enough to deter Inspectors from bringing cases before him. For example, one case which Pollard was about to try was withdrawn when the victim accepted an offer of compensation on the advice of the Worsted Inspector. It is possible that the settlement was considered by the Inspector to be preferable to a court case made uncertain by a notoriously obstructive magistrate, and, in fact, the proportion of Pollard's cases which were settled before the trial is more than double the average (December 1866 WCMB). Certainly Inspectors were keen to avoid particular magistrates – one Inspector going so far as to refuse to divulge to an obstructive magistrate that he worked for the Worsted Committee for fear that the prosecution would then fail (*Bradford Observer* 10 December 1846).

Disagreements over the application of the Worsted Acts may have been expected as part and parcel of the traditional and well-documented antagonism between landed and manufacturing elites. However, since some of the magistrates who most happily applied the Factory Acts were also manufacturers, such easy assumptions cannot be made. Indeed, an examination of how Factory Act cases were judged has been one of the methods by which historians have attempted to determine the limits of judicial bias. Although a consensus has not been arrived at, the vigorous debate which has been conducted, notably between Bartrip and Carson, has helped to frame some of the questions which this chapter will attempt to answer (see Carson 1970, 1979; Bartrip and Fenn 1983; Nardinelli 1985; Bartrip 1985; Peacock 1985).

However, for modern historians to decide with certainty that those magistrates with manufacturing interests, or those who sat on the Worsted Committee, acted in unison in convicting a disproportionately high proportion of those accused of illegal appropriation, the newspapers would have had to record the occupation of each presiding magistrate. This they did not do. Even less satisfactorily, the newspapers did not always give the names of the magistrates they quoted, which means that their occupations cannot be derived from other sources. One last weakness in the newspaper and Worsted Committee Minute Books is that both sources display conscious or unconscious bias. The Inspectors' reports in the minute books have an obvious bias in discrediting magistrates who rejected their evidence. The editor of the *Bradford Observer* wished to print exciting or controversial items. For example, when Pollard fined a manufacturer seventy-five pounds for not boxing-off a roving machine, the newspaper anticipated the incredulity and indignation of many of its readers at the severity of the fine (*Bradford Observer* 12 March 1846). Similarly Pollard's other attacks on manufacturing and Worsted Committee interests were printed since they were of interest to the paper's readers. Despite the limitations of both the Worsted Committee registers and newspaper sources, there is the strong suggestion that the 'strange alliance' between the magistrates and the Worsted Committee was cemented by an interest in the punishment of workplace offenders (Heaton 1965, p. 426).

Co-operation between the two agencies even reached a stage where the magistrates once asked for the Committee's advice before sentencing an offender. The accused had already been convicted for the possession of appropriated oil, but the magistrates had not enforced the conviction 'in wishing the opinion of the Committee'. The Committed, 'resolved to write to the Magistrates that the Committee feel obliged by their courtesy and leave the matter in their hands, having the fullest confidence that they will deal with the case with justice to all parties' (29 March 1949 WCMB 56D.88/1/4).

Alone among modern commentators, Firth alleges that the co-operation of the magistrates could not be relied upon (Firth 1990:145). He cites Henry Wickham as one who constantly thwarted the wishes of the Worsted Committee, yet Soderlund (1992) has talked of the warm relationship between the Committee and Wickham, who, after all convicted approximately eight hundred appropriators between 1777 and 1781 (Wickham averaged 182 convictions per year between 1777 and 1781, see Soderlund 1992, pp. 423–4). The West Riding petty sessions magistrates and the Worsted Committee seem at the very least to have recognized a common disciplinary language, even if that language was not spoken by all magistrates. But clearly it has not been possible to examine the issue of judicial impartiality by use of qualitative data alone. The next section will turn to more fruitful sources.

Judicial bias against workplace appropriators

Unfortunately Soderlund (1992) does not state how many magistrates were also members of the Worsted Committee in the eighteenth century, nor does he analyse the occupational structure of the local magistracy. However, when this work is undertaken for the nineteenth-century magistrates, some significant statistics are revealed. The Worsted Acts required two magistrates to sit in judgement, and in 77 per cent of the prosecutions brought by the Worsted Committee at least one of the magistrates was a manufacturer, while 21 per cent were judged by two manufacturers. In certain areas the concentration of manufacturers was far higher. At East Morley petty sessions in Bradford, for example, 80 per cent of the magistrates were worsted manufacturers. In addition, between 1844 and 1876, 27 per cent of the magistrates who tried appropriation cases were also members of the Worsted Committee.

Moreover, in approximately 3 per cent (22 cases) of all prosecutions brought by the Worsted Committee, both magistrates were Committee members, and in three-quarters of those cases, both magistrates had attended the Worsted Committee meeting immediately preceding the trial. Not only did those magistrates have an implicit interest in the case as manufacturers, but they had already discussed the case with the Worsted Inspector and the victim of the appropriation. Indeed the Committee would not have proceeded had there not been a good likelihood of conviction. Unless the potential arbiters of the case sat at Committee meetings blindfolded, with their hands over their ears, they would have had at the very least a good knowledge of the case before it reached the courts. Since a significant proportion of the magistrates who heard appropriation cases were manufacturers in the same industry as the prosecutor, sat on a committee which decided whether to prosecute offenders, and had an indirect commercial interest in the outcome of the case, it would seem that the legal principles described by us earlier were not adhered to. Indeed, attempts to complain that magistrates had a direct interest in appropriation cases were ignored (*Bradford Observer* 21 April 1864). But this would only seem to matter if magistrates exerted undue influence over the outcome of trials. What evidence is there that this was the case?

The statistics taken from the Worsted Committee Registers and portrayed in the table below are somewhat surprising given the previously described historiography. There was no completely consistent link between abnormally high conviction rates and 'manufacturing magistrates'. Conviction rates were 12 per cent below average in the small number of cases in which neither of the magistrates was a textile manufacturer, and were 5 per cent above average when at least one of the two adjudicators was such a manufacturer. However, cases in which both magistrates were textile masters had only average conviction rates, and most surprising of all, when both magistrates belonged to the Worsted

Committee, the conviction rate was only 73 per cent. This was approximately 3 per cent lower than the conviction rates of summary cases involving either Joshua Pollard or William Murgatroyd, two magistrates notoriously antagonistic to the Worsted Committee, and 10 per cent below the overall average.

Despite the weight of qualitative evidence, and the opinions of historians previously discussed, no consistent causal link between the occupation of the magistrates and the conviction rate of appropriators can therefore be established through statistical analysis – the occupation of the magistrate had some impact but is not a clear predictor of the likelihood of conviction. Did more subtle factors exist which affected the statistics?

David Philips, in his study of the Black Country, makes two important points about the treatment of appropriators (Philips 1976, 1977). First, he asserts that the fact that offenders were tried summarily before two local JPs was a great encouragement to industrialists to prosecute appropriators in large numbers. Second, he argues that the composition of the magistracy had an impact on the proportion of convictions. Applying these points to the West Riding, it is true that the convenience of petty sessions suited manufacturers. Also, if newspapers and Worsted Committee records are to be believed, manufacturers were convinced that appropriators were best tried by fellow manufacturers. However, it cannot be definitely established that the occupational profile of the local magistracy encouraged the prosecution of workplace offenders. Unfortunately, Philips did not analyse the conviction rate of each occupational group of magistrates. When this analysis is carried out on West Riding statistics, the occupation of the magistrate does not appear to have had a systematic effect on the conviction rate of appropriators, although there is limited evidence that the absence of a textile manufacturing magistrate may have reduced conviction rates in such cases.

Occupation and Combination of Magistrates	**Conviction Rate (%)**	**No. cases**
A textile manufacturer plus one non-textile manufacturer	88	123
Both textile manufacturers	82	246
Both Worsted Committee members	73	22
Neither textile manufacturers	70	26
All cases in which magistrate's occupation is known	82	417

Figure 7.3 Conviction rate by combination of magistrates (%), 1844–1876.

There are a number of possible explanations for the apparent lack of occupational bias in the magistrates' treatment of appropriators. First, almost all of the magistrates in the textile districts may have made assumptions about the characters of factory employees which led the majority of magistrates to convict them in large proportions (Plint 1851, pp. 82–130, 144–58). Worsted Committee members, manufacturers, magistrates and employers of all kinds may have shared not only similar views on the nature of appropriation but also informal and formal social networks (for a description of the close relationship between manufacturers in the 1820–30 period, see Myatt 1980, p. 33). These associations obviously could not 'bind' elites together into a homogenous whole, whose members thought and acted the same way. Undoubtedly intra-judicial tensions must have arisen at times which possibly explain the relatively low conviction rate of non-textile manufacturers. Trade competition and personal rivalries between various magistrates could also have been a factor. One report by an Inspector reveals as much:

> The plain fact of the matter was an old score or grudge Luccock (the presiding magistrate) has against us which prevented him doing us justice. A former case I had against Mewlay Dye Works in which Luccock had at that time an interest in that business and it appears it has not left his memory (September 1868 WCMB).

Nevertheless, generally it can be assumed that magistrates of all occupations disapproved of appropriation whomever the victim, and shared with the Worsted Committee many of the underlying assumptions concerning the protection of manufacturers' property. Membership of the Worsted Committee involved more than attending an annual dinner, however. Most members attended the quarterly meetings over long periods of time, where they discussed the best ways of prosecuting appropriation. Only a quarter of the Committee members left voluntarily over a forty-year-plus period, with 16 per cent dying, and 59 per cent attending regularly from 1840 to 1880. Committee members were dedicated and diligent men who willingly gave up their time and energy to prosecute appropriation. Why then did they convict a lower than average proportion of appropriators?

Either the Committee JPs were cautious in their judgements, and showed leniency to defendants, since they anticipated and indeed experienced bitter criticism from prominent sections of West Riding society, or there may have been mechanisms which acted to pre-select the cases that were heard before particular magistrates. If the weakest prosecution cases were arranged to be judged by

Worsted Committee members, then the rate of conviction may not have been relatively low, but relatively high. This would only be possible if petty sessions could be managed in this way, which seems unlikely since any magistrate who cared to turn up could sit in on a case. Nevertheless, when sessions were held in magistrates' houses, or in at least one instance inside a magistrate's factory, it may not have been impossible (Wakefield Petty Sessions, *WYAW* P7/2).

Fortunately, there are more likely explanations than envisaging the scenario of Worsted Committee members separating the wheat from the chaff before quickly dragging the weakest cases over to sessions to be judged before another magistrate turned up. Only 5.2 per cent of workplace appropriation cases were judged by two Worsted Committee members sitting together in a summary hearing. It may be that Worsted Committee members strove to avoid such situations lest they be accused of bias against working people. When this situation was unavoidable, perhaps because only two eligible magistrates turned up to sessions that day, and they both belonged to the Worsted Committee, they probably took great pains to apply the law in a transparently fair way. Indeed, two Worsted Committee members, sitting together, may have demonstrated more leniency, when that was possible, than other combinations of magistrates were inclined to do.

If the relatively low conviction rates, in cases where two Worsted Committee magistrates presided, is puzzling, it must be remembered that the generally high conviction rates in workplace appropriation cases are much easier to explain. The editor of the *Bradford Observer* stated in 1853, 'there can be no doubt that the provisions of the Worsted Acts are exceedingly harsh and oppressive, and that for a very venial fault, and sometimes for no fault at all, men have been subjected to its severe discipline' (*Bradford Observer* 3 February 1853). In other words, the framing of the Worsted Acts ensured a high conviction rate. It must be remembered that, even if manufacturers and non-manufacturers acted in concert, they still convicted higher proportions of defendants in Worsted Act cases than they did defendants facing comparable charges. The magistrates who judged many appropriation cases had only to establish that the accused could not prove ownership of a piece of cloth for the case to be made. Only if magistrates set their face against a prosecution could a case fail. To avoid a successful appeal by the Worsted Committee against the decision, magistrates had to find justifiable doubt in the prosecution's case. Since only a few magistrates were interested in seeking out this doubt, most cases were decided in the Committee's favour, with no need to overtly display any occupational bias the magistrate may have had.

The personal costs of conviction

Sarah, wife of Eli Wigglesworth, was dragged out of bed by two policemen at two in the morning on 9 May 1850. She was charged with neglecting her work under the Worsted Acts and taken to Bradford Police Station to await her trial. Despite her husband's protestations that she was too ill to be out of the house, and that he would answer the charge in her stead, the police kept them both for a number of hours before relenting and letting them go home to answer a summons instead. This must have had a considerable impact on the couple and their neighbours who witnessed the scene. The main impacts on those charged under the Worsted Acts would have been longer-term.

As previously discussed, workplace offenders could be dismissed and blacklisted. This could have also applied to those formally charged with theft, but, additionally they would have to find a significant amount of money to pay the fine. Raising £20 at short notice was a tricky task, and it appears that often it necessitated selling possessions, having 'whip-rounds' among friends, family and neighbours or taking loans and handouts from wherever they could be found. Nevertheless, with no immediate income and poor prospects of finding employment as a convicted thief in a land watched over by a Committee of employers, many convicted workers must have been forced to leave the area to try their luck in an area where they were not known. Some convicted workers perhaps changed their names and identities, as well as their employment, in order to start new lives after being fined, or indeed after coming out of prison as many ex-convicts did (Godfrey et al. 2010). For it must be remembered that many hundreds of workers could not raise the funds the court demanded, and paid their debts by spending a month in prison.

8

Changing Notions of Customary Right, Morality and Control in the Factory System

In 1972, the labour and crime historian Peter Linebaugh concluded that:

> The attack on the mixed form of the wage required not just the extension of the criminal sanction but the reorganization of the labour process to enforce it. The construction of docks and factories in the textile industry achieved direct control over labour, and were promoted, in part, to secure this end [moreover] apparent 'technical' improvements received widespread application both because they permitted greater productivity and because they removed possibilities of embezzling materials (Linebaugh 1972, p. 9).

It is true that the factory system removed some opportunities for appropriating an employer's materials, as Linebaugh suggests. Short-reeling and the 'weight offences' were eradicated by virtue of the change to centralized production methods, for example. However, Linebaugh's inference that the factory attacked the mixed wage, and allowed the imposition of a cash-wage system against the wishes of the employees, warrants closer scrutiny. Was the factory system partly established to, and largely successful in, curtailing workplace appropriation and replacing the law as the major weapon against employee 'theft'? Did notions of customary entitlement die off with the move to factory production, or were they simply transplanted in new surroundings?

The defence of their customary rights by workers in the eighteenth-century domestic textile industries was almost always based on the maintenance of established traditions. When the factory system was established, which required dislocation from traditional work practices, and the emigration of many workers from their villages to the new factory districts, this lineage of traditional rights may have been broken. It may be that these rights were reinterpreted or reinvented in an industrial context by the first and subsequent generations of factory workers, but the successful establishment of a new set of customary rights cannot be assumed. In fact there is little recorded evidence that factory textile workers defended or even recognized the existence of customary rights. In the quarter sessions depositions, neither those who pleaded guilty nor those who pleaded innocent attempted to justify their appropriations by recourse to traditional entitlements. In the eighteenth century, tradition had been waved like a totem at employers and magistrates, and customary acts of appropriation in the countryside and in the work context were staunchly and vocally defended as established rights (Thompson 1991, pp. 1–15).

Convincing evidence that these notions survived beyond the eighteenth century is lacking, however. What appears to happen in the nineteenth-century industrial districts is that the popular code of customary rights was either replaced or buttressed by a framework of agreed practices which placed strong emphasis on fairness and morality rather than tradition (Jones 1992.124). This framework encompassed what was morally correct in a wider social and political context, as well as the proper relationship between employee and employer.

Workers may have legitimated appropriation to themselves by reference to either custom, or fairness, or both, but in court they relied solely on moral arguments, for example, the appropriator who observed in court 'It's a shame they take me to court for taking so little, when they have so much' (September 1844, Sheffield QS1/183/12). Workers who explained to the magistrates that they had turned to workplace appropriation because of impoverishment rather than 'greed' were also obliquely referring to issues of morality and necessity, not custom. This situation may have arisen because the invoking of traditional entitlement had ceased to be a successful defence strategy in court by the mid-nineteenth century. However, it must be remembered that beliefs concerning workplace loyalties, traditions and duties, or concerning the obligations owed to one's work-colleagues, which existed in the eighteenth century, were re-affirmed and strengthened by the union movements of the nineteenth century. Although it may not have suited those tried for workplace appropriation to justify their behaviour by recourse to tradition, notions of customary right may still have existed deep in their hearts and minds.

The effectiveness of control – did the factory eradicate workplace appropriation?

Linebaugh, and others, who believe that the establishment of the factory system meant the end of the mixed wage, seem to uncritically accept that the factory system was established to eradicate the taking home of workplace materials by the workers, and that the operation of workplace perquisites was ended once industrial capitalism was founded. These historians draw on a broader set of 'social control' theories about the coming of the factory developed by Marxist historians.

The critical aspect of these 'social control' arguments is that the capitalist's search for greater efficiency led both to mechanization, and the establishment of centralized production areas in order to facilitate greater control over labour. The development of the factory therefore accomplished four aims in Dickson's opinion: first, the suppression of 'embezzlement'; second, control over the pace of production (Dickson 1981, pp. 41–95, 71–83); third, the centralization of labour which both facilitated machine technology and allowed the control of the worker's adverse reaction to new machinery; lastly, it made capitalists indispensable to production because the factories needed large and frequent capital investments. Although the first two aims were explicitly concerned with labour control, Dickson (1981) rightly saw the other aims as also being primarily work discipline measures. The origins of the factory were therefore embedded in the desire to control labour, and this desire inevitably spawned supervisors and surveillance techniques in the workplace. Marglin asserts that this explains why factories were established with the kind of technology already in place in much of the cottage textile industry, and also why many factories did not mechanize until years after their establishment (Marglin 1976). After all, Gott's mill in Leeds, a huge and highly developed complex, was managed for twenty-five years without mechanization taking place in any key area of production.

The alternative 'technological imperative' argument is not without its defenders, however. Landes (1987), for example, has attacked the 'social control' thesis on a number of grounds. First, he argues that the specialization of labour and the introduction of machinery created a level of profit which was sufficient for factories to eclipse other forms of production. Second, he asserts that capitalists performed tasks which labour could not (aside from supplying the capital investment), therefore making themselves indispensable to any successful form of production. To summarize his argument, the factories became dominant for the savings that were inherent in the mechanization and specialization of production tasks, so long as labour was under the supervision of employers or their agents. Recently, Pollard (1963), Berg (1984) and Hudson (1992) have adopted a more measured response to the debate, arguing that both mechanization (combined with the specialization and division of labour) and social control were motivating forces behind the move to factory production. But what implications do these theories have for surveillance in the factory?

The debate, which has been presented by the protagonists as a 'technology versus discipline' duality, is actually a debate about the *relative* importance of the two main impetuses to factory production. For example, *all* of the theorists in this debate believe that workplace indiscipline, especially appropriation, was rife in the domestic system, and also that the factory engendered and increased managerial control over the workforce. Landes agrees that centralization of labour facilitated supervision, and that manufacturers could not 'afford the embezzlement that invariably occurs with unsupervised labour'; see Landes (1987, p. 603) and also Giddens (1992, p. 66).

This consensus is supported by contemporary documents. The *Committee on the Woollen Manufacture* (1806) concluded that the dispersed work organization of the domestic system minimized the opportunities for surveillance over the workforce (vol. III, 268, pp. 10–12), and by 1842 Chadwick noted that the factory system had maximized the effects of internal networks of social control (*1842 Report on the Sanitary Condition of the Labouring Population and on the Means of its Improvement*, vol. X, 327: 241–4). Similarly, both manufacturers and employees linked together centralization, mechanization and labour discipline. For example, the words of one domestic spinner, who commented that, 'when they steyl tops in that way . . . they bring a bad name on us all; an set't maisters o'thinking abaht them machines, folks talk so much abaht' were similar in tone to the comments of a factory master, spoken at the trial of his employee in 1850 (Room 1882, p. 10). He reportedly stated that 'the prisoner had recently applied for an advance in wages, but such conduct as this afforded poor encouragement to those who employed to accede to such requests. In fact the conduct of the men would drive them to get combing machines, as no profits in the world could stand being robbed in this way' (*Leeds Mercury* 23 February 1850).

It would be churlish to ignore the technological imperatives of the factory system. The move towards large mechanically integrated production processes did allow for economies of scale, and these machines needed to be housed inside large buildings. But it would also be naïve to conclude that this was the only, or indeed the main, reason for the move to a factory system. If the employers had not seen the benefits of centralization in terms of labour control, and/or as a foil to appropriation, then the domestic system with its unspecialized and dispersed labour force could have continued as the primary form of work organization unhindered for many decades more than it did (Hudson believes that domestic organization was economically viable until at least the 1860s, [Hudson 1992, pp. 9–37]). However, the assumption that centralization and the concomitant surveillance systems were a panacea to cure employee indiscipline must be questioned.

Marglin's ideas, and those of the other 'control' theorists, rely on three points. First, that manufacturers perceived there to be a problem of control in the domestic organization of industry. Second, that they recognized the factory as a possible solution to these problems. Third, that the factory offered the best way to overcome labour discipline problems. Evidence presented in this book supports the first two assumptions. The manufacturers were critically aware of the scale and persistence of appropriation in the eighteenth-century textile industries. Whether they immediately saw the factory or centralized workshop as the natural solution to their losses is not so clear. Indeed, the length of time taken by various manufacturers to move to factory production, after noting the seemingly devastating losses due to 'embezzlement' in the existing domestic organization, seems to cast doubt on this, as does the continued use of the criminal and civil codes against labour. Indeed, Chapter 2 has shown that appropriation from the industrial workplace continued until at least 1880, which suggests that the factory was not completely successful in carrying out one of its primary aims – the eradication of workplace appropriation.

In some respects there appears to have been a consensus of views about the problem of workplace 'theft', and unanimity of action against appropriation, across employers of large scale businesses in the nineteenth century, whether they were manufacturing firms or service providers. London dairies and bus companies, and the Black Country industrialists, all used the power to prosecute appropriators as a discretionary tool. In similar fashion to the West Riding factory owners, they chose to prosecute only when the economic climate favoured such an action – when the sanction of dismissal was made impotent by periods of high employment (Davis 1987, p. 407). However, there were significant differences between the prosecution policies of the West Riding factory owners and those of other nineteenth-century large-scale employers.

In London, service sector masters used prosecution as a last resort, and tolerated workplace appropriation since it could be used to justify their paying low wages to their employees (Davis 1987, pp. 400, 407). This was not the case in the West Riding. There the wages were also low, but appropriation was considered to be too economically damaging to business enterprise to be tolerated (see Chapter 3). If not prosecution, then a punishment of near equivalent severity was sought by foremen and employers. Moreover, in the Black Country the prosecution of workplace offenders rose throughout the nineteenth century, and especially in the 1835–60 period, whereas in the West Riding the opposite appears to have been true.

Philips advances two explanations for the dramatic rise in prosecutions for 'industrial theft' around the mid-century. First, that the 1855 Criminal Justice Act made prosecution cheaper and easier, which encouraged employers to use the law to enforce their campaign against workplace perquisites. Second, that the change in the social composition of the magistrates' benches, which meant that fellow industrialists were increasingly likely to hear appropriation cases, encouraged greater numbers of prosecutions. These points are not entirely convincing, first, because the 1855 CJA could only have had an impact in the last five years of the period Philips examines. Second, because, in the West Riding, summary process had been open to potential prosecutors for all of the nineteenth century, yet the rate of prosecution appears to fall in the period 1840 to 1880. Thus, although the move to summary process caused an increase in Black Country prosecutions in the mid-nineteenth century just as the Worsted Acts did in the West Riding nearly eighty years earlier, it cannot be assumed that the increase would continue at the same rate, or even 'level off' at a rate higher than had existed previously. Lastly, Philips gives no evidence that the Black Country employers were right to think that the local benches became more sympathetic to their campaigns against offending workmen.

By comparing conviction rates in workplace appropriation cases with the occupations of the magistrates involved, Chapter 7 has shown that the social composition of West Riding petty sessions benches did play a part in determining the fate of workplace appropriators once they had reached the court. When a suspected offender was tried by a bench which included at least one textile manufacturer, he or she was slightly more likely to be convicted. However, these minor differences must not obscure the more central facts. First, the conviction of eight out of every ten suspected appropriators by magistrates of all occupations, manufacturing or non-manufacturing, illustrates the efficiency of the factory security systems, which provided a high standard of evidence against the accused. More importantly, the high conviction rate for workplace appropriators reveals how easily convictions under the Worsted Acts could be achieved. The mere possession of material which could not be accounted for was likely to lead an employee into deep trouble.

Sociologists and historians have sometimes tried to suggest that paternalism and coercion were the only strategies employers had to control the workforce. Indeed, the control of labour appears mystical to some. Giddens, for example, is unspecific about the control of 'free' labour in the factory, despite his discussion of the daily 'imprisonment' of labour within the capitalistic workplace (Giddens 1995, p. 139). All neglect the awesome power of the criminal code, yet how can 'the absence of legal enforcement of unfree work', be 'not only one of the marked characteristics of the new capitalism, but one of its most seminal ideas' (Giddens 1995, p. 136), when not only the master and servant but also the Worsted Acts were on the statute books? Certainly until the mid-century the criminal law was central to the control of workplace appropriation in the West Riding.

When the Worsted Committee was fully operational, there were nearly two hundred cases of workplace 'theft' per year that were thought serious enough to be pursued in court. Such prosecutions were a considerable boon to the employers. The extension of criminal sanctions into the workplace, with the strong possibility of a period of imprisonment in Wakefield gaol, not only punished workplace offenders but also strengthened the authority of the factory supervisory structure. The criminal code, in the shape of the Worsted Acts, first, brought in the State to legitimize employer authority and bear the cost of punishment, although it is difficult to see how the public benefited from the protection of the private entrepreneur. Second, it allowed the threat of imprisonment to be used to intimidate employees in ways which other punishments could not. This is true of all of the criminal legislation aimed against appropriation, including the felony statutes. The Worsted Acts, moreover, had other advantages. They facilitated the prosecution of workplace appropriators when the evidence was insufficient to gain a felony conviction, and they enabled prosecutors to achieve higher conviction rates than under the felony statutes. To take a simple example of this, in 1851, one Inspector recorded that he was not sure that he could gain a conviction for felony over an offender, so he successfully applied the Worsted Acts (*Bradford* Observer 12 June 1851). They also gave the West Riding mill owners wide-ranging discretionary powers. They could prosecute or decide not to do so. Furthermore, they could choose whether to risk a prosecution for felony at quarter sessions, which entailed a more severe penalty for the guilty, or to use the Worsted Acts at petty sessions with their more certain chance of success and their still considerable penalties.

There was still a significant use of the criminal law to control labour after the re-organization of the Worsted Committee in 1853. For example, approximately eight hundred suspects were taken to petty sessions by the Committee between 1853 and 1876 (an average of thirty-five prosecutions a year). However, the use of the law declined steadily throughout the mid- to late-nineteenth century. There are a number of explanations for this decline. First, the reduction in the number of Worsted Inspectors, and the concordant reduction in the territory which came under their supervision, certainly had a significant effect on the number of prosecutions. In the ten years after the 1853 cut backs, the Committee prosecuted only around a third of the number they had in the decade before 1853. Had the Committee continued throughout the nineteenth century at full strength, the decline in prosecutions might not have been so marked. However, it can be assumed that the occupational profile of prosecuted offenders would have been different, and would have been increasingly dominated by receivers of appropriated property, waste-dealers, pawnbrokers and so on, rather than factory workers. This is because the factories' internal authority structures were continually strengthened during the nineteenth century. The techniques of supervision were refined, and served to deter appropriation, although they could not eradicate it completely, as Chapter 2 has shown.

Last, the willingness of foremen and employers to use informal modes of punishment increased considerably once the Worsted Committee had ceased to be a convenient prosecution agency. Price (1986) is right to note the various kinds of coercive managerial practices, and Joyce (1980) the fostering of a paternalistic relationship between capital and labour. Both coercion and paternalism were present in many factories at different times depending both on the strategies of control favoured by the foremen and the state of trade. The model of control adopted inevitably affected the fate of detected appropriators at work. Since prosecution did not automatically follow the discovery of workplace 'theft' there may have been a huge number of acts of appropriation which were dealt with inside the factory for every one which ended up in court. It is possible that, after the mid-century, the proportion of workplace appropriations which were prosecuted fell, this change coming within a general decrease in the incidence of workplace 'thefts'.

It must be remembered that the three possible reactions to the detection of workplace 'theft' – tolerance for the sake of good industrial relations, prosecution of the offender or the administration of some form of informal punishment – were not discrete. Offenders could experience any combination of these outcomes. It is not hard to imagine, for example, that an apprentice could be physically chastised, dismissed from employment and then have an embargo placed on his future employment in the district's mills. The administration of particular punishments was not an arbitrary decision, however. While men were likely to be taken to the courts for punishment, women and younger workers were more likely to receive informal penalties. These last two groups of workers were often subject to physical sanction and dismissal, but were usually spared the ordeal of a trial, and the possibility of a punitive fine or a period of imprisonment. Clearly a differential punishment structure imposed penalties of varying severity on particular groups of workers.

The social meaning of workplace appropriation and the Worsted Acts

It is impossible to speak of a homogeneous group of industrial employers (Rodgers 1977, pp. 141–69). There were marked differences in the attitude of small workshop masters, and large and small factory owners. Furthermore, within these groups there were variations of response to trade conditions, and competitive rivalry which were dependent on the size and organization of the company (Hudson 1992, p. 42). For example, it is possible that the larger textile masters pioneered the factory system because they had the most widely dispersed production networks, the capital to invest in machines and premises and the greatest potential losses from appropriation. The Worsted Committee was certainly dominated by large scale employers. In practice, the Inspectors prosecuted the appropriation of all materials covered by the Worsted Acts, including wool, whenever they came across it. For example, Koditchek listed the leading firms and largest employers in Bradford in the 1833 to 1851 period (Koditchek 1990, pp. 596–7). The Bradford members of the Worsted Committee feature heavily in that list. Indeed, of the eight Bradford Committee members, Anderton was the smallest manufacturer, yet he employed over eight-hundred workers. Moreover, the aim of the Committee was to both deter appropriation and eradicate the trade in appropriated goods between workers and small manufacturers.

As previously stated, the trade in appropriated goods could give smaller manufacturers the chance of survival in lean times, and hope to foremen that they could set themselves up as masters, as many did. Curtailing this trade therefore removed an incentive for the larger manufacturers' employees to appropriate, but also wounded and killed off potential trade rivals. The Worsted Committee was not chary of prosecuting manufacturers, if the prosecuted did not have influence in any of the political and religious groupings which dominated Bradford politics. After all, the prosecution of a manufacturer helped to establish an unbiased image for the Committee among the populace in the same way as that of Earl Ferrers is supposed to have done for the Bloody Code (Hay 1975, p. 34).

The power resting in the hands of the Worsted Committee could therefore diminish rivals, discipline employees and help to reduce production losses. Equally, the Worsted Committee had powers which no other employer, local political faction or later nineteenth-century prosecution associations enjoyed. They appeared to the local population to have a peculiar symbolic 'ownership' of the law.

It was the apparent monopoly that Bradford's worsted manufacturers had over the administration of one particular set of laws, as much as the 'harshness' of the Worsted Acts which prompted criticism of the Committee in the local newspapers. Indeed, aside from some criticism in 1853, when the *Bradford Observer* editorial pronounced that 'there can be no doubt that the provisions of the Worsted Acts are exceedingly harsh and oppressive, and that for a very venial fault, and sometimes for no fault at all, men have been subjected to its severe discipline', most of the criticism centred around the legitimacy of the Committee (*Bradford Observer* 3 February 1853).

> In times gone by, the Act has not seldom been made the means of cruel persecution. On one occasion an intelligent non-Bradfordian asked the lawyer for the defence whether his client had been wrongly convicted in defiance of all forms of English law, to which the lawyer replied the man was rightly convicted under the Worsted Act – the only law which threw the burden of proving his innocence on the supposed criminal [*in this he was wrong, since the Game laws, some of the acts which criminalized customary rights in the countryside, such as wood gathering, and the offence of infanticide, all threw the burden of proving their innocence onto the accused. Of course, these were exceptional laws, and the majority of statutes conformed to the common law doctrine of presumed innocence*].

The report of these cases, and of meetings of the Worsted Committee, with its congratulatory statements of shameful injustice can only be read with indignation . . . Only its local obscurity, and the helplessness of those who suffer from it, have hitherto prevented the Act from being effaced as an accidental indignity and outrage on the principles of Justice (*Bradford Observer* 14 and 15 May 1879).

As might be expected, criticism from sources outside the industry, who, unlike parliament itself, had no power over the Committee, was brushed aside. In 1879, for example, the Worsted Committee clerk saw only an enlarged role and a glorious future for the Committee (*Bradford Observer* 17 and 22 May 1879). The Committee continued to vigorously defend both itself and the Worsted Acts. For example, the 1888 Master and Servant Act was intended to repeal all of the acts the Committee enforced except 22 Geo II. c.27. The Committee sent pamphlets and a deputation to the Home Secretary to explain the importance of the acts, which he then accepted (23 July, 24 September 1888 WCMB). It was, of course, essential that the Acts were defended since this was the source of the Committee's legitimacy. The Committee never accepted anything but the most minor tinkering with the Acts (such as the reduction of fine from £20 to £5 in 1888), for if new legislation was passed, a mid- to late-nineteenth-century parliament was unlikely to allow the Committee to administer it. By 1880 the Committee was increasingly viewed by local newspapers, and by parliament, as anachronistic to a mature capitalist society, but 'local obscurity' and the influence of local power elites postponed its abolition until 1968 when the Worsted Acts were superseded by the 1968 Theft Act.

Workplace appropriation, in causing the existence of a committee to oversee its eradication, had helped to define a powerful elite group (which already existed, and interacted within other elite groupings). Indeed, becoming a member of the Committee was important in defining oneself as a member of the 'elite'. However, appropriation had no less an effect on the self-perceptions of the employees, and it is important that this book does not conclude without another reference to how appropriation from work affected factory workers' lives.

We have considered the financial importance of appropriation to workers' lives, but what of the experiential aspects of workplace appropriation? Aside from its importance to the household economy, appropriation also helped to define 'identity' in the workplace (Gay du 1996). Sometimes this meant that people who toiled in factories, or parts of a factory, where appropriation was difficult, perceived themselves as actors in an alienating process over which they had little control. For others, appropriation offered the illusion, if not the reality, that they had some control over the work process in which they participated. As this book has proved, examining the daily work experiences of factory appropriators is problematic, and they stand even now only imperfectly revealed. Partly this is because one cannot weigh the symbolic and economic benefits of appropriation – it meant different things to different people. Nor can one portray a typical appropriator since the generalizations are fractured by gender, status and occupation. It must be remembered that much of the knowledge about workplace appropriators has been obtained from sources concerned with the prosecution process. Some information can be gained about those appropriators who were punished in ways other than formal prosecution from business records and the Worsted Committee minute books. Obviously, however, very little can be known of those whose appropriations were undiscovered. Nevertheless, illegal appropriation, as a practice subject to various formal and informal control mechanisms, and as a regular experience for many workers, has been made more understandable.

The factory, discipline, surveillance and power

The assumption that capitalism established a monolithic ideological hegemony has been challenged (Ignatieff 1983a, 1983b; Stedman-Jones 1971, 1983), but theories concerning the asymmetricality of power relations within the factory, and the part that appropriation played in reducing the power imbalances, have remained relatively unexamined. However, as this book has demonstrated, factories were not watertight vessels. Acts of appropriation at work may have both served to psychologically undermine the over-bearing nature of surveillance and proved to the workforce that they had some control over their lives within the factory, albeit small and exercised with a considerable risk of meaningful punishment. The wonder is that an historical study of factory appropriation has not previously served to discourage and undermine some historians' confidence in the success of capitalist forms of control. Paradoxically, it is the more socialist historians who attribute more power to capitalism than it actually possessed, see Linebaugh (1991), Hay (1975). However, if the factory was partly envisaged as a tool of surveillance, how does the rise of the factory system fit into the general progression towards the 'surveillance society', which some assert was constructed in the nineteenth century (see Foucault 1977; Melossi and Pavarini 1981; Lyon 1994; Dandeker 1990; O'Neill 1986)?

The factory was not a 'total institution' in the same way that the prisons, barracks and the asylums were. The factory system acted on workers inside the factory, but also interacted with external forms of social control, and existed within a totality of both regulated and unregulated human experience. It impacted on both police and penal development, although not in the direct way that Melossi and Foucault assert. For example, the policing of labour in the factory was more sophisticated and less costly to society, but was essentially concerned with a different agenda to the county and borough police. Factory discipline was privatized, and the development of supervision inside the factory was different to the development of the police. However, it is true to say that both agencies were analogous both in terms of hierarchical organization and having recourse to a set of 'rules or laws'. Similarly, the factory did not consciously imitate the prison, nor the prison the factory, but both evolved from ideas concerning the commodification of space. Giddens stated that 'the commodification of time, and its differentiation from further processes of the commodification of space, hold the key to the deepest transformations of day-to-day social life that are brought about by the emergence of capitalism' (Giddens 1995, p. 131). Clearly, the factory acted upon the will or the character of the worker in unknown ways, which may have been of benefit to society. In a reciprocal way, the external forces of law and order may have both pacified society, and prevented damage to the capitalists' property after working hours. However, whereas capitalists were willing to pay all the costs of direct supervisory control inside the factory, they were unwilling to pay disproportionately for control outside the factory. Moreover, they may have been unwilling to pay at all for (as they might have seen it) the unnecessary policing of 'public' areas from which they gained little.

This study has done nothing to contradict the view that factories were established mainly for reasons of surveillance, but it has suggested that the resulting surveillance was incomplete. Moreover, it has shown that even when surveillance was effective, the reaction which followed was mediated through the beliefs and policies of employers and supervisors, as well as the interactions between supervisors and workers. The 'factory', if that term can be taken as shorthand for these changes in the supervision and physical organization of labour, did have a significant effect on appropriation, although it was probably less affected than other customary practices, such as the setting of one's own pace of work. The West Riding textile employers, mainly worsted masters, used a plethora of measures against workplace indiscipline – including specific legislation, private police agencies, internal supervisory structures and the physical geography of workplace organization. These measures had great symbolism, and were arguably effective in combating time-wasting and helping to shape a factory culture in which work indiscipline was disapproved of by workers and employers alike. Nevertheless, workplace appropriation remained, and ebbed and flowed with economic conditions despite the fact that long-term strategic changes in the way that the industry was organized tended to curtail a good deal of appropriation. Among the most important of those changes were the growing sophistication of supervision within the factory and the concordant growth in 'management theory', the decline of the domestic industry which provided a market for some embezzled goods, and the tendency towards larger factories which squeezed smaller rivals out of business. But appropriation had too many benefits and too few disincentives for employees to ignore. The three thousand men and women who were prosecuted by the Committee between 1844 and 1876 stand testament to that. Yet, even that high number only included those who suffered the most formal legal sanction and many thousands more may have been dismissed from work, or suffered informal workplace punishments.

9

Conclusion

We aimed at the outset of our study to address four major research questions:

First, did workplace appropriation, which was widespread in the eighteenth-century domestic industries, continue at the same level in the nineteenth-century factory system, where a more disciplined environment existed?

From our study, despite the apparent ease with which convictions could be gained under the Worsted Acts, the rate of prosecution seems to have fallen in the textile heartland of the West Riding because the organization of the factory potentially offered greater control both over the labour process and over the departure of employees at the end of their shift than, for example, coalfields and ironworks could. Although the prosecution figures cannot be taken as a true indicator of the decline in workplace appropriation, because informal sanctions supplemented the use of the law on many occasions, three things can be stated. First, the factory, with its internal hierarchy of supervision, its rule books and work disciplines did manage to curtail many forms of appropriation, and caused a decline in the incidence of workplace 'theft'. Second, the internal orderings of the factory were strongly enforced, and where they were thought insufficiently powerful, the criminal law was used against labour throughout the nineteenth century in the West Riding. Last, the Worsted Acts served as a symbol of the power of capital over labour, and endowed employers, and particularly the Worsted Committee, with a considerable degree of authority both in the factory and in the wider society.

Second, what form did appropriation take, and which groups within the factory exercised opportunities to take home workplace materials?

Chapter 3 has shown the varying degrees which appropriation could take within the newly emergent factory system, ranging from small-scale poverty alleviation measures amounting to a few pence per week through to larger-scale collusion between employees of larger mills and owners of smaller concerns. Gender differences in regard to opportunity and methods of appropriation have also been investigated, as have the responses of both employees and employers to times of adversity and plenty.

Third, how was appropriation controlled by both internal and external agencies, and what legal and organizational weapons were used against workplace appropriators?

In Chapters 2 and 4 we have discussed the numerous ways in which employees and their agents attempted to control workplace appropriation, together with the panoply of both criminal and civil law that could be ranged against the transgressor. It has become apparent that the worsted manufacturers employed a vast range of methods against workplace appropriation with varying degrees of success. The changing role of the Worsted Committee has also been detailed and debated.

Fourth, how did private policing such as that practised by the Worsted Inspectorate develop generally in the eighteenth and nineteenth centuries, and what was its relationship with public policing forms such as the Parish Watch and the New Police?

Chapter 5 has illustrated how both private and public policing developed throughout the late-eighteenth and nineteenth century not in a simple, teleological process, but rather in a piecemeal and *ad hoc* manner. We have demonstrated that the Worsted Inspectorate was not the only privately funded policing body, and also discussed the often complex relationship between the Inspectorate and the newly emergent publicly funded police forces at both county and borough level.

Finally, in this study we have raised important questions about the interaction between private and public forms of control, about the changing relationship between law and capitalism and about industrial change and the disciplining of working people. Our study has helped to focus criminological attention on one neglected area of research. In doing the latter, one further question is raised: is workplace appropriation criminological 'property'?

The subjects of criminological research are diverse, but can be listed thus: law-breaking, the construction and contravening of normative orderings and the operation of both the administration of the law and the state's instruments of control and punishment. Appropriation would seem to have a resonance in many of those areas of research, except in one important respect. The behaviour of criminological subjects – those who break the law, or who deviate from societal norms – are marked out as 'special', extraordinary and deviant. Yet factory appropriation was endemic to that production system. The appropriation of materials was as likely to have accorded with the internal normative orderings constructed by the workforce, as to have contravened them. The 'offence' was committed by people who were seen, and who saw themselves, as normal. Thompson said, of the eighteenth century, that 'Crime – in the sense of being on the wrong side of the law – was, for vast numbers of undifferentiated people, normal' (Thompson 1972, p. 9). For the nineteenth century we can now echo that this has been the study of ordinary people in routine work situations: a history of what many considered to be everyday normal human activity.

The prosecuted may have been only a proportion of those who were punished for appropriation, and a smaller proportion of those who appropriated workplace materials. Yet, what has been most surprising has been the importance of the criminal code to manufacturers. Despite the changes in production methods and productive methods, from the development of a centralized and later mechanized factory system to a mature capitalist system, and from laissez-faire employment practices to unionization, the Worsted Acts maintained their centrality to labour control until the 1850s. Even after the peak of mid-century activity, the Worsted Acts and their enforcers remained significant. The nineteenth century was the period when capitalism 'came of age', but in one of the most strategic industries, a reliance on eighteenth-century legislation, private policing and coercive supervision in the factory remained.

Glossary of Technical Terms

Alpaca	hair of the llama used with worsted for superfine lightweight cloths the use of which was pioneered by Titus Salt
Baize	heavy *woollen* cloth, well-*felted*, and usually raised on both sides
Bobbins	round spools used for holding yarn
Botany Wool	wool from New South Wales used for *worsted* superfines
Broadcloth	originally any cloth made on the broad loom, but later a fine cloth, chiefly made in Leeds they became unfashionable after 1830
Burling	the process by which vegetable matter was removed from finished cloth. In most cases the term was applied to the rectification of faults in the cloth caused by the *weaving* process
Burling Iron	the iron tool used for *burling*
Carding	the preliminary treatment before *spinning* to open and mix the wool, originally the process was completed by hand cards covered with wire
Combing	the preparatory process for long wools whereby the short fibre *noil* was removed allowing the *top* to be spun into *worsted*
Commission combers	person working on commission for *top* makers and other owners of raw material
Condensers	the final part of *carding* involving either the ring *doffer* or tape condenser
Cop	the yarn package obtained on the *mule*
Corve	basket for receiving coal in mines – later put on railway bogies
Cropping	another term for *shearing*
Devil	the machine which tore up rags in the manufacture of *shoddy* or *mungo*
Doffer	the person who controls the *carding* rollers
Doffing Comb	the implement which removed material from the roller
Dolly	a scouring machine
Doubling	the process of *spinning* where yarns are twisted together
Drafting	the attenuations of *slubbings* in *drawing* and/or *spinning*
Drawing	process mainly used in *worsted spinning* to draw out the combed *top* into a sliver, but sometimes used to describe the mending of *worsteds*

Drawloom	old loom used in *fancy worsteds*
Drying	material was periodically soaked in all branches of the textile industry
Extract	lowest type of waste from the production of *shoddy*
Fancy Worsteds	fine *worsted* cloth mainly produced in the Huddersfield area
Fearnought	machine fitted with spiked rollers used for opening and mixing the wool ready for *combing*
Felting	the matting together of wool fibres
Fent	short, sometimes damaged, piece of cloth
Fettling	cleaning of waste from the *carding* machines
Flock	short lengths of wool formed during the *cropping* process
Flying Shuttle	device for driving the *shuttle* quickly across the loom
French Worsted	worsteds made from *Merino wool*, first imported around the mid-century
Fulling	the cleaning and thickening of *woollen* cloth by beating and washing
Fustic	yellow dye
Gig Mill	raising machine
Hank	a length of *reeled* yarn
Heavy Woollens	cloth made from *shoddy*, *mungo* or *extract*
Hosiery	stockings and socks, usually *woollen*
Indigo Dye	the most common type of dye
Jacquard Loom	loom used in the weaving of *fancy* goods
Jenny	*spinning* machine invented by Hargreaves
Laps	waste produced in the *drawing* of *worsted*
Mending	the repairing of cloth after *weaving*
Merino Wool	fine wool from Merino sheep
Milling	the *fulling* of cloth, mechanized in the nineteenth-century
Mohair	wool of the angora goat
Mule	spindle draft *woollen spinning* machine
Mungo	material made from tearing *felted woollen* cloth
Nap	surface of the *woollen* cloth which is raised and sheared off
Noble Comb	*combing* machine popular in Bradford
Noils	short fibre from the *worsted combing* process, which was an important raw material for *woollen* manufacture
Piece	a length of finished cloth (28 yards long in hand weaving and 70 yards in power-loom weaving)
Piecer	the *mule* operator
Piecing	tying the broken ends together in the *spinning* process
Pulling	the process of reducing rags to mere fibre
Rack	another word for the *tenter* frame
Rag Grinding	process by which rags were reduced to a fibrous state for re-use

Raising	raising up the *nap* of the cloth
Reeling	the process of unwinding the yarn from the *cops* on which it was spun onto *bobbins*
Roving Frame	last machine in the *worsted drawing* process
Rovings	slivers of wool which then go into the *drawing* processs
Say	cheap *worsted* cloth
Scribbling	first part of the *carding* process, the wool is opened and given to the carder
Scribbling Mill	machine used for *scribbling*
Self-Acting Mule	machine designed by Roberts to improve the *spinning mule*
Shearing	alternative word for *cropping*
Shoddy	material which has been *pulled*
Shuttle	the part which carries *weft* across the *loom*
Slubbing	the joining together of the *slubs* made by *carding*
Slubbing Billy	machine which twisted *slubbings* taken off the *carding* machine before passing them to the *spinning jenny*
Spinning	the manufacture of yarn
Staple	a collection of *woollen* fibres
Teasels	plant head used in the first half of the nineteenth-century for raising the surface of the cloth
Tenter	machine which dried the cloth
Throstle	the combined *bobbin* and fly-spinning frame
Thrums	surplus ends of the *warp*
Tops	the slivers of fibre created by the comb during the production of *worsted, tops* could be described as the raw material of *worsted* manufacture
Warehousemen	originally meaning those who held a stock of wool for sale, more usually used in the nineteenth-century for those who worked in the stores and warehouses of the factory, they were similar in status to the foremen
Warp	the lengthwise threads in the cloth
Water Frame	*spinning* frame driven by water-power
Weaving	the interlacing of *warp* and *weft*
Weft	the threads that run across the cloth
Willey	machine used to wash and open the wool
Woollens	properly cloth made from short wool, but commonly used to cover both *woollens* and *worsteds*
Wool Staplers	persons who bought wool from the farmers and sold it to manufacturers
Worsteds	sometimes called stuffs, long wool where the top of the wool was spun into yarn
Worsted Mule	roller and spindle draft *mule*

Bibliography

Abram, W. A. (1868), 'Social conditions and political prospects of the Lancashire workman', *Fortnightly Review*, October: 426–41.

Allott, A. (1980), *The Limits of Law*. London: Butterworths.

Anon. (n.d.), *History of the Leeds Police*. Leeds.

— (n.d.), *This Century's Progress*. London.

— (1732), *A Treatise of Feme Coverts, or the Lady's Law*. London: B. Lintot.

— (1831), *The Factory Child: A Poem*. London.

— (T.E.) (1632), *The Lawes, Resolutions of Women's Rights*. London.

Appleby, P. (1995), *A Force on the Move: The Story of the British Transport Police*. Malvern: Images.

Ashton, T. S. (1954, reprinted 2003), *Capitalism and the Historians*. London: Routledge.

— (1955, reprinted 2006), *An Economic History of England: The Eighteenth Century*. London: Routledge.

Atiyah, P. S. (1979), *The Rise and Fall of Freedom of Contract*. Oxford: Clarendon Oxford University Press.

Baines, E. (1870), 'An Account of the Woollen Manufacture of England', Past and Present.

Baker, J. H. (1979), *An Introduction to English Legal History*. London: Butterworths.

Baker, R. Smith (1868), 'Social results of the employment of girls and women in factories and workshops', *TNAPSS*, 12: 344–7.

Barrie, D. G. (2008), *Police in the Age of Improvement: Police Development and the Civic Tradition in Scotland, 1775–1865*. Cullompton: Willan.

Bartleet, R. S. and Jordan, R. C. R. (1868), 'Social results of the employment of girls and women in factories and workshops', *TNAPSS*, 12: 442–5.

Bartrip, P. W. J. (1985), '"Success or Failure?": the prosecution of the early Factory Acts', *Economic History Review*, 38(3): 432–27.

Bartrip, P. W. J. and Fenn, P. T. (1983), 'Regulation and the Factory Inspectorate', *Journal of Sociology and Law*, 10(2, Winter): 201–22.

Beattie, J. M. (1975), 'The criminality of women in eighteenth-century England', *Journal of Social History*, 8: 80–116.

— (1986), *Crime and the Courts in England, 1660–1800*. Oxford: Oxford University Press.

— (2001), *Policing and Punishment in London 1660–1750: Urban Crime and the Limits of Terror*. Oxford: Oxford University Press.

— (2012), *The First English Detectives: The Bow Street Runners and the Policing of London, 1750–1840*. Oxford: Oxford University Press.

Behagg, C. (1990), *Politics and Production in the Early Nineteenth Century*. London: Routledge.

Berg, M. (1985), *The Age of Manufactures, 1700–1820*. London: Fontana.

Berg, M. and Hudson, P. (1992), 'Rehabilitating the Industrial Revolution', *English Historical Review*, XLV(I): 24–50.

Berg, M. (1984), 'The power of Knowledge, comments on Marglin's "Knowledge and Power"', in F. H. Stephen (ed.), *Firms, Organization and Labour, Approaches to the Economics of Work Organization*. London: Macmillan, pp. 165–75.

Bicknell, P. B. (1877), *The New Police Manual*. London: Shaw and sons.

Bischoff, J. A. (1842), *A Comprehensive History of the Woollen and Worsted Manufacturies and the Natural and Commercial History of Sheep from the Earliest Records to the Present Period*.

Blackstone, W. (1765–9), *Commentaries on the Laws of England*, 4 volumes. Oxford: Clarendon.

Blaugh, M. (1961), 'The productivity of capital in the Lancashire cotton industry during the nineteenth-century, *English Historical Review*, 13: 358–81.

Bottomley, M. (1988), 'Women and industrial militancy in the 1875 heavy woollen dispute', in T. A. Jowettand A. J. McIvor (eds), *Employers and Labour in the English Textile Industry*. London: Routledge, pp. 171–86.

Box, S. (1987), *Recession, Crime and Punishment*. London: Palgrave Macmillan.

Bradley, H. (1989), *Men's Work, Women's Work, A Sociological History of the Sexual Division of Labour*. Cambridge: Cambridge University Press.

Brogden, M. (1981), 'All Police is Conning Bastards: Policing and the problem of consent', in B. Fryer, A. Hunt, D. McBarnet and B. Moorhouse (eds), *Law, State and Society*. London, pp. 202–28.

— (1987), 'The emergence of the police: the colonial dimension', *British Journal of Criminology*, 27(1): 4–14.

Brown, L. (1985), *Victorian News and Newspapers*. Oxford: Oxford University Press.

Bull, G. S. (1838), *The Ten Hour Bill*. London.

Burn, R. (1837), *The Justice of the Peace and Parish Officer*, 6 volumes, 28th edition. London: S. Sweet.

Burnett, J, Mayall, D. and Vincent, D. (1984), *The Autobiography of the Working Class. An Annotated Critical Biography*. New York: New York University Press.

Bushaway, R. W. (1982), 'From custom to crime: wood gathering in eighteenth and early nineteenth century England, a focus for conflict in Hampshire, Wiltshire and the South', in J. Rule (ed.), *Outside the Law: Studies in Law and Order, 1650–1850*. Exeter: Exeter University Press, pp. 65–101.

Bushaway, R. W. (1982), *By Rite: Custom Ceremony and Community in England 1700–1880*. London: Junction Books.

Busfield, D. (1989), 'Skill and the Sexual Division of Labour in the West Riding Textile Industry 1850–1914', in J. Jowitt and T. McIvor (eds), *Employers and Labour in the English Textile Industry 1850–1939*. London: Routledge, pp. 153–70.

Calvert, I. (1910), *Commercial Yearbook of the Leeds Chamber of Commerce*. Leeds.
Carlen, P. (1985), *Criminal Women*. London: Blackwell.
— (1988), *Women, Crime and Poverty*. Milton Keynes: Open University Press.
Carlyle, T. (1829), 'Signs of the Times', *Edinburgh Review*, 49: 439–59.
Carson, W. G. (1970), 'White-collar crime and the enforcement of factory legislation', *British Journal of Criminology*, 10: 383–98.
— (1979), 'The conventionalization of early factory crime', *International Journal of the Sociology of Law*, 7: 37–60.
Chapman, S. D. (1967), *The Early Factory Masters: The Transition to the Factory System in the Midlands Textile Industry*. Newton Abbot: David & Charles.
Chapman, S. J. (1904), *The Lancashire Cotton Industry, A Study in Economic Development*. Manchester: Manchester University Press.
Clapham, J. H. (1906), 'Industrial Organisation in the Woollen and Worsted Industries in Yorkshire', *Economic Journal*, 16: 515–52.
— (1910), 'The Transference of the Worsted Industry from Norfolk to the West Riding of Yorkshire', *Economic Journal*, 20: 195–210.
Clay, J. (1846), *The Prisoner Set Free: The Narrative of a Convict in the Preston House of Correction*. Preston: H. Oakey.
Cockerell, H. A. L. and Green, E. (1976), *The British Insurance Business 1547–1970*. London: Heinemann.
Collier, F. (1965), *The Family Economy of the Working Classes in the Cotton Industry, 1784–1833*. Manchester: Manchester University Press.
Connell, E. J. and Ward, M. (1980), 'Industrial Developments, 1780–1914', in D. Fraser (ed.), *A History of Modern Leeds*. Manchester: Manchester University Press, pp. 142–76.
Cox, D. J. (2010), *'A Certain Share of Low Cunning': A History of the Bow Street Runners 1792–1839*. Cullompton: Willan.
Critchley, T. A. (1978), *A History of the Police in England and Wales*. London: Constable.
Cudworth, W. (1885), *The Condition of the Working Class*. Bradford.
— (1887), *The Condition of the Industrial Working Class of Bradford and District*. Bradford.
Curthoys, M. (2004), *Government, Labour and the Law in Mid-Victorian Britain*. Oxford: Oxford University Press.
Dandeker, C. (1990), *Surveillance, Power and Modernity*. Cambridge: Cambridge University Press.
Davidoff, L. and Hall, C. (1987), *Family Fortunes: Men and Women of the English Working Class, 1780–1850*. London: Hutchinson.
Davis, J. (1984), 'Law breaking and law enforcement: the creation of a criminal classin mid-Victorian London', unpublished Ph.D thesis. Boston: Boston College.
— (1987), 'The thief non-professional: Workplace appropriation in nineteenth-century London', *Bulletin for the Society for the Study of Labour History*, 52: 41.

— (1989), 'Prosecutions and Their Context: The use of the criminal law in laternineteenth-century London', in D. Hay and F. Snyder (eds), *Policing and Prosecution in Britain, 1750–1850*. Oxford: Oxford University Press, pp. 397–426.

Dickson, D. (1981), *Alternative Technology*. London: Fontana Collins.

Dinsmor, A. (2000),'Glasgow Police Pioneers', *Journal of the Police History Society*,15: 9–11.

Ditton, J. (1972), 'The Problems of Time: Styles of time management and schemes of time manipulation amongst machine-paced workers', *Working Paper Two*. Durham: Durham University.

— (1977a), *Part-time Crime*. London: Macmillan.

— (1977b), 'Perks, pilferage and the fiddle: The historical structure of an invisiblewage from the eighteenth-century up to the present day', *Theory and Society*, 4: 39–71.

— (1979), *Controlology, Beyond the New Criminology*. London: Macmillan.

Dodd, W. (1842), *The Factory System Illustrated*. London: J. Murray.

Duncan, R. (1984), *Textiles and Toil: The factory system and the industrial working class in nineteenth-century Aberdeen*. Aberdeen: Aberdeen City Library.

Dutton, H. I. and King, J. E. (1982), 'The limits of paternalism: the cotton tyrants of North Lancashire, 1836–54', *Social History*, 7(1): 59–74.

Eastwood, D. (1997), *Government and Community in the English Provinces 1700–1870*. Basingstoke: Macmillan.

Elliot, A. (1976), 'The establishment of municipal government in Bradford, 1837–1857', unpublished Ph.D thesis. Bradford University.

— (1982), 'Municipal government in Bradford in the mid nineteenth-century' in D. Fraser (ed.), *Municipal Reform in the Industrial City*. Leicester: Leicester University Press, pp. 111–61.

Elliot, R. (1868), 'What are the principal causes of crime, considered from a social pointof view', *TNAPSS*, 12: 324–37.

Emmerichs, M. (1991), 'Five Shilling and Costs: Petty Offenders in Late VictorianNorthampton', unpublished Ph.D thesis. University of Pennsylvania.

Emsley, C. (1982), 'The Bedfordshire Police, 1840–56: a case study of the workings of the Rural Constabulary Act,' *Midland History*, volume, 7: 73–92.

— (1983), *Policing and its Context 1750–1850*. London: Macmillan.

— (1991), *The English Police: A Political and Social History*. London: Longman.

— (1996a), *The English Police: A Political and Social History*, 2nd edition. London: Longman.

— (1996b), 'Albion's Felonious Attractions: Reflections upon the history of crime in England', in C. Emsley and L. A. Knafla (eds), *Crime Histories and Histories of Crime, Studies in the Historiography of Crime and Criminal Justice in Modern History*. London: Greenwood, Westport CT, pp. 67–85.

— (2004), *Crime and Society in England 1750–1900*, 3rd edition. London: Longman.

— (2009), *The Great British Bobby: A History of British Policing from 1829 to the Present*. London: Quercus.

— (2010), *Crime and Society in England 1750–1900*, 4th edition. London: Longman.
England, R. 'Investigating murders in Northern England, 1800–1824', *Criminal Justice History*,VI (1985): 105–24.
Evans, C. (1990), 'Unemployment and the making of the feminine during the Lancashire cotton famine', in P. Hudson and W. R. Lee (eds) *Women's Work and Family Economy in Historical Perspective*. Manchester: Manchester University Press, pp. 248–70.
Faithfull, E. (1862), *On some of the drawbacks connected with the present employment of women: a paper read before the National Association for the promotion of social science, in London, June 11th, 1862*. London: E. Faithfull/Victoria Press.
Fang, H. (1930), *Triumph of the Factory System in England*. Tiensin: Porcupine Press.
Feltes, D. (1977), 'To saunter. To hurry: Dickens, time and industrial capitalism', *Victorian Studies*, 20: 245–67.
Field, S. (1990), '"Without the Law?" Professor Arthurs and the early Factory Inspectorate', *Journal of Law and Society*, 17(4, Winter): 445–68.
Finer, A. and Savage, G. (1965), *The Selected Letters of Josiah Wedgwood*. New York: Born and Hawes.
Firth, G. (1990), *Bradford and the Industrial Revolution*. Leeds: Ryburn.
Fletcher, G. (1976), 'The Metamorphosis of Larceny', *Harvard Law Review*, 89(3 January): 449–530.
Flinn, M. W. (1952), *The Law Book of the Crowley Ironworks*. Woodbridge: Boydell and Brewer.
Foster, D. (1971), 'The changing social and political composition of the Lancashire magistracy, 1821–1851', unpublished Ph.D. University of Lancaster.
Foster, J. (1977), *Class Struggle in the Industrial Revolution*. London: Weidenfeld and Nicholson.
Foucault, M. (1977), *Discipline and Punish: The Birth of the Prison*. London: Penguin.
Fraser, D. (1973), 'Areas of Urban Politics: Leeds 1830–1880', in H. J. Dyos and M. Wolff (eds), *The Victorian City: Images and Realities*, volume 2. London: Routledge Kegan and Paul.
— (1980), *A History of Modern Leeds*. Manchester: Manchester University Press.
Franklin, A. (1979), 'Criminality in the workplace: A comparison of male and female offenders', in F. Adler and R. J. Simon (eds), *The Criminology of Deviant Women*. Boston: Houghton Miffler, pp. 196–211.
Freifeld, M. (1986), 'Technological change and the "self-acting" mule: A study of skill and the sexual division of labour', *Social History*, 5: 319–43.
Friedman, D. (1995), 'Making Sense of English Law Enforcement in the Eighteenth Century', *The University of Chicago Law School Roundtable* (Spring/Summer): 475–505.
Garrett, E. M. (1988), 'Before their time: Employment and family formation in a northern textile town', unpublished Ph.D. University of Sheffield.
Gatrell, V. A. C. and Hadden, T. B. (1972), 'Criminal Statistics and their Interpretation', in E. A. Wrigley (ed.), *Nineteenth Century Society: Essays in the Use of Quantitative*

Methods for the Study of Social Data. Cambridge: Cambridge University Press, pp. 336–96.

Gatrell, V. A. C. (1980), 'The decline of theft and violence in Victorian and Edwardian England', in V. A. C. Gatrell, B. Lenman and G. Parker (eds), *Crime and the Law*. London: Europa, pp. 238–337.

Gatrell, V. A. C. (1992), 'Crime, Authority and the Policeman State' in F. M. L. Thompson (ed.), *Cambridge Social History of Britain*, volume III. Cambridge: Cambridge University Press, pp. 243–310.

Gatrell, V. A. C., Lenman, G., and Parker, G. (1980), *Crime and Law: The Social History of Crime in Western Europe since 1500*. London: Europa.

Giddens, A. (1992), *The Nation State and Violence*. Oxford: Oxford University Press.

— (1995), *A Contemporary Critique of Historical Materialism*, 2nd edition. Basingstoke: Palgrave Macmillan.

Giles, C. and Goodall, I. H. (1992), *Yorkshire Textile Mills, 1770–1830*. London: HMSO.

Gillet, H. (2001), *Guide to the Archives of the Bank of England*, 2nd edition. London: Bank of England.

Godfrey, B., Cox, D. J. and Farrall, S. (2010), *Serious Offenders*. Oxford: Clarendon, Oxford University Press.

Graz, N. S. B. (1930), *Industrial Evolution*. London: Holt and Company.

Gregory, D. (1984), *Regional Transformation and the Industrial Revolution: A Geography of the Yorkshire Woollen Industry*. London: Macmillan.

Griffin, E. (2012), 'Patterns of Industrialisation', in M. Hewitt (ed.), *The Victorian World*. London: Routledge.

Grüttner, M. (1982), 'Working class Crime and the Labour Movement: Pilfering in the Hamburg Docks 1888–1923', in R. Evans (ed.), *The German Working Class 1888–1933: The Politics of Everyday Life*. New York: Taylor and Francis, pp. 57–79.

Gay, P. de (1996), *Consumption and Identity at Work*. London: Sage.

Hall, J. (1952), *Theft, Law and Society*, 2nd edition. New York: Bobbs-Merrill.

Hammick, J. T. (1867), 'On the judicial statistics of England and Wales, with special reference to the recent returns relating to crime', *Journal of the Statistical Society of London*, 30(3): 375–426.

Hanagan, M. (1989), *Nascent Proletarians, Class Formation in Post Revolutionary France*. Oxford: Oxford University Press.

Harding, R. and Jenkins, R. (1989), *The Myth of the Hidden Economy*. Milton Keynes: Open University Press.

Harris, B. (1969), *The Criminal Jurisdiction of Magistrates*. London: B. Rose.

Hart, J. (1956), 'The Reform of the Borough Police, 1835–6', *English Historical Review*, 70: 411–22.

Hartley, M. and Ingelby, J. (1976), *Life and Tradition in West Yorkshire*. Otley: Dalesman.

Hartwell, R. M. (1961), 'The rising standard of living in England, 1800–1850', *Economic History Review*, 3: 397–416.

— (1970), 'Business management in England during the period of early industrialization' in R. M. Hartwell (ed.), *The Industrial Revolution*. Oxford: Oxford University Press, pp. 28–41.

Hastings, R. (1980), 'Private Law-Enforcement Associations', *The Local Historian*, 14(4): 226–31.

Hawkings, D. (2003), *Fire Insurance Records for family and local historians 1696 to 1920*. London: Francis Boutle.

Hay, D. (1975), 'Property, authority and the criminal law', in D. Hay, P. Linebaugh, and J. G. Rule (eds), *Albion's Fatal Tree*. London: Allen Lane, pp. 17–54.

— (1983), 'Manufacturers and the criminal law in the later eighteenth-century: Crime and "Police" in South Staffordshire', *Past and Present Colloquium on Police and Policing*. Unpublished.

— (1989), 'Prosecution and Power: Malicious Prosecution in the English Courts, 1750–1850' in D. Hayand F. Snyder (eds), *Policing and Prosecution in Britain, 1750–1850*. Oxford: Oxford University Press, pp. 343–95.

— (2004), 'England, 1562–1875: The law and its uses', in D. Hay and P. Craven (eds), *Masters, Servants, and Magistrates in Britain and the Empire, 1562–1955*. University of North Chapel Hill and London, pp. 59–117.

Hay, D. and Snyder, F. (1989), 'Using the Criminal Law, 1750–1850, policing, Private Prosecution, and the State', in D. Hay and F. Snyder (eds), *Policing and Prosecution in Britain, 1750–1850*. Oxford: Oxford University Press, pp. 4–52.

Head, G. (1836), *A Home Tour through the Manufacturing Districts of England in the Summer of 1835*. London: John Murray.

Heaton, H. (1965), *The Yorkshire Woollen and Worsted Industries from the Earliest Times up to the Industrial Revolution*. Oxford: Oxford University Press.

Heidensohn, F. (1985), *Women and Crime*. New York: New York University Press.

Henry, S. (1978), *Controlling the Hidden Economy*. Oxford: Oxford University Press.

Hill, B. (1989), *Women, Work and Sexual Politics in Eighteenth-Century England*. Oxford: Oxford University Press.

Hobson, J. (2011), *Cathedral Bobbies: A Testament to the Constables who Safeguard Some of Our Great Cathedrals*. Mirfield: Mirfield Publications.

Hobsbawm, E. (1986 edition), *Labouring Men. Studies in the History of Labour*. London: Weidendeld and Nicolson.

Hobsbawm, E. J. (1957), 'The British standard of living, 1790–1850', *Economic History* Review, 10(1): 46–68.

— (1968), 'Customs, Wages and Workload', in E. Hobsbawm (ed.), *Labouring Men, Studies in the History of Labour*, 2nd edition. London: Weidenfeld and Nicholson, pp. 340–70.

— (1986), *Labouring Men: Studies in the History of* Labour, 2nd edition. London: Weidenfeld and Nicholson.

Hodgson, J. (1879), *Textile Manufacture and the other Industries in Keighley*. Keighley: A. Hey.

Hollis, P. (1979), *Women in Public, 1850–1900. Documents of the Victorian Women's Movement*. London: Allen and Unwin.

Hopkins, E. (1979), *A Social History of the English Working Class, 1815–1945*. London: Edward Arnold.

— (1982), 'Working hours and conditions during the Industrial Revolution: A re-appraisal', *English Historical Review*, 35: 52–66.

Horning, D. (1970), 'Blue-collar theft: Conceptions of property, attitudes towards pilferingand work group norms in a "modern" plant', in E. Smigel and H. Ross (eds), *Crimes Against Bureaucracy*. New York: Van Nostrand Reinhold Co., pp. 46–64.

Horrell, S. and Humphries, J. (1995), 'Women's labour force participation and the transition to the male-breadwinner family, 1790–1865', *Economic History Review*, XLVIII: 89–117.

Horsfall-Turner, J. (1904), *The Annals of Wakefield House of Correction for Three-Hundred Years*. Bingley: Harrisons and Sons.

Hostettler, J. (1992), *The Politics of Criminal Law Reform in the Nineteenth-Century*. Chichester: Barry Rose.

Hudson, P. (1975), *The West Riding Wool Textile Industry: A Catalogue of Business Records*, Edington: Pasold Research Fund.

— (1983), 'From Manor to Mill', in M. Berg et al. (eds), *Manufacture in Town and Country before the Factory*. Cambridge: Cambridge University Press, pp. 124–44.

— (1986), *The Genesis of Industrial Capital: A Study of the West Riding Wool Textile Industry, c. 1750–1850*. Cambridge: Cambridge University Press.

— (1992), *The Industrial Revolution*. London: E. Arnold.

Ignatieff, M. (1979), *A Just Measure of Pain. The Penitentiary and the Industrial Revolution*. London: Macmillan.

— (1983a), 'Total Institutions and the Working Classes. A Review Essay', *History Workshop Journal*, 15(Spring): 167–73.

— (1983b), 'State, Civil Society and Total Institutions: A Critique of recent Social Histories of Punishment', in D. Sugarman (ed.), *Legality, Ideology and the State*. London: Academic Press, pp. 75–105.

Ittmann, K. (1995), *Work, Gender and Family in Victorian England*. New York: New York University Press.

James, J. (1857), *A History of the Worsted Manufacture in England*. London: Longman, Brown, Green, Longman, and Roberts.

Jenkins, D. and Yoneyama, T. (eds) (2000), *The History of Insurance*, 8 volumes. London: Pickering and Chatto.

Jenkins, J. G. (ed.) (1972), *The Wool Textile Industry in Great Britain*. London: Routledge.

Jenkins, D. T. (1973), 'Early Factory Development in the West Riding of Yorkshire 1770–1880', in D. T. Jenkins (ed.), *Textile History and Economic History: Essays in Honour of Miss Julia de Lacy Mann*. Manchester: Manchester University Press, pp. 247–66.

— (1975), *The West Riding Wool Textile Industry, 1770–1835: A Study of Fixed Capital Formation*. Wiltshire: Erdington.

Jenkins, D. T. and Ponting, K. T. (1982), *The British Wool Textile Industry, 1770–1914.* London: Heinneman.

Jerrard, B. (1993), 'Early Policing in Gloucestershire', *Transactions of the Bristol and Gloucestershire Archaeological Society for 1992*, C: 221–40.

John, A. V. (1978), 'Colliery legislation and its consequences: 1842 and the women minersof Lancashire', *Bulletin of the John Rylands Library*, LXI(I): 78–114.

Johnston, E. (1867), *Autobiography: Poems and Songs of Emily Johnston, "The Factory Girl"*. Glasgow.

Johnston, H. (2005), 'Policing, Punishment and Social Institutions in the nineteenth century: the role of the Shropshire Magistracy', in D. Cox and B. Godfrey (eds), *Cinderellas and Packhorses: A History of the Shropshire Magistracy.* Almeley: Logaston, pp. 43–64.

Johnson, J. (1777), *Laws Respecting Women*. London: J. Johnson.

Johnston, L. (1992), *The Rebirth of Private Policing.* London: Routledge.

Jones, D. (1973), 'The Liberal press and the rise of Labour: A study with particular reference to Leeds and Bradford, 1850–1895', unpublished Ph.D thesis. University of Leeds.

Jones, D. V. L. (1982), *Crime, Protest, Community and Politics in Nineteenth Century Britain*. London: Routledge.

— (1983), 'The new police, crime and people in England and Wales, 1829–88', *Transactions of the Royal Historical Society*, 33: 151–68.

— (1992), *Crime in Nineteeenth Century Wales*. Cardiff: University of Wales Press.

Jones, T. and Newburn, T. (1998), *Private Security and Public Policing*. Oxford: Clarendon Oxford University Press.

Jowitt, A. J. and McIvor, J. A. (eds) (1988), *Employers and Labour in the English Textile Industry 1850–1939*. London: Routledge.

Jowitt, A. J. and Wright, C. (1982), *Victorian Bradford; essays in honour of Jack Reynold.* Bradford: Bradford City Libraries.

Joyce, P. (1980), *Work, Society and Politics: The Culture of the Factory in Later Victorian England.* Manchester: Harvester Press.

Karstedt, S., Levi, M. and Godfrey, B. (eds) (2006) 'Markets, Risk and 'White-collar' Crimes: Moral Economies from Victorian times to Enron', *Special Edition of The British Journal of Criminology*, 46/6.

Kelly, M. (1987), 'Western Civilization's first detectives', *Police Studies*,10(1, Spring): 36–41.

King, P. J. R. (1989a), 'Gleaners, farmers and the failure of legal sanctions in England 1750–1850', *Past and Present*, 125: 116–50.

— (1989b), 'Prosecution Associations and their impact in eighteenth-century Essex', in D. Hay and F. Snyder (eds), *Policing and Prosecution in Britain, 1750–1850*. Oxford: Oxford University Press, pp. 171–209.

— (1996), 'Female offenders, work and life-cycle change in late-eighteenth-century London', *Continuity and Change*, 11(1): 61–90.

King, P. (2000), *Crime, Justice, and Discretion in England 1740–1820*. Oxford: Oxford University Press.

— (2006), *Crime and Law in England, 1750–1840*. Cambridge: Cambridge University Press.

Knipe, J. P. (1970), 'Justices of the Peace in Yorkshire', Unpublished Ph.D thesis. University of Wisconsin.

Koditchek, T. (1990), *Class Formation and Urban Industrial Society, 1750–1850*. Cambridge: Cambridge University Press.

Kohl, J. G. (1844), *Ireland, Scotland and England*. London: Chapman and Hall.

Kynnersley, T. C. S. (1858), 'The incentives to crime presented by marine store dealers, and how to repress them', *TNAPSS*, 13: 361–63.

Lambert, W. R. (1975), 'Drink and work – discipline in industrial South Wales, 1800–1870, *Welsh Historical Review*, 7: 289–306.

Landes, D. S. (1987), '"What do bosses really do?"', *Journal of Economic History*, XLVI: 585–623.

Langbein, J. (1983), 'Albion's fatal flaws', *Past and Present*, 98: 96–120.

Lazonick, W. (1978), 'The subjection of Labour to Capital: the rise of the capitalist system', *Review of Radical Political Economics*, 10(1, Spring): 1–31.

— (1979), 'Industrial relations and technological change: the case of the self-actingmules', *Cambridge Journal of Economic History*, 3: 231–62.

Lea, J. (1979), 'Discipline and capitalist development' in B. Fine, R. Kinsey, J. Lea, S. Piciotto and J. Young (eds), *Capitalism and the Rule of Law*. London: Hutchinson, pp. 100–17.

Linebaugh, P. (1972), 'Eighteenth-Century Crime, Popular Movements and Social Controls', *Bulletin for the Society for the Study of Social History*, 37: 9–11.

— (1991), *The London Hanged*. London: Allen Lane.

— (2003), *The London Hanged, Crime and Civil Society in the Eighteenth-Century*, 2nd edition. London: Allen Lane.

Lipson, E. (1921, reprinted 1965), *The History of the Woollen and Worsted Industries*. London: Routledge.

Little, C. and Sheffield, C. P. (1983), 'Frontiers and Criminal Justice: English Prosecution Associations and American Vigilantism in the Eighteenth and Nineteenth Centuries', *American Sociological Review*, 48: 796–808.

Lloyd, A. (1995), *Doubly Deviant, Doubly Damned*. Harmondsworth: Penguin.

Lloyd-Baker, T. B. (1860), 'Abstracts and Inferences founded upon the Official Criminal Returns of England and Wales for the years 1854–1859, with special reference to the results of the Reformatories', *TNAPSS*, 11 December: 427–54.

Lobban, M. (2012), '"Private law" and the *laissez-faire* state' in M. Hewitt (ed.), *The Victorian World*. London: Routledge.

Locker, J. and Godfrey, B. (2006), Ontological boundaries and temporal watersheds in the development of white-collar crime', *British Journal of Criminology Special edition*,

'Markets, Risk and 'White-Collar' Crimes: Moral Economies from Victorian times to Enron', 46(6): 976–93.

Lowe, W. J. (1983), 'The Lancashire Constabulary, 1845–70: The Social and Occupational Function of a Victorian Police Force', *Criminal Justice History*, IV: 41–62.

Lown, J. (1990), *Women and Industrialization: Gender at Work in the Nineteenth-Century*. Cambridge: Cambridge University Press.

Lyon, D. (1994), *The Electronic Eye: The Rise of Surveillance Society*. Cambridge: Cambridge University Press.

MacDonell, J. (1894), 'Statistics of Litigation in England and Wales since 1859', *Journal of the Royal Statistical Society*, 57(3): 452–523.

Magrath, I. (1988),'Protecting the interests of the trade: Wool textile employers' organizations in the 1920s', in J. A. Jowitt and A. J. McIvor (eds), *Employers and Labour in the English Textile Industry*. London: Routledge, pp. 44–64.

Mander, G. P. (1934), 'The Wolverhampton "Association"', *The Wolverhampton Antiquary*,11(1): 60–3.

Marglin, S. (1976), '"What do bosses do?" the origin and function of hierarchy in capitalist production', in A. Gorz (ed.), *The Division of Labour: The Labour Process and Class Struggle in Modern Capitalism*. London: Harvester Press, pp. 13–54.

— (1984), 'Knowledge and Power' in F. H. Stephen (ed.), *Firms, Organization and Labour, Approaches to the Economics of Work Organization*. London: Macmillan.

Mars, G. (1983), *Cheats at Work. An Anthropology of Workplace Crime*. London: Unwin.

Marx, K. (1906), *Capital, A Critique of Political Economy*, 3rd edition. London: Modern Library.

McClelland, K. (1987), 'Time to work, time to live: some aspects of work and the reformation of class in Britain, 1850–80', in P. Joyce (ed.), *The Historical Meanings of Work*. Cambridge: Cambridge University Press, pp. 180–209.

McConville, S. (1981), *A History of English Prison Administration, 1750–1877*, Volume 1. London: Routledge.

McIvor, A. (1988), 'Work, wages and industrial relations in cotton finishing, 1880–1914', in J. A. Jowett and A. McIvor (eds), *Employers and Labour in the English Textile Industries, 1850–1939*. London: Routledge, pp. 127–52.

McKendrick, N. (1961), 'Josiah Wedgwood and Factory Discipline', *Historical Journal*, 4: 30–55.

Melling, J. (1980), 'Non-Commissioned Officers: British employers and their supervisoryworkers, 1880–1920', *Social History*, 5: 183–221.

Melossi, D. and Pavarini, M. (1981), *The Prison and the Factory. The Origins of the Penitentiary System*. London: Macmillan.

Milne, J. D. (1870), *The Industrial and Social Position of Women*. London: Chapman and Hall.

Morris, R. J. (1990), *Class, Sect and Party: the making of the British Middle Class: Leeds 1820-50*. Manchester: Manchester University Press.

Munsche, P. (1981), 'The Gamekeeper and English Rural Society', *Journal of British Studies*, XX(2, Spring): 82–105.

Myatt, P. (1980), *The Rise of the Bradford Worsted Industry*. Bradford: Emerald Group.

Napier, W. (1857), *The Life and Opinion of General Sir Charles Napier*. London: John Murray.

Nardinelli, C. (1985), 'The successful prosecution of the Factory Acts: A suggested explanation', *Economic History Review*, 38(3): 428–30.

Neale, R. S. (1966), 'The standard of living, 1780–1844: A regional and class study', *Economic History Review*, 19: 590–606.

Neff, W. F. (1966), *Victorian Working Women: An Historical and Literary Study in British Industries and Professions, 1832–50*. London: Cass.

Nelson, D. (1975), *Managers and Workers: Origins of the Twentieth-century Factory System in the United States, 1880–1920*, University of Wisconsin Press; 2nd Revised edition.

Newburn, T. (1996), 'Comparative reflections on policing', paper presented to the Department of Criminology, Keele University.

Newbery, M. (1992) *Picking up Threads: The Complete Reminiscences of a Bradford Mill girl*. Bradford: Bradford Libraries.

— (1993), *Picking Up Threads: Reminiscences of a Bradford Mill Girl*. Bradford: Bradford Libraries.

Nicholson, J. (1831) *The Factory Child*. London: Whittaker, Treacher and Arnot.

O'Neill, J. (1986), 'The Disciplinary Society: From Weber to Foucault', *British Journal of Sociology*, 37(1): 42–60.

Paley, R. (1989), '"An Imperfect, Inadequate and Wretched System"? Policing London before Peel', *Criminal Justice History*, X: 95–130.

Paley, W. (1818), *The Principles of Moral and Political Philosophy*, Volume 1, 21st edition. London: Baldwyn & Co.

Parkes, B. R. (1862), 'The balance of popular opinion in regard to women's work', *TNAPSS*, 24: 808–9.

Peacock, A. E. (1985), 'Factory Act Prosecutions: A hidden consensus', *Economic History Review*, 38(3): 431–6.

Philips, D. (1976), 'The Black Country Magistracy, 1835–1860. A changing elite and the exercise of its power', *Midland History*, 3(3): 161–89.

— (1977), *Crime and Authority in Victorian England*. London: Croom Helm.

— (1980), '"A New Engine of Power and Authority". The Institutionalisation of Law Enforcement in England, 1780–1830', in V. A. C. Gatrell, G. Lenman, and G. Parker (eds), *Crime and the Law: The Social History of Crime in Western Europe since 1500*. London: Europa Publications, pp. 155–89.

— (1989), '"Good Men to Associate and Bad Men to Conspire": Associations for the Prosecution of Felons in England 1760–1860', in D. Hay and F. Snyder (eds), *Policing and Prosecution in Britain, 1750–1850*. Oxford: Oxford University Press, pp. 113–70.

Pike, L. O. (1876), *A History of Crime in England, From the Accession of Henry VII to the Present Times*, 2 volumes. London: Smith, Elder and Co.

Pinchbeck, J. (1930, reprinted 1969), *Women Workers and the Industrial Revolution*. London: A. M. Kelly.

Plint, T. (1851), *Crime in England, its Relation, and Extent, as Developed from 1801 to 1848*. London: Charles Gilpin.

Plummer, A. and Early, R. E. (1969), *The Blanket Makers, 1669–1969. A History of Charles Early and Marriot (Witney) Ltd*. London: Taylor and Francis.

Pollard, S. (1963), 'Factory Discipline in the Industrial Revolution', *Economic History Review*, 16: 254–71.

— (1993), *The Genesis of Modern Management*. Hampshire: Gregg Revivals.

Price, R. (1986), *Labour in British Society*. London: Taylor and Francis.

Pritchard, T. S. (1875), *The Jurisdiction, Practice and Procedure of the Quarter Sessions in Judicial Matters*. London: H. Sweet.

Radzinowicz, L. (1948), *A History of English Criminal Laws*, 4 volumes. London: Stevens and Sons.

Randall, A. (1972), *The Kettering Worsted Industry of the Eighteenth Century*. Kettering: Northamptonshire Record Society.

— (1990–2), 'Peculiar Perquisites and Pernicious Practices. Embezzlement in the West of England Woollen Industry, c.1750–1840', *International Review of Social History*, 35: 194–219.

— (1991), *Before the Luddites. Custom, Community and Machinery in the English Woollen Industry, 1776–1809*. Cambridge: Cambridge University Press.

Rediker, M. (1989), *Between the Devil and the Deep Blue Sea. Merchant Seamen, Pirates and the Anglo-American Maritime World*. Cambridge: Cambridge University Press.

Reid, D. (1986), 'The Decline of Saint Monday 1766–1876', *Past and Present*, 71: 76–101.

Reiner, R. (1985), *The Politics of the Police*. London: Wheatsheaf.

— (2000), *The Politics of the Police*, 3rd edition. Oxford: Oxford University Press.

Reynolds, E. (1998), *Before the Bobbies: The Night Watch and Police Reform in Metropolitan London: 1720–1830*. Basingstoke: Macmillan.

Richardson, C. (1976), 'The Irish in Victorian Bradford', *The Bradford Antiquary*, 4: 294–316.

Robb, G. (2006), 'Women and white-collar crime: Debates on gender, fraud and the corporate economy in England and America, 1850–1930', British Journal of Criminology Special edition, *'Markets, Risk and 'White-Collar' Crimes: Moral Economies from Victorian times to Enron'*, 46(6): 1058–73.

Roberts, I. (1881), *The Life of Israel Roberts, 1827–1881*. York.

Roberts, J. S. (1978), 'Drink and Industrial Work Discipline in Nineteenth Century Germany', *Journal of Social History*, 3: 25–38.

Rodgers, R. (1977), 'Mid-Victorian employers' attitudes', *Social History*, 2(1): 77–80.

Roethlisberger, F. J. (1944–5), 'The Foreman: Master and Victim of Double Talk', *Harvard Business Review*, 28: 283–98.

Room, J. (1882), *Notes from the Logbook of a Late Worsted Inspector*. Keighley: Herald Office.

Rose, S. O. (1988), 'Gender antagonisms and class conflict; exclusionary strategies of male trade unions in nineteenth-century Britain', *Social History*, 13: 191–208.

— (1992), *Limited Livelihoods, Gender and Class in Nineteenth-Century England.* London: Psychology Press.

Rudé, G. (1985), *Criminal and Victim in Early Nineteenth-Century England.* Oxford: Oxford University Press.

Rule, J. (1981), *The Experiences of Labour in Eighteenth-Century Industry.* London: Croom Helm.

— (1986), *The Labouring Classes in Early Industrial England, 1750–1850.* London: Longman.

— (1992), *The Vital Economy. England's Developing Economy, 1714–1815.* London: Longman.

Rusche, G. and Kircheimer, O. (1939), *Punishment and Social Structure.* New York: Russell and Russell.

Samuel, R. (1972), 'Industrial Crime in the Nineteenth Century', *Society for the Study of Labour History Bulletin*, 25: 7–8.

Schubert, A. (1981), 'Private Initiative in Law Enforcement: Associations for the Prosecution of Felons, 1744–1856', in V. Bailey (ed.), *Policing and Punishment in Nineteenth Century Britain.* London: Croom Helm, pp. 25–41.

Schultze-Gaevernitz, V. (1893), *Social Peace: A Study of the Trade Union Movement in England.* London: Swan Sonnenschein.

Scoresby, W. (1846), *The Condition and Prospects of the Female Operatives: A Sermon preached at the Parish Church to the Bradford Female Factory Operatives, on Sunday 15th November, 1846.* London: James Nisbit.

Seccombe, W. (1982), 'Patriarchy stabilized; the construction of a male breadwinner wagenorms in nineteenth Britain', *Social History*, 11(1): 53–76.

Sellin, T. (1951), 'The Significance of the Records of Crime', *Law Quarterly Review*, LXV: 489–504.

Sharpe, J. A. (1984), *Crime in Early Modern England 1550–1750.* London: Longman.

Sigsworth, E. M. (1958), *Black Dyke Mills, A History.* Liverpool: Liverpool University Press.

Silver, A. (1967), 'The demand for order in civil society: a review of some themes in the history of urban crime, police and riot', in D. J. Bordua (ed.), *The Police: Six Sociological Essays.* London: Wiley, pp. 1–24.

Simon, D. (1954), 'Masters and Servants', in J. Saville (ed.), *Democracy and the Labour Movement, Essays in Honour of Dona Torr.* London: Lawrence and Wishart, pp. 160–200.

Smith, A. (1910), *Wealth of Nations*, 2 volumes, 3rd edition. London: Dent (Everyman edition).

Smith, G. (1974), *Bradford's Police.*Bradford: City of Bradford Police.

Smith, S. A. (1993), 'Workers and Supervisors: St.Petersburg, 1905–17, and Shanghai, 1895–1927', *Past and Present*, 139: 131–77.

Smith, V. (1990), *All Muck and Nettles, the Early Life of Burler and Mender No. 57.* Bradford: Bradford Libraries.

Snyder, F. and Hay, D. (1987), 'Comparisons in the social history of the law: labour and crime', in F. Snyder and D. Hay (eds), *Labour Law and Crime: An Historical Perspective.* London: Taylor and Francis, pp. 1–41.

Soderlund, R. (1992), 'Law, crime and labour in the worsted industry of the West Riding of Yorkshire, 1750–1850', unpublished Ph.D thesis. University of Maryland.

— (1993), '"For the Protection of Manufacturer's Property": Policing the Workplace in the Yorkshire Worsted Industry in the Age of Liberal Capitalism, 1810–45', Paper given to the annual meeting of the North American Labour History Conference.

South, N. and Scraton, P. (1981), 'Capitalist discipline, private justice and the hidden economy', *Occasional Papers in Deviance and Social Policy*, 2. Middlesex.

South, N. (1987), 'Law, Profit and "Private Persons", Private and Public Policing in English History', in P. C. Shearing (ed.), *Private Policing.* California: Sage, pp. 72–109.

Speed, M., Burrows, J. and Bamfield, J. (1994), *Retail Crime Costs, 1993–94 Survey.* Northampton: British Retail Consortium.

Spitzer, S. and Scull, A. (1977), 'Privatization and Capitalist Development: The case of the private police', *Social Problems*, 25(1): 18–29.

Stedman-Jones, G. (1971), *Outcast London: A Study in the Relationship between Classes in Victorian Society.* Oxford: Oxford University Press.

— (1983), *Languages of Class: Studies in English Working-Class History, 1832–1983.* Cambridge: Cambridge University Press.

Steinfeld, R. (2001), *Coercion, Contract and Free Labour in the Nineteenth Century.* Cambridge: Cambridge University Press.

Steinmetz, W. (ed.) (2000), *Private Law and Social Inequality in the Industrial Age: Comparing Legal Cultures in Britain, France, Germany and the United States.* Oxford: Oxford University Press.

Stephen, J. (1890), *A General View of the Criminal Law in England.* London: Macmillan.

Stephen, J. F. (1883), *A History of the Criminal Law of England*, 3 volumes. London: Macmilln, p. 280.

Stevenson, S. J. (1986), '"The Criminal Class": Legislation, labelling and prosecution in the late nineteenth century', paper presented to the Urban History Group, Economic History Society Conference, Cheltenham, April.

Storch, R. D. (1976), 'The Policeman as Domestic Missionary: Urban Discipline and Popular Culture in Northern England, 1850–80', *Journal of Social History*, 9: 481–509.

— (1981), 'The Plague of Blue Locusts: Police Reform and Popular Disturbances in Northern England, 1840–1857,' *International Review of Social History*, 10: 61–90.

Styles, J. (1982), 'An Eighteenth-Century Magistrate as Detective': Samuel Lister of Little Horton', *Bradford Antiquary*, New Series Part XLVII October: 98–117.

— (1983), 'Embezzlement, Industry and the Law in England, 1500–1800', in M. Berg, P. Hudson and M. Sonescher (eds), *Manufacture in Town and Country before the Factory.* Cambridge: Cambridge University Press, pp. 189–99.

— (1987a), 'The Emergence of the Police – Explaining Police Reform in Eighteenth and Nineteenth Century England', *British Journal of Criminology*, Winter: 15–22.

— (1987b), 'Policing a Female Workforce: The Worsted Inspectors, 1760–1810', *Bulletin for the Society for the Study of Labour*, 52: 39–40.

Sugarman, D. and Rubin, G. R. (1984), 'Towards a new history of law and material society in England, 1750–1914', in D. Sugarman and G. R. Rubin (eds), *Law, Economy and Society, 1750–1914. Essays in the History of English Law*. London: Professional Books, pp. 1–186.

Sutton, J. (2002), 'The Staffordshire Society for the Apprehension of Felons', *Staffordshire Studies*,14: 32–52.

Sweeney, T. (1985),'The extension and practice of Summary Jurisdiction in England, c.1790–1860', unpublished Ph.D. Cambridge.

Swift, R. (1988a), 'Urban policing in early Victorian England: a reappraisal', *History*, 73: 211–37.

— (1988b), *Police Reform in Early Victorian York, 1835–56*. York: University of York.

— (1992), 'The English urban magistracy and the administration of justice during the early nineteenth-century: Wolverhampton, 1815–60', *Midland History*, 17: 75–92.

Tabor, M. C. (1862), 'On the condition of women as affected by law', *TNAPSS*, 25: 910–11.

Taylor, D. (2010), *Hooligans, Harlots, and Hangmen: Crime and punishment in Victorian Britain*. Santa Barbara: Praeger.

Tebbutt, M. (1983), *Making Ends Meet: Pawnbroking and Working-Class Credit*. Leicester: Leicester University Press.

Thomas, C. (1994), 'The Origins and Development of British Transport Police', in *Police History Society Journal*, 9: 31–6.

Thompson, E. (1972), 'Crime and capitalism,' in *Bulletin for the Society for the Study of Social History*, 37: 9–11.

Thompson, E. P. (1963), *The Making of the English Working Class*. Harmondsworth: Penguin.

— (1967), 'Time, work-discipline and industrial capitalism', *Past and Present*, 38: 56–97.

— (1975), *Whigs and Hunters, The Origins of the Black Act*. Harmondsworth: Penguin.

— (1991), *Customs in Common*. Harmondsworth: Penguin.

Thompson, F. M. L. (1963), *English Landed Society in the Nineteenth Century*. London: Routledge.

— (1988), *The Rise of Respectable Society. A Social History of Victorian Britain*. London: Fontana.

Tobias, J. J. (1967), *Crime and Industrial Society in the Nineteenth Century*. London: Batsford.

— (1979), *Crime and Police in England, 1700–1900*. Dublin: Gill and Macmillan.

Trainor, R. H. (1993), *Black Country Elites, The Exercise of Authority in an Industrialized area 1850–1900*. Oxford: Oxford University Press.

Tunzelmann, G. N. Von (1978), *Steam Power and British Industrialism to 1860*. Oxford: Oxford University Press.

Ure, A. (1853, reprinted 1967), *The Philosophy of Manufactures, or an Exposition of the Scientific, Moral and Commercial Economy of the Factory System of Great Britain*. London: Longmans.

Valenze, D. (1995), *The First Industrial Women*. Oxford: Oxford University Press.

Veneziani, B. (1986), 'The Evolution of the Law of Contract', in B. Hepple (ed.), *The Making of Labour Law in Europe*. London: Mansell Publishing.

Wadsworth A. P. and Mann, J. de Lacy (1931), *The Cotton Trade and Industrial Lancashire 1600–1780*. Manchester: Manchester University Press.

Wakefield, E. G. (1831), *Facts Related to the Punishment of Death in the Metropolis*. London: James Ridgway.

Walby, S. (1986), *Patriarchy at Work*. Cambridge: Cambridge University Press.

Walklate, S. (1995), *Gender and Crime*. London: Prentice Hall.

Weinberger, B. (1981), 'Law Breakers and Law Enforcers in the Late Victorian City: Birmingham 1867–1877', unpublished Ph.D thesis. University of Warwick.

Whipp, R. (1987), '"A time to every purpose": an essay on time and work', in P. Joyce (ed.), *The Historical Meanings of Work*. Cambridge: Cambridge University Press, pp. 210–36.

Wiener, M. J. (1990), *Culture, Law and Policy in England, 1850–1914*. Cambridge: Cambridge University Press.

Williams, T. W. (1793–5), *The Whole Law relating to the Duty and Office of a Justice of the Peace*, 4 volumes. London: Robinson and Kearsley.

Wilson, S. (2006), 'Law, Morality and Regulation: Victorian Experiences of Financial Crime, Markets, Risk and "White-Collar" Crimes: Moral Economies from Victorian Times to Enron', *Special Issue of British Journal of Criminology*, 46(6): 1073–91.

Woods, D. C. (1982), 'The operation of the master and servant act in the Black Country, 1858–1875', *Midland History*, 7: 93–115.

Wray, D. E. (1949), 'Marginal men of Industry: The Foreman', *American Journal of Sociology*, 54: 298–301.

Yarmie, A. H. (1984), 'British employers' resistance to grandmotherly government, 1850–80', *Social History*, 9(2): 141–69.

Zangerl, C. H. E. (1971), 'The Social Composition of the County Magistracy in England and Wales, 1831–1887', *Journal of British Studies*, XI(November): 113–25.

Zedner, L. (1991), *Women, Crime and Custody in Victorian England*. Oxford: Oxford University Press.

Zehr, H. (1976), *Crime and the Development of Modern Society*. London: Croom Helm.

Index